Great Philosophers And Thinkers on Education

J.C. Aggarwal
S. Gupta

SHIPRA

(2014, 2010, 2008, 2007 Rev. Ed., 2006)

Rs. 1250; US$ 50

ISBN: 978-81-7541-733-5

2021 Impression

Great Philosophers and Thinkers on Education

Published by:

SHIPRA PUBLICATIONS
LG 18-19, Pankaj Central Market,
I.P. Ext., Patparganj, Delhi 110092, India
Ph.: +91 11 22236152, 9650028065, 9810522367
Email: info@shiprapublication.com
www.shiprapublication.com

Preface

Believe nothing, merely because you have told it, or because it is traditional or because you yourselves have imagined it. Do not believe what your teacher tells you merely out of respect for your teacher. But whatever after due consideration and analysis you find it to be conducive to the good, the benefit, the welfare of all beings, that doctrine, believe and cling to and take it as your guide.

— *The Buddha*

The field of education has grown enormously. Philosophers and thinkers on education throughout the world continue to enrich the professional literature with their important contributions. In such a scenario, it is rather difficult for any single person to find his way through the wilderness of this huge mass of literature or to reach an indefinitely large number of authorities in the normal course. To meet with this limitation, we have here endeavoured to get together within the cover of a single volume inspiring thoughts of some of the great philosophers and thinkers on education. In addition, brief notes on several other philosophers and thinkers are given and a list of Thinkers on Education in UNESCO series is also attended.

The most important characteristic of this work is that it presents the deeply penetrating and subtle thoughts of the masterminds in a simple and easy to understand language and style. It includes publications and contribution of each educator to education.

While studying such works, it must be remembered that the views of great persons do not in the least absolve us from the duty of thinking and reflecting for ourselves. They are splashes of inspiration which reveal to us certain aspects of truth and reality that may have remained invisible without them. But that is all. We cannot live for them or even by them. We should also look within ourselves for light.

A word about selection. We have tried to include philosophers and thinkers on education who have attained a certain measure of celebrity in this field. We are aware we have missed a some other great names partly for our inability to locate the source of information and partly for the non-availability of information on account of our limited resources. We regret our unintentional omissions. It is also possible that some of the readers may not agree to our selection. Nevertheless, a choice had to be made.

The authors extend their warm thanks to all the publishers and authors whose works they have made use of and quoted. Special mention may be made of the various issues of '*Prospects*' published by International Bureau of Education/UNESCO.

We thank Prof. K.S. Chalam, Member, UPSC, New Delhi and former V.C. of Dravidian University, A.P., for his contribution on B.R. Ambedkar. The authors are grateful to Shri Yudhvir Singh of the Association of Indian Universities and Smt. A. Biswas for providing some documents.

It is hoped this book would serve as a reliable handy source of information for a cross section of population interested in educational thought and practices.

J.C. Aggarwal
S. Gupta

Contents

1

A.N. Whitehead (1861-1974)

A.N. Whitehead, an Englishman, was an educator, mathematician and philosopher. Whitehead was born in Ramsgate, England. He taught at Cambridge University and London University until 1924 when he joined the faculty of Harvard University in the United States. Whitehead's writings on mathematics, logic, and the theory of knowledge laid the groundwork for his philosophical classic, *Process and Reality* (1929). This book explains that process and growth are the fundamental ideas which lead us to understand God, nature and our own experiences.

Bertrand Russell was one of his most favourite students.

Publications

1. *Principles of Mathematics* (joint author with Bertrand Russell).
2. *Science and the Modern World.*
3. *Process and Reality.*
4. *Aims of Education.*

Concept of Philosophy

According to Whitehead, there was an intimate relationship between philosophy and environment. He wrote, "The doctrine I am maintaining is that neither physical nature nor life can be understood unless we fuse them together as essential factors in the composition of really real things. There is a unity—of the body and soul—into one person. Philosophy begins in wonder, and at the end when philosophic thought has done its best, the wonder remains".

For Whitehead, the educated man has general culture and expertise in some speciality. His general culture is intellectual, aesthetic and moral. Learning should not just be the storing of inert ideas, or a sharpening of supposed faculties, but should be an active assimilation of general ideas.

These ideas should be tested, applied to life and interrelated as much as possible to give an understanding of the present. To achieve this, not too much should be taught, but it should be taught thoroughly.

Purpose of Education

The students are alive, and the purpose of education is to stimulate and guide their self-development. It follows as a corollary from this premise, that the teachers also should be alive with living thoughts. (Aims of Education p. v)

Education is the acquisition of the art of the utilisation of knowledge. (Aims of Education p. 6)

Culture is activity of thought, and receptiveness to beauty and humane feeling. Scraps of information have nothing to do with it. A merely well informed man is the most useless bore on God's earth. What we should aim at producing is men who possess both culture and expert knowledge in some special direction. (Aims of Education p. 1)

When one considers in its length and in its breadth the importance of this question of the education of the nation's young, the broken lives, the defeated hopes, the national failures, which result from the frivolous inertia with which it is treated, it is difficult to restrain within oneself a savage rage. In the conditions of modern life the rule is absolute, that the race which does not value trained intelligence is doomed. Not all your heroism, not all your social charm, not all your wit, not all your victories on land or at sea, can move back the finger of fate. (Aims of Education p. 22)

Concept of Education

It must never be forgotten that education is not a process of packing articles in a trunk. Such a simile is entirely inapplicable. It is, of course, a process completely of its own peculiar genus. Its nearest analogue is the assimilation of food by a living organism: and we all know how necessary to health is palatable food under suitable conditions. (Aims of Education p. 51)

I do not share in this reverence for knowledge as such. It all depends on who has the knowledge and what he does with it. That knowledge which adds greatly to character is knowledge so handled as to transform every phase of immediate experience. (Aims of Education p. 49)

The pupils have got to be made to feel that they are studying something, and are not merely executing intellectual minuets. (Aims of Education p.15)

Knowledge does not keep any better than fish. You may be dealing with knowledge of the old species, with some old truth; but somehow or other it must come to the students, as it were, just drawn out of the sea and with the freshness of its immediate importance. (Aims of Education p. 147)

Contents or Subject Matter of Education

There is only one subject matter for education, and that is life in all its manifestations. Instead of this single unity, we offer children—Algebra, from which follows Geometry, from which nothing follows; Science, from which nothing follows; History, from which nothing follows; a couple of

Languages, never mastered; and lastly, most dreary of all, Literature, represented by plays of Shakespeare, with philological notes and short analyses of plot and character to be in substance committed to memory. (Aims of Education p. 10)

The sense for style... is an aesthetic sense, based on admiration for the direct attainment of a foreseen end, simply and without waste. Style in art, style in literature, style in science, style in logic, style in practical execution have fundamentally the same aesthetic qualities, namely, attainment and restraint. The love of a subject in itself and for itself, where it is not.

You may not divide the seamless coat of learning. What education has to impart is an intimate sense for the power of ideas, for the beauty of ideas, and for the structure of ideas, together with a particular body of knowledge which has peculiar reference to the life of the being possessing it. (Aims of Education p. 18)

Characteristics of the National System of Education

There are three main methods which are required in a national system of education, namely, the literary curriculum, the scientific curriculum, the technical curriculum. But each of these curricula should include the other two. What I mean is, that every form of education should give the pupil a technique, a science, an assortment of general ideas and aesthetic appreciation, and that each of these sides of his training should be illuminated by the others. (Aims of Education p. 75)

Mere literary knowledge is of slight importance. The only thing that matters is, how it is known. The facts related are nothing. Literature only exists to express and develop the imaginative world which is our life, the kingdom which is within us. It follows that the literary side of a technical education should consist in an effort to make the pupils enjoy literature. It does not matter what they know, but the enjoyment is vital. The great English Universities, under whose direct authority school children are examined in plays of Shakespeare, to the certain destruction of their enjoyment, should be prosecuted for soul murder. (Aims of Education pp. 88-9)

The antithesis between a technical and a liberal education is fallacious. There can be no adequate technical education which is not liberal, and no liberal education which is not technical; that is, no education which does not impart both technique and intellectual vision. In simpler language, education should turn out the pupil with something he knows well and something he can do well. This intimate union of practice and theory aids both. The intellect does not work best in a vacuum. (Aims of Education p. 74)

1. The Stages of Mental Development

Whitehead mentions the following three stages of mental development:

One: *Romance.* Romance is considered as the first apprehension of vividness and novelty – the child's first contact with knowledge – through observation and experience of the world and objects around him.

Two: *Precision.* Precision is the stage of grammar, language and science, where width of relationships is subordinate to exactness of formulation.

Three: *Generalisation.* Generalisation is the third stage of synthesis.

A return to romance with the advantage of classified ideas and relevant techniques: the final success of precise training... Education should repeat these cycles.

2. Curriculum

Whitehead has advocated the following principles of curriculum construction:

1. Each school must develop its own curriculum.
2. The sequence of subjects should be determined by the readiness, interest and the abilities of the learners.
3. There is no one course of study which gives general culture and another which gives special knowledge.
4. The main ideas to be introduced into the child's education should be a few but important. They may be thrown into every combination possible.
5. The theoretical ideas should always find important applications within student's curriculum.
6. Subjects should not be taught in isolation.
7. The ultimate aim of the curriculum in education should be to acquire Style. Style is the product of careful study and constitutes the morality of mind in the ultimate analysis.

3. Scientific Education

Whitehead considers a scientific education as mainly training in observing natural phenomena and in knowing and deducing laws of the sequence of these phenomena. The firsthand observation is the essence of science and first hand knowledge obtained by observation is the ultimate basis of all branches of science.

4. Technical Education

Technical education is based on scientific knowledge. The other aspects of technical education are its artistic nature, aesthetic appreciation and creativity. Technical training is broader than ultimate specialisation. Technical training should give students the power of adaptation to varying demands suiting the needs of the society. The skills learnt should be flexible.

Technical studies include (1) Biology, (2) Commerce, (3) Chemical Techniques, (4) Geometrical Techniques, (5) Mechanical Techniques, (6) Physical Science, (7) Social Sciences.

For example *Artistic Crafts*, *Carpentry* and *Steel making plastics* all need knowledge of Geometrical Techniques as well as Physics. *Agriculture* requires Biology and Chemical Techniques. *Cooking and Food Catering* require Biology, Physics and Chemistry.

Value Education

Value education cannot wait and must be introduced early.

5. Methods of Instruction

1. There is no royal road to learning through generalisations. Education is a patient process of the mastery of details minute by minute, hour by hour and day by day.
2. Too many subjects should not be taught at a time.
3. What is taught, should be taught thoroughly.
4. Powers of the mind—activity, delicacy, receptivity and responsiveness to stimulus must be utilised in whatever is being taught.
5. In scientific training, 'to prove' is the worth of an idea.
6. Self-development is the ultimate objective of all teaching.
7. The teachers should stimulate the students to think over what is taught and to develop their own individual thought and ideas over and above.
8. Spoon-feeding must be avoided.

6. Technical and Liberal Education

There is no conflict between a liberal education and technical education. Technical education cannot be adequate without liberal education. Likewise there is no liberal education without technical education. True education must strike a harmonious balance between technical education and liberal education.

7. Role of Teachers

Teachers should keep their imagination alive and teach all the subjects with creativity and imagination. They must develop creativeness in the students so that students develop into thinking beings. They must be prepared 'how to learn' by their own efforts.

8. Examinations

Whitehead was a great critic of the prevailing system of examination. His views on examinations were as under:

1. Students should not be subjected to any system of external examinations. He observed, "Uniform external examinations are deadly. They kill the best part of culture. We are dealing with human beings, not with dead matter".
2. No examination system is valid unless every question directly asked of a student is either framed or modified by the actual classroom

subject teacher. Whitehead wrote, "No system of external examinations which aims at examining individual scholar can result in anything but educational waste".

3. The best way of examinations consists of frequent assignments and tests designed by their own teachers.

9. Inspection

According to Whitehead, it is the schools and not the students in the classroom who should be inspected.

10. School Autonomy

Whitehead was of the view that each school should issue its own certificates and diplomas to its students, based on its own curriculum.

The schools should be treated as individual units and should maintain their own high standards.

Whitehead's Contribution to Education

Whitehead is the forerunner of several reforms and movements in education. Some of his ideas are quite radical. He does not believe in any curriculum prescribed by any other authority outside the school. In the same way he was in favour of evaluation of the students by their own teacher. His concept of school autonomy is quite revolutionary in nature.

Whitehead advocated self-discipline and self-development through self-effort.

2

Abraham Lincoln (1809-1865)

From log cabin (a sort of small hut) to the White House (Presidential Residence) – Thus case Abraham Lincoln to become the President of the USA (1861-1865). Abraham's father was a farmer and carpenter. Since his childhood, Lincoln was fond of reading, and constantly borrowed books from his neighbours. Lincoln became a successful attorney. He became known to the institution of slavery. In 1846, he became a member of the United States House of Representatives and in 1861 he became the 16th US President.

Educational Thought

The following extracts from the Letter which he wrote to the headmaster of a school in which his son was studying indicate his views on education.

He will have to learn, I know, that all men are not just, all men are not true. But teach him also that for every scoundrel there is a hero; that for every selfish politician, there is a dedicated leader.

Teach him that for every enemy there is a friend. It will take time, I know, but teach him if you can, that a dollar earned is of more value than five pound.

Teach him learn to lose and also to enjoy winning.

Steer him away from envy, if you can.

Teach him the secret of quiet laughter.

Let him learn early that the bullies are the easiest to lick.

Teach him, if you can, the wonder of books, but also give him quiet time to ponder over the external mystery of birds in the sky, bees in the sun, and flowers on a green hill-side.

In school, teach him it is far more honourable to fail than to cheat.

Teach him to have faith in his own ideas, even if everyone tells him they are wrong.

Teach him to be gentle with gentle people and tough with the tough.

Try to give my son the strength not to follow the crowd when everyone is getting on the band wagon.

Teach him to listen to all men but teach him also to filter all he hears on a screen of truth and take only the good that comes through.

Teach him, if you can, how to laugh when he is sad.

Teach him, there is no shame in tears.

Teach him to scoff at cynics and to beware of too much sweetness.

Teach him to sell his brawn and brain to the highest bidders; but never to put a price tag on his heart and soul.

Teach him to close his ears to a howling mob, and to stand and fight if he thinks he is right.

Teach him gently, but do not cuddle him because only the test of fire makes fine steel.

Let him have the courage to be impatient, let him have the patience to be brave.

Teach him always to have sublime faith in himself because he will always have sublime faith in mankind.

This is a big order; but see what you can do. He is such a little fellow, my son."

Significant Quotes

Those who deny freedom to others, deserve it not for themselves; and, under a just God, can not long retain it. (*The Collected Works of Abraham Lincoln* edited by Roy P. Basler, Volume III, "Letter To Henry L. Pierce and Others (April 6, 1859), p. 376)

"As I would not be a slave, so I would not be a master. This expresses my idea of democracy". (*Ibid*, Vol. II, p. 532)

"Let us have faith that right makes might, and in that faith, let us, to the end, dare to do our duty as we understand it". (*Lincoln's Coper Institute Address*, February 27, 1860)

"All men are created free and equal". (*Ibid*, Vol. II, p. 502)

"With malice towards none, with charity for all, with firmness in the right as God gives us to see the right, let us strive on to finish the work we are in; to bind up the nation's wounds; to care for him who shall have borne the battle, and for his widow and his orphan—to do all which may achieve and cherish a just and lasting peace, among ourselves, and with all nations". (*Lincoln's Second Inaugural Address*, March 4, 1865)

"The probability that we may fall in the struggle ought not to deter us from the support of a cause we believe to be just; it shall not deter me". (*Ibid* Vol. I, p. 178)

"Leave nothing for tomorrow which can be done today". (*Ibid*, Vol. II, p.81)

"The dogmas of the quiet past are inadequate to the stormy present. As our case is new, so we must think anew, and act anew". (*Lincoln's Second Annual Message to Congress*, December, 1862)

3

Abul Kalam Azad (1888-1958)

Abul Kalam Azad was a great intellectual and philosopher whom Gandhiji considered as a person of the calibre of Plato, Aristotle and Pythagoras. He was one of the prominent freedom fighters of India, President of the Indian National Congress (1923-1940) and the first Education Minister of Independent India.

Publications: India Wins Freedom[1]

Philosophy of Life: Concept of Man

The concept of man which the East has evolved regards man as not merely an animal superior to all earthly creatures but as essentially different from them in nature. Man is not the first among equals but is a being which is higher than any other creature. He is not only a progressive animal, but reveals in his being the lineaments of God Himself. In fact, his nature is so high and elevated that nothing higher is conceivable by human reason. In the words of the *Chhandogya Upanishad*:

"That is Reality. That is *Atman* (Soul). That art thou".

This doctrine has also been beautifully expressed in Arabic which means:

"He who knows himself knows God".

It will be readily agreed that there can be no higher concept of man. God marks the highest limit of human thought. By identifying man with God, the Eastern concept of man elevates him to godhead. Man has, therefore, no other goal, but to re-establish his identity with God. He, thus, becomes superior to the entire creation.

We must, however, admit that while the conception of man in both Vedanta and Sufism gives him a lofty status, neither of these philosophies can escape the charge that if, on the one hand, they set no limit to human capacity, they, on the other hand, imply an element of fatalism that circumscribes man's power. The explanation of this paradox is to be found in their concept of the relation of man to God. Since man is an emanation of divinity, whatever man does is ultimately God's doing: whatever happens is

1. First published Pothumously, January 1959 with a preface by Humayon Kabir.

due to the will of God. From this, it is, but another step to think of man as a mere toy in the hands of fate

(*Inaugural Speech at the Symposium on the Concept of Man and Philosophy of Education in the East and the West*, New Delhi, December 13, 1951)

Philosophy of Education

Experience has shown that education can profoundly affect the development of individuals and, through individuals, of societies. If the individual is not an integrated personality, society cannot be harmonious. The function of education in the modern world is therefore to build up integrated individuals in an integrated society and the concept of both the East and the West must contribute to such a development (Ibid).

Religious Education in Schools

After the World War I, a new approach had begun to assert itself, and the intellectual revolution brought about in the wake of the World War II gave it a decisive shape. At first it was considered that religions would stand in the way of the free intellectual development of a child but now it has been admitted that religious education cannot altogether be dispensed with. If national education was devoid of this element, there would be no appreciation of moral values or moulding of character on human lines. It must be known to you that Russia had to give up its ideology during the last World War. The British Government in England had also to amend its educational system in 1944.

So far as India is concerned, the problem presents itself in an entirely different shape. Europe and America felt the need of religious education as it was observed that without religious influences people became over-rationalistic. But in so far as they are working in Indian life we have to face the other side of the coin. We have no fear that people will become ultra-rationalist. On the contrary we are surrounded by over-religiosity. Our present difficulties, unlike those of Europe, are not creations of materialistic zealots but of religious fanatics. If we want to overcome them, the solution lies not in rejecting religious instruction in elementary stages but in imparting sound and healthy religious education under our direct supervision so that misguided credulism may not affect the children in their plastic stage.

It is obvious that millions of Indians are not prepared to see that their children are brought up in an irreligious atmosphere and, I am sure, you, too, will agree with them. What will be the consequence if the Government undertakes to impart purely secular education? Naturally people will try to provide religious education to their children through private sources. How these private sources are working today or are likely to work in future is already known to you. I know something about it and can say that not only in villages but even in cities the imparting of religious education is entrusted to teachers who though literate are not educated. To them religion means nothing but bigotry. The method of education, too, is such in which there is no scope for broad and liberal outlook. It is quite plain, then, that the children will not be able to drive out the ideas infused into them in their early stage whatever modern education may be given to them at a later stage. If we want to safeguard the intellectual life of our country against this danger, it becomes all the more necessary for us not to leave the imparting of early religious education to private sources. We should rather take it under our direct care and supervision. No doubt, a foreign government had to keep itself away from religious education. But a National Government cannot divest itself of undertaking this responsibility. To mould the growing mind of the nation on the right lines is its primary duty. In India we cannot have an intellectual mould without religion.

(*Presidential Speech at the Fourteenth Session of the Central Advisory Council of Education*, New Delhi, January 13, 1948)

Women's Education

I need hardly say that all our educational programme will ultimately depend upon the proper education of women. If women take to education, more than half of our problems will be solved. Educated mothers will mean children who can be easily made literate.

(*Central Institute of Education*, December 19, 1947)

Status of Women

Providing education to women without giving them freedom and forcing them to conformity to the veil will not only be useless but injurious and baneful.

(*Inaugural Address at the UNESCO Seminar on Rural Adult Education*, Mysore, November 02, 1949)

Medium of Instruction

I hold that there is no place for English as the medium of instruction in future in India, but at the same time there should be no precipitate action that may damage the cause of education. I hold that the replacement of English as a medium of instruction should be gradual and stage-by-stage so that there is the least possible interruption or interference with the process of education in the country.

Agricultural Bias to School Education

The universities have always and in all countries played a leading part i transforming the quality of life of the people. In order to perform thi function successfully, the universities must base their programmes on th real needs of the country. Until now, our university education has prove inadequate because, among other faults, it has ignored agriculture, which is the basis of Indian life. I would therefore appeal to all educationists to have this deficiency overcome by giving an agricultural bias to our school education and introducing agricultural education in the universities and practical work in farms. In addition, schools and colleges in the rural and semi-rural areas must encourage all students — whatever be their subjects of study — to devote a part of their normal scholastic routine to work on the land. For schools and colleges in cities and towns, I would suggest their adoption of villages where students may participate in a programme of complete reconstruction of village life.

(*Speech at a meeting of the Vice-Chancellors of the Indian Universities and Others*, New Delhi, November 3, 1951)

Delinking Degrees from Jobs

Is the present exaggerated emphasis on university degrees as a qualification for government service justified? The fact that a university degree is a necessary condition for government service has led people to look upon university degrees as a passport to government service. Those who join universities do so not to cultivate talent but to secure this passport. This state of affairs has had its repercussions on our universities also. Consciously or unconsciously an atmosphere was created which inevitably brought their standards down... We know that in other countries government servants are not recruited in this fashion... Why should we continue to regard the university degree as a passport to service? ... We have, of course, to bear in mind, that, so far as professional services are concerned, the acquisition of a university degree will continue to be necessary.

(*Broadcast from AIR*, New Delhi, September 30, 1953)

4

Annie Besant (1847-1933)

An Irish lady, coming from an aristocratic family, Annie Besant made India her home after coming here in 1893. She became a great lover of Hinduism and claimed that she was a Hindu in her former birth; she wore the Hindu costume and adopted Hindu way of life. She was a great free thinker, a captivating orator and organiser. She was the President of the Theosophical Society of India from 1907 till her death. She played a leading role in the freedom struggle of India and was the President of the Indian National Congress in 1918. Her name is associated with the Home Rule Movement (Movement for Self Rule in India).

ANNIE BESANT'S CONTRIBUTION TO EDUCATIONAL THOUGHT AND PRACTICES

Publications

Among her important publications on education, mention may be made of the following:

Education as a National Duty (1903)
The Education of Indian Girls (1906)
Principles of Education (1915)
Education for the New Era (1914)
Theosophical Education Report (1917)

Many-Sided Education

Education according to her should make man a good citizen of free and spiritual commonwealth of humanity. She observed: "What do we find in modern India? An education directed to one part of the body's nature only developing the intelligence, training the intellect, but leaving entirely the spiritual nature and the moral or emotional nature... Such an education can never build up a true man of the world, able to discharge his duties in the world... What sort of nation can you have where the education given to its young is but one quarter what it should be?" Annie Besant describes the all round education in these words: "I look forward to a time when every child shall receive, in the national schools, the elements of a literary, scientific, artistic and technical education. No boy or girl should leave the school ignorant of our literature or of the wonders of science. He should delight in beauty. He should also learn some definite means of breadwinning, let it be tailoring, cookery or any trade or profession. Every pair of hands should be able to do at least some thing well by which an honest living may be earned".

Not Looking for West

Annie Besant wrote: "Let us not look to the West for power in our education. Let us cease to believe that education of the West is the ideal for the East. Far from it, for some parts of the body, we may well go to the West. But for the soul never—only with an education full of Indian unity, full of Indian simplicity, full of Indian purpose, that is of Indian life, can India be herself".

Scheme of Education

According to Annie Besant, following should be the scheme of national education.

1. Education during the first period from birth to seven should be chiefly physical. The body should be given a balanced nutrition in order to secure a healthy development.
2. The second period from seven to fourteen is chiefly emotional. Hence education during this period should be directed towards training and controlling of emotions.
3. Third period from 14-21 years is "the period of rapid intellectual development. Logic and mathematics should be taught intensively. The sense of duty to one's fellowmen should be taught through Civics and Social Studies. Literature, Philosophy and Economics should occupy an important place. Sciences such as Biology, Physiology and Psychology should be mastered. Various aspects of Arts should also be included in the curriculum.

Faith in the Old Gurukula System

She wrote: "Here is an Indian ideal that it would be well to revive. India must have a few representatives (of the ancient *Ashram*) if she is to rise to her former level in supreme intellectual and spiritual achievement". She laid a great stress on the ideal of *Brahmacharya* for a student.

Role of the Teacher

Annie Besant holds that a teacher has to be not only a friend of the body of the child but also of his soul. The teacher must respect the individuality of the child and must not force him into line with his own standard.

Promotion of Women's Education

Annie Besant did a pioneering work in women's education. She organised several groups to strive for the furtherance of girls' schools and colleges in many parts of India where facilities for girl's education did not exist.

Vocational Education

Dr. Besant was a strong advocate for vocational education. Specialisation in some chosen field should prepare the student for his future career in life.

Mother Tongue as the Medium of Instruction

She advocated the use of mother tongue as the medium of instruction. She said, "Nothing denationalises a people as the imposition upon them of a foreign tongue, dominating their life and thought".

Establishment of Educational Institutions and Organisations

She set up organisations like the 'Sons and Daughters of India', 'Scouts and Guides' for inculcating the spirit of selfless service. She formed several schools and colleges. The Central Hindu School and College (Benaras) was established by her in 1898. She launched a plan for the establishment of Benaras Hindu University. Pt. Madan Mohan Malaviya was also a moving figure behind this project.

5

Aristotle (384-322 B.C.)

Aristotle, an ancient Greek philosopher is regarded as one of the encyclopaedic writers in the entire range of the European thought. His ideas on ethics and politics are still considered as works studying. He is widely quoted by scholars in their writings. Aristotle was the disciple of Plato. He served as a tutor to Alexander of Macedonia.

Aristotle was the head of the Lyceum (a type of higher education institution). In the field of education, he had made a very valuable contribution.

Aristotle's scheme of education is to be found in the Seventh and Eighth Books (Chapters) of his monumental publication *Politics*. Aristotle considered education as a branch of political science or politics.

Philosophical Thought Regarding Life

According to Aristotle there can be three possible types of life:

1. The lowest type is the sensuous life—life of pleasures and gratification.
2. Higher than this is the life of the warrior and the politician. Aristotle considers this type of life praiseworthy if led among a community of freemen.
3. Aristotle criticises the despotic and tyrannical life which derives pleasure in subjugating people who do not deserve enslavement. He appreciates the political life among equals based on the principle of reciprocity.

Aristotle praises as the highest, the life of the self-sufficient philosophers contemplating eternal truth. "The life of the reason is the highest because reason is the essence of man and is divine in its nature".

Philosophy of Realism and Its Implications

Aristotle never considered man to be completely evil or wicked. He believed that in man there are elements of both self-love and social instinct. In case he is not trained in the art of just, decent and socialised existence then the beastly instincts dominate in him but if he gets training, then he can rise.

Aristotle divides the soul of man into two parts – the irrational and the rational. The irrational part is trained by the cultivation of moral virtues. Moral virtues are acquired by the repetition of the corresponding acts. Although these acts cannot be prescribed exactly, still they must avoid excess and defect. Thus, Aristotle was a great believer in the ethical mean or moderation (‘*Madhyam*’) way: The mean is difficult to achieve but can be grasped by perception.

According to Aristotle a completely happy man is he who acts in accordance with complete virtue and possesses physical prowess, technical competence, mental virtuosity and morality. He advocates the doctrine of golden mean which implies that a virtuous man would be neither super-normal nor sub-normal but justly and wisely normal. Thus his philosophy was of *realism*.

Aristotle follows a middle path in relation to the State and the citizen. His virtue is relative in the sense that the citizen has to act according to the canons of that particular constitution wherein the person is born and resides. But this does not imply, according to Aristotle, that the citizens should perform those actions in which oligarchs and democracies delight but that they should perform those actions by which the existence of an oligarchy or democracy is made possible.

Except for military training other branches of education should receive the maximum degree of autonomy from State interference. This aspect also conforms to *realism*. Aristotle observes that necessary, useful and profitable actions are also essential but they are not ends in themselves.

Aristotle wants the development of physical strength by gymnastic training but is opposed to mere athleticism acquired by the neglect of other virtues.

According to Aristotle, courage and endurance are needed for business and action, philosophy or wisdom for leisure, and temperance and justice are needed for both action and leisure.

MAIN FEATURES OF ARISTOTLE’S EDUCATIONAL PHILOSOPHY AND PRACTICES

Meaning and Aim of Education

According to Aristotle, education is the process of systematic training and instruction whereby the citizen may be enabled to realise the synthesis of the ideals of the best man and the best citizen. Aristotle states that the goods of the mind cannot be attained without an adequate supply of goods of the body. Thus education implies ‘creation of a sound mind in a sound body’.

Education, according to Aristotle is the art of acquiring happiness and not the pursuit of pleasure.

Aristotle, however, lays more emphasis on making an individual a good human being. “In the virtue of each, the virtue of all is involved”. In his book *Politics* Aristotle dealt with the individual rather than social aspect of education.

Three Stages in the Development of the Individual and Functions of Education

Aristotle points out the following three stages in the development of the individual:

1. The period of physical growth.
2. The period of irrational appetites or passions.
3. The period of reason.

Correspondingly education has three aspects:

(i) Education of the body, *i.e.*, physical development.
(ii) Education of character.
(iii) Education of the intellect.

Curriculum

In accordance with the three functions of education Aristotle prescribed the following curriculum:

(a) *Gymnastic and Drill* for the development of the body not to make brainless athlete but to ensure a sound bodily condition. He wrote in *Politics*: "It is grace and not brute strength that should count for most, for it is not the wolf or any of the lower animals that can engage in any fine and dangerous contest, but the good man".

(b) *Inculcation of good habits* without which the irrational soul of the child may be led astray by pleasures from wrong things. This implies training of character.

(c) *Music* for supplying occupation for leisure. According to Aristotle, "Music is able to modify the character of the soul".

(d) *Study of biology and natural history* followed by a study of metaphysics for the intellectual education of the young.

(e) *Art and literature, science and religion* for teaching the man business of war and peace, the useful and the fine.

Curriculum for Different Stages/Ages

1. First Seven Years: Stress on physical education.
2. Seven to Fourteen years: Reading and writing. Music etc.
3. Fourteen to Twenty One Years: Arithmetic, Biology and Geometry, Metaphysics, etc.
4. After Twenty Years of Age: Politics, Religion and Psychology for administrative work, war and peace.

Habit Formation

Aristotle attaches great importance to habits in the realisation of the moral nature of man and accordingly gives it a fundamental place in education. Habit is defined by him in his book *Metaphysics*: "Having a habit means a disposition to that which is either well disposed or ill disposed, and either in itself or with reference to something else, e.g., health is a habit, for it is such a disposition. We speak of a habit if there is a portion of such a disposition, and even the excellence of the parts is a habit of the whole thing".

Training in habit formation must come earlier than rational training. From the very early years Aristotle wants the children to be habituated to hard life.

Moral Education/Training

According to Aristotle, the main categories of moral virtues are courage, friendliness, justice, liberality, magnificence, magnanimity, temperance, and truthfulness. Aristotle would like to include ready wit as a moral virtue. He calls upon the educators to control the use and circulation of stories etc. in order that from the very childhood the future citizens may learn temperance. Temperance is a cardinal virtue in Aristotle's book *Ethics*. Aristotle states that moral training is not complete in itself. It is for the growth of intellectual enlightenment.

Significance of the Teaching-Learning of Music: Aristotle lists the following merits of music:

1. Music is a source of harmless pleasure.
2. Music provides recreation.
3. Music has a purgative influence – *Katharsis*.
4. Music is needed for forming character because it habituates the mind to the love of that which is good and noble.
5. Music provides intellectual enjoyment in leisure.

Aristotle is opposed to professional competence in music. He only wants an amateurish understanding of music. He is against passion-exciting music.

EVALUATION OF ARISTOTLE'S VIEWS

Aristotle was a realist; he observed what education is and emphasised that the way children ought to be instructed should be very clear to the instructors/teachers. Education would differ according to the nature of the State.

Aristotle's views on the teaching and training of moral virtues are quite relevant even today. He is fully justified in stressing 'habituation' for the practice of moral virtues.

Aristotle is mindful of the synthesis of knowledge and happiness.

Aristotle was a *realist* and his *realism* is manifest in his approach to life and educational ideas and practices. He fully took note of the prevailing scenario and accordingly formulated his scheme of education.

6

Aurobindo Ghose (1872-1950)

Aurobindo was born in an educated middle class family of Calcutta (Kolkata) in Bengal on August 15, 1872. At the age of 7, he went to England and lived there for 14 years. He received his education at Cambridge. Besides English, he mastered Latin and Greek and learnt French, German, Italian and Spanish.

Aurobindo was a very brilliant student. At the age of 18, he passed the entrance examination of the Indian Civil Service (ICS)—the most coveted service during the British rule. He, however, did not appear in the riding test. This was perhaps on account of his hatred for the foreign rule.

Literary and Cultural Activities: On his return to India in 1893, he joined service in the Princely State of Baroda (Vadodara). He became the Professor of English at Baroda College. He devoted himself to cultural and literary activities. He learnt Bengali, Gujarati, Marathi and Sanskrit. He drank deep in the culture and philosophy of India. He began yoga also.

Political Work—A Revolutionary: In response to the call of the Indian National Congress, he joined as the Principal of Bengal National College at Calcutta (now Jadavpur University). He became an active freedom fighter. He was disappointed with the moderate leaders of the Indian National Congress. He even justified an armed revolt against the British rule. He was considered one of the most dangerous leaders by the British Government.

He started the Bengali daily *Yugantar* and an English daily *Bande Mataram* to promote revolutionary ideas. He played a notable role against the Partition of Bengal (1905). He was arraigned in 1908 in connection with the Alipore Bomb case. He was acquitted after one year.

Freedom Fighter—Revolutionary Turned Philosopher and Seer: During one year in jail he spent most of his time in yoga, meditation and study of religious, philosophical and spiritual literature. It led to a transformation in his life. In 1910, he left his political activities and went to Pondicherry (a French settlement in India at that time) and spent the remaining forty years (1910-1950) at his Ashram at Pondicherry. He devoted himself to study, and writing. He advocated moral and spiritual regeneration. He propounded theories of education which catered to Indian needs. He set up an International Ashram and International Centre of Education at Pondicherry and started several educational and social activities. He also started a new experiment known as Aurovill as a city of human unity.

Important Publications on Education and Allied Subjects

1. *A System of National Education*
2. *Sri Aurobindo and the Mother on Education*
3. *The Human Cycle*
4. *Ideal of Human Unity*
5. *The Life Divine*
6. *Riddle of the World*
7. *The Savitri*
8. *Essays on Geeta*
9. *On the Vedas*
10. *Eight Upanishads*

Most Prominent Features of Philosophy

1. Everyone has in him something Divine.
2. The task is to find it, develop it and use it.
3. This Divine can be obtained by a spiritual discipline, called yoga.
4. Aurobindo's concept of yoga is not that of a *sanyasi* who turns away from life in order to turn towards God.
5. Yoga is for the ordinary man, while he carries on his worldly pursuits.
6. If a merchant wishes to follow *yoga,* he regards his work as Divine; he does not use unfair practices to earn money.
7. If a student, looks for higher values, he must observe *Brahmacharya* (self-control).

Main Ideas on Education

1. Aims of Education

1. According to Sri Aurobindo, "The chief aim of education should be to help the growing soul to draw out which is best and make it perfect for a noble cause"
2. The education should enable an individual to realise his inner self which is a part of the universal consciousness. The individual has to enter into right relationships not only within himself but also with the people of his country and with the universal society to which he belongs.

The human race is composed of people or nations and a nation is composed of individuals. The nations make the universal humanity.

2. Functions of Education

Following are the chief functions of education:

(i) To bring out the real man.

(ii) To build the powers of the human mind and spirit, *i.e.,* the evoking of knowledge, character and culture.
(iii) To enable the individual to establish a clear continuity between the past, present and the future.
(iv) To enable the individual to establish right relations with life.

3. Nature of the Child and Principles of Teaching

Shri Aurobindo attaches great importance to the divine gift inherent in the children. Accordingly, he has stated the following three principles of teaching:

The first principle of true teaching is that nothing can be taught. The teacher is not an instructor or task master, he is a helper and guide.

The teacher's work is to suggest and not to impose on the mind of the students. He does not actually train the mind of his student but helps him to perfect his mind and encourages him every way in this process. Thus he does not impart knowledge, but shows the way how knowledge can be acquired. Knowledge is within the pupil and the pupil has to help himself to bring it out, but he needs help. Somebody must tell him where it is and how it can be 'habituated to rise to the surface'. Teacher alone can do this work.

The second principle is that the mind has to be consulted in its growth. The idea of hammering the child into the shape desired by the parent or teacher is a barbarous and ignorant superstition. Sri Aurobindo wrote, "It is wrong and rather immoral to force adult will on the child. The divine in the child should not be ignored and mutilated. To force the nature of the child to abandon its own *Dharma* is to do permanent harm".

The third principle of teaching is to work from the near to the far, from the known to the unknown. Man's nature is moulded by his soul's past, his heredity and his environment. The past is the foundation, the present is the material and future is the aim and each must find its due and natural place in any national system of education.

4. Main Principles of Learning

(i) Concentration is the first principle of learning.
(ii) *Abhyasa* or steady natural practice is the second principle of learning.

5. Moral Education

This should be on the following methods:

(i) Personal examples of the teachers and elders.
(ii) Study of books having lofty examples.
(iii) *Satsanga i.e.,* good company.
(iv) Suggesting and not commanding and imposing.

6. Discipline

Chitta Shuddhi, i.e., purification of the mental and moral habits should be the basis of discipline. This means to discriminate between right and wrong impressions and to absorb right ones in the mind.

Sri Aurobindo advises teachers not to be arbitrary, despotic, impatient and ill tempered.

7. Physical Education

Perfection is the true aim of education and physical development is an integral part of perfection. Moreover without physical development, *Dharma* cannot be performed. Only a healthy body can contain a healthy mind. As the Sanskrit saying goes, *Shariram khalu dharmasadhanam* (the body is the means of fulfillment of *dharma*).

8. Curriculum

It should include the following;

(i) Physical development studies
(ii) Mental development studies
(iii) Cultural development studies
(iv) Vital sciences relating to preservation of body etc.
(v) Vocational development studies
(vi) International understanding programmes

9. Teacher—A Guide and Helper

Sri Aurobindo observes: "The teacher is not an instructor or task-master; he is a helper and guide. His business is to suggest and not to impose. He does not actually train the pupil's mind, he only shows him how to perfect his instruments of knowledge and helps and encourages him in the process. He does not impart knowledge to him; he shows him how to acquire knowledge for himself. He does not call forth the knowledge for himself. He does not call forth the knowledge that is within. He only shows him where it lies and how it can be habituated to rise to the surface"

National System of Education

Prevailing Defects in Education: Shri Aurobindo found the following defects in the prevailing system of education:

1. It was de-nationalising.
2. It was degrading.
3. It was impoverishing the mind; soul and character.
4. It was bad in kind.

Main Characteristics of the National System of Education: Aurobindo pointed out the following elements:

(i) Human and spiritual values are complementary and supplementary.
(ii) Education does not become national by tagging the word 'national' to the system.

(iii) Education should pay due attention to modern knowledge and scientific progress.
(iv) Mere knowledge of science does not make us educated in the true sense. This must be related to powers of the human mind and spirit.
(v) There should be a balanced understanding of the national and international relationships of universal humanity.

Contribution to Education

The Ashram School: The school was originally started in 1943 for the children of Sri Aurobindo's disciples. It expanded gradually from a Primary School to a full-fledged High School. There are resident as well as day-students.

The International Centre of Education: The objectives underlying the centre are:

1. To evolve a system of education for making it dynamic, ideal for society.
2. To organise an environment which may provide inspiration and facilities for the exercise and development of the five aspects of personality—the physical, the vital, the mental, the psychic and the spiritual.
3. To emphasise the unity of all knowledge.
4. To develop the sense of oneness of mankind.
5. To discover and prepare for the role India has to play in the formation of the new international harmony.

Select Quotes on Education

1. "To bring out the real man is the first business of education".
2. "The chief aim of education should be to help the growing soul to draw out which is best and make it perfect for a noble cause".
3. "The best method of moral education is by personal example, daily converse and the books read from day-to-day".
4. "Perfect liberty would be desirable for the child".
5. "The teacher is not an instructor or task master; he is a helper and guide".
6. "Indeed, if the education is to have its maximum result, it must begin even before birth".
7. "The true basis of education is the study of the human mind".
8. "The idea of hammering the child into the shape desired by the parent or teacher is a barbarous and ignorant superstition".
9. "The education of the intellect divorced from the perfection of the moral and emotional nature is injurious to human nature".

Integral Education

Meaning of Integral Education: According to Sri Aurobindo, integral education is that which helps to bring out to full advantage, makes ready for the full purpose of life and scope of all that is in the individual man, which at the same time helps him to enter into his right relation with life, mind and soul of the people to which he belongs and with the great total life, mind and soul of humanity of which he himself is a unit and his people or nation, a separate and yet inseparable member".

The human body, mind and intellect combine together to form a magnificent machine; we call it a machine for want of a better world but it is superior to any other equipment built by man. Education must integrate these elements to serve its real purpose.

Two-fold Bases of Integrated Education

1. Individuality is one whole.
2. Humanity is one. There are no inconsistencies in the East and the West.

1. Individuality is One Whole

(a) *Harmonious Development of Three Dimensions of Individuality*: Body, mind and soul have their significance when they are harmoniously developed as they constitute the whole individuality. Likewise individual's intellectual development must develop in relation to his moral, emotional and spiritual nature and vice versa. In other words integral education must develop all the dimensions of the individuality of the person. According to Sri Aurobindo, there should be a balanced and harmonious development of all the aspects of human personality—cognitive (knowledge), conative (skills) and affective (attitudes and values). An individual thus becomes an integrated individual.

(b) *Socio-economico-politico Integration:* Neither man has been regarded as a pre-eminently reasoning animal so that education should aim at developing only his mental capacities, nor has he been seen as an economic, political and social being only so that education should train him as a productive and disciplined member of the society. These, no doubt, are aspects and characteristics of human being but they do not define the whole of the real man. The real man is not only a bundle of selfish interests, nor alone an intellectual entity, nor merely a social being. He is something more. Beyond the physical and mental bounds there is spiritual existence. Sri Aurobindo said, "India has seen always in man the individual a soul, a portion of the divinity enwrapped in mind and body".

(c) *Different Aspects of the 'Self' but 'Self' is One:* Man is the conscious manifestation of the universal spirit. We may distinguish in man different aspects of his being, mental, intellectual, ethical, practical, aesthetic, physical and the like but all these have been as powers of a 'self' that manifests through them and yet they are not all the 'self'.

(d) *No Concentration on Academic Perfection Alone:* The study of mind is fundamental in education. Any system of education which concentrates on academic perfection of the child with disregard to his mind is destined to fail. It would rather hamper the intellectual growth than producing an integrated mind.

2. Oneness of Humanity

Sri Aurobindo immersed himself in *Vedanta* and *Yoga.* Instead of seeing conflict or finding inconsistencies between the East and the West, he evolved a synthesis of both. He also synthesised 'Spirit' and 'Matter', 'Science' and '*Vedanta*'.

3. Multiple Cells of One

Sri Aurobindo considers all forms in the universe as multiple cells of one consciousness and the *Yoga* as the means through which one may come into contact with the true 'self' and unite the separate parts of oneself and also can see the divine in others.

4. Inner as Well as Outer Realisation

Aurobindo says that we must aim not only at an inner realisation but an outer realisation also—the establishment of the Kingdom of God not only within the heart but also in the world of human affairs.

Task of Integral Education

What really is the task of integral education? Sri Aurobindo said that there are three things that education must take into account:

1. The man
2. The nation or people
3. Universal humanity.

Education must enable us to understand the interrelationship among these three.

Stages or Phases of Integral Education

According to Aurobindo, education to be integral must have the following aspects relating to the five principal activities of the human being:

1. The physical
2. The vital
3. The mental
4. The psychic
5. The spiritual

Sri Aurobindo stated that usually these stages or phases of education succeed each other in a chronological order following the growth of the individual. This, however, does not mean that one stage should replace another until another is complete but that all must continue, complementing each other till the end of life.

Five Stages or Phases of Integral Education

(1) Physical Education	(2) Vital Education	(3) Mental Education	(4) Psychic Education	(5) Spiritual Education

1. *Physical Stage of Education:* It includes:
(1) Total harmonious and integrated development of the body.
(2) Physical discipline, *i.e.,* control of various part of the body.
(3) Freedom from diseases.

2. *Vital Stage of Education:* The vital education has two elements:
(1) Development and utilisation of senses.
(2) Becoming conscious and gradually controlling them.
Thus vital education is very important in training senses.

3. *Psychic Stage of Education*: The word 'psychic' implies sensitiveness relating to non-material. Psychic education, therefore, implies education which includes development of non-material values. In the words of Mother, an outstanding disciple of Sri Aurobindo, "One thing is absolutely indispensable, the will to discover". Psychic is related to Yoga.

4. *Mental Stage of Education*: Mental education has the following aspects:
(1) Development of power of attention and concentration.
(2) Development of the capacity to expand mental horizon.
(3) Development of the capacity to enrich mental horizon.
(4) Development of the capacity to organise ideas around a central theme.
(5) Development of reasoning power so as to accept desirable thoughts and reject undesirable ones.
(6) Development of the power to accept or reject ideas coming from different quarters.
(7) Development of the power to get inspiration from the higher regions of the being.

5. *Spiritual Stage of Education*: This is the highest level of education. It is also called 'super-mental education'. This stage is reached after one develops physical, vital, mental and psychic elements. According to Mother, "It will, by its all powerful action, work not only upon the very substance of which they are built and upon the environment in which they live". This requires deep and intensive insight and persistent efforts. This leads to 'eternal bliss'.

Measures for Achieving the Ends of Integral Education

Following are the measures suggested by Sri Aurobindo:

1. *Role of the Teacher*: According to Aurobindo, "The teacher is not an instructor or task master; he is a helper and a guide. His business is to suggest".

2. *Principles of Education*: Sri Aurobindo enumerated the three principles:

a. The teacher's work is to suggest and not to impose principles on the minds of the students.
b. The second principle is that the child has to be consulted in the growth.
c. The third principle is to work from the near to the far.

3. *Discipline*: Aurobindo wrote, "If education is to bring out to full advantage all that is in the individual child, we should first generate a safe custody of all that is in the individual. The divinity in man is not to be insulted".

4. *Moral Training*:

a. It should be through personal example of the teacher,
b. '*Sadhna*' should be the basis of moral training,
c. It should be based on practical opportunities,
d. It should come through *Yoga*.

5. *Immense Faith in the Potentialities of the Child*: Teacher must have an immense faith in the capacity of the child.

6. *Physical Education*: Perfection or integral development is the true aim of all culture. Therefore, the physical part of it cannot be left aside. Sri Aurobindo refers to the old Sanskrit adage *Sariram Khalu Dharma – Sadhanam* – the body is the means of fulfilment of 'dharma'.

7. *Curriculum at the International Centre, Pondicherry*: It includes:

a. Psychic and spiritual studies.
b. Academic subjects
c. Physical and health education
d. Cultural activities like art, music, drama
e. Vocational training
f. Education for international understanding

8. *Basic Principles of Integral Teaching-Learning*: Integral teaching-learning process involves the following elements:

a. *Sense Training*: Sense training is developed through observation of natural phenomenon under the guidance of the teacher.
b. *Developing Power of Investigation*: Observation plays an important role in developing power of investigation.
c. *Training of Memory and Mind*: Training of memory and mind is done by equipping the students to note similarities and dissimilarities.
d. *Training in Making Judgements*: The above factors provide suitable training in making judgements.
e. *Training of Logical Faculty*: This depends upon:
   (i) Ascertaining correctness of facts.
   (ii) Collecting accurate data.
   (iii) Sifting facts by eliminating false elements.

6. *Training of Imagination*: Training of imagination depends upon the following three elements:

a. Forming correct images.
b. Developing power of creative thinking.
c. Training in appreciating the existence of truth, goodness and beauty of soul in all existing things.

7. *Training of Language*: This is done through appropriate methods of teaching and also through concrete things.

8. *Free Environment*: Sri Aurobindo has stressed the significance of free environment under the guidance of the teacher.

Summing up: To understand the concept of integral education as propounded by Sri Aurobindo, we must understand the interrelationship among the different elements within the man, the nation and the universal humanity. We must see the synthesis among these.

7

A.P.J. Abdul Kalam (1931-)

Thinking is the capital
Enterprise is the way
Hard work is the solution

—*A.P.J. Abdul Kalam*

An outstanding saint-scientist, prominent humanist philosopher and captivating author and orator. A.P.J. Abdul Kalam, son of a common boat-owner, has risen to the Office of the President of India by virtue of his extraordinary intellect, devotion to work and honesty and integrity in personal and public life. He has the unique distinction of receiving honorary doctorates from thirty universities and country's highest civil honour Bharat Ratna (1997) before becoming the President of India.

He received secondary education at the Schwartz School, a missionary institute in Ramanathapuram and B.Sc. degree from St. Joseph's College, Tiruchirapalli. Thereafter he studied Aeronautical Engineering at the Madras Institute of Technology (MIT), regarded as the crown jewel of technical education in South India at that time.

Abdul Kalam is responsible for the development of India's first Satellite Launch Vehicle, the SLV-III development and operationalisation of strategic missiles and their weaponisation and for building indigenous capability in critical technologies.

Abdul Kalam joined the Defence Research and Development Organisation (DRDO) in 1958 and in his forty-year career as a scientist, achieved many milestones. He later joined the ISRO (Indian Space Research Organisation) where he succeeded in putting the 35-kg Rohini-I Satellite on a low-earth orbit with the help of SLV-III (Satellite Launch Vehicle). After spending 19 fruitful years in ISRO, he returned to DRDO to head the country's Integrated Missile Development Programme, which culminated in the successful launch of the Agni and Prithvi missiles.

"Do things yourself. Do not indulge in shortcuts by importing equipment", thundered the great scientist after the famed Pokhran-2 nuclear blasts in 1998. A strong advocate of this philosophy, he distributed newspapers at a young age to help with household expenses.

He is perhaps the only educational philosopher who has interacted with nearly a lakh children in interactive 'Question-Answer Sessions'.

Here an attempt is made to provide the essence of his philosophy of life in brief and its impact on education. It is felt that a comprehensive account of his contribution to education is needed at the hands of a competent person.

Publications

1. *India 2020: A Vision for the New Millennium* with Y.S. Rajan.
2. *Wings of Fire: An Autobiography* with Arun Tiwari.
3. *Ignited Minds: Unleashing the power within India.*
4. *My journey.*
5. *Development in Fluid Mechanics and Space Technology.*
6. *Envisioning an Empowered Nation.*

PHILOSOPHY OF LIFE

Glory of God

"Each individual creature on this beautiful planet is created by God to fulfill a particular role. Whatever I have achieved in life is through His help, and an expression of His will. He showered His grace on me through some outstanding teachers and colleagues, and when I pay my tributes to these fine persons, I am merely praising His glory. All these rockets and missiles are His work through a small person called Kalam". (*Wings of Fire* pp. XVI)

Faith in God

"We have identified five areas to transform India – education and health care, agriculture, information and communication, infrastructure and critical technology. Along with these five, you need a sixth one – faith in God and developing people through spirituality. This is very important. We need to first generate a moral and spiritual atmosphere. We need people who live by laws of the scriptures and bear faith in God". (*Ignited Minds*, pp. 75)

Efficacy of Prayer

"One of the most important functions of prayer, I believe, is to act as a stimulus to creative ideas. Within the mind are all the resources required for successful living. Ideas are present in the consciousness, which when released give scope to grow and take shape, can lend to succeed events. God, our creator, has stored within our minds and personalities, great potential strength and ability. Prayer helps us to tap and develop these powers". (*Wings of Fire*, pp. 33)

Spiritual Wisdom

"Our spiritual wisdom has been our strength. We survived as a nation the onslaught of invaders and the numbing effects of colonisation. We have also learnt to adjust to the rifts and divisions in our society. But in the process of all the adjustment, we also lowered our aims and expectations. We must regain our broad outlook and draw upon our heritage and wisdom to enrich our lives. The fact that we advance technologically does not preclude spiritual development. We need to home-grow our model of development based on our inherent strengths". (*Ignited Minds*, pp. 99)

Vision of Developed India by 2020 or Even Earlier

"What does the developed nation status mean in terms of the common man. It means the major transformation of our national economy to make it one of the largest economies in the world; where the countrymen live well above the poverty line, their education and health is of high standard, national security reasonably assured, and the core competence in certain major areas gets enhanced significantly so that the production of quality goods, including exports, is rising and thereby bringing all round prosperity for the countrymen. What is the common link needed to realise these sub-goals? It is the technological strength of the nation which is the key to reach this developed status". (*India 2020*, p. 22)

Type of People Needed for a Developed India

Three types of people are needed — *punya atma* (virtuous people), *punya neta* (virtuous leaders) and *punya adhikari* (virtuous officers). If the people of the three types were to increase in our society, then India would become the Jagadguru (World leader). (*Ibid.*, p. 76)

Education and Spirituality

"Spirituality must be integrated with education. Self-realisation is the essence. Each one of us must become aware of our highest self. We are links of a great past to a grand future. We should ignite our dormant inner energy and let it guide our lives. The radiance of such minds embarked on constructive endeavour will bring peace, prosperity and bliss to this nation". (*Ignited Minds*, p. 20)

Need for Role Model for Children

"I have been asked during the course of meeting 40,000 high school students so far. (This relates to the year 2000. Since then he has met several thousand students more). The questions reflect the children's innocence, but most of all they show how strongly they feel the desire to live in a strong and prosperous nation. I realised from these sessions how important it is for them to have role models". (*Ibid.*, p. 20)

Role Model for Children: Meeting with Students in Tripura

"Whether we are aware of it or not, from childhood onwards, through various phases of life, we adopt role models. When you are growing up, say till the age of fifteen, the best role model I can think of would be your father, your mother and your school teacher. They, to my mind are the people who can impart the best guidance during this period". (*Ibid.*, p. 24)

Provision of First-Rate Education

"Kuppu and Karuppan in our book *India 2020 – Vision for the New Millennium* as mentioned earlier in my talk, represent about 60 per cent of India's population. These two have the urge and the willingness to work hard. But because of the lack of education they are unable to utilise the available opportunities for better employment or to improve their standard of living. People like Kuppu and Karuppan have to break out of their educational handicap. The lack of educational opportunities and their poor quality of life perpetuates their poverty."

"Educated parents will never like to have uneducated children as their future generation. Is it not true? Non-availability of preventive health care further weakens their bodies and, therefore, their capabilities. Can we break this vicious circle?"

"Prof. Indiresan, who led the TIFAC (Technology Information, Forecasting and Assessment Council) panel to identify the driving forces and impedances, has tried to point the way out. Indians should be provided access to first-rate education and skill. This cannot be done by the prevalent methods of village schools or other schools and institutions in towns and cities. We have to create clusters of villages with excellent internal connectivity through roads and communications which are linked to nearby urban centres. These rural clusters would have quality centres of education and health support facilities. People can easily commute between the villages and acquire the best skills and education. Their access to well-equipped health care centres will be the necessity. These centres would have the knowledge base to advise them on preventive health care methods. The teachers or medical personnel in these quality centres would also have access to other experts in India and even abroad through communication connectivity. Let us not forget India's excellent achievements in technological expertise; what is required is good political and managerial leadership all over the country to implement this mission. Let not the children and grandchildren or Kuppus and Karuppans be handicapped. We can achieve an India without such handicaps by 2020."

Who Can be the Role Models for the Young Generation?

"Mother, father and elementary school teachers play a very important part as role models. When the child grows the role models can be national leaders of quality and integrity in every field including politics, the sciences, technology and industry". (*Ignited Minds*, p. 39)

Student-Teacher Relationship

"The teacher, the child's window to learning and knowledge has to play the role model in generating creativity in the child... Education and the teacher-student relationship have to be seen not in business terms but with the nation's growth in mind." (*Ibid.*, p. 26)

Message to Children: Why Dream?

Meeting with students at St. Mary School, Dindigul in Tamil Nadu – Answer to a student of his question, "You always give a message to dream. Tell me why dream".

"Dream transforms into thoughts. Thoughts result in actions. Friends, if there are no dreams, there are no revolutionary thoughts, if there are no thoughts, no actions will emanate. Hence parents and teachers should allow their children to dream. Success always follows dreams attempted though there may be some setbacks and delays". (*Ibid.*, p. 28)

Education of the Unprivileged Children

He has a burning desire to provide suitable educational opportunities borne out from his writings. In *Wings of Fire*, (p. 166), he writes, "On October 15 (1991), I turned sixty. I looked forward to retirement and planned to open a school for the less privileged children. My friend, Prof. P. Rama Rao, who was heading the Department of Science and Technology in the government of India, even struck up partnership with me to establish what he called the Rao-Kalam School. We were unanimous in our opinion that carrying out certain missions and reaching certain milestones, however, important they may be or however impressive they might appear to be, is not all there to life. But we had to postpone our plan as neither of us was relieved from our post by the Government of India".

Need for Ignited Youth Minds: Need of the Hour

"A developed India, by 2020 or even earlier is not a dream. It need not even be a mere aspiration in the minds of many Indians. It is a mission we can all take up – and accomplish.

Ignited youth minds, we feel, are a powerful resource. This resource is mightier than any resource on the earth, in the sky and under the sea. We must all work together to transform our 'developing India' into a 'developed India' and the revolution required for this effort must start in our minds". *India 2020: A New Vision for the New Millennium*

Clarion Call to the Youth to Remember

A.P.J. Abdul Kalam has an abiding faith in the young. He exhorts them with these words: "... However underprivileged or small, need not feel disheartened about life. Problems are part of life. Suffering is the essence of success. As someone said –

God has not promised
Skies always blue,
Flower-strewn pathways

All our lives through;
God has not promised
Sun without rain,
Joy without sorrow
Peace without pain.
But God has promised
Strength for the day,
Rest for the labour
Light, for the way.
(*Wings on Fire*, pp. 67)

Three Visions of Dr. A.P.J. Abdul Kalam

'I have three visions for India. In 3000 years of our history, people from all over the world have come and invaded us, captured our lands, conquered our minds. From Alexander onwards, the Greeks, the Portuguese, the British, the French, the Dutch, all of them came and looted us, took over what was ours. Yet we have not done this to any other nation. We have not conquered anyone. We have not grabbed their land, their culture, their history and tried to enforce our way of life on them. Why? Because we respect the freedom of others. That is why my first vision is that of FREEDOM. I believe that India got its first vision of this in 1857, when we started the war of independence. It is this freedom that we must protect and nurture and build on. If we are not free, no one will respect us.'

'My second vision for India is DEVELOPMENT. For fifty years we have been a developing nation. It is time we see ourselves as a developed nation. We are among top 5 nations of the world in terms of GDP. We have 10 per cent growth rate in most areas. Our poverty levels are falling, our achievements are being globally recognised today. Yet we lack the self-confidence to see ourselves as a developed nation, self-reliant and self assured. Isn't this right?'

'I have a third vision. India must stand up to the world. Because I believe that unless India stands up to the world, no one will respect us. Only strength respects strength. We must be strong not only as a military power but also as an economic power. Both must go hand-in-hand.' (*source*: Website)

Inspiring Quotes

- Children are our precious wealth
- We will give equal importance to male and female children in providing education and rights for growth of our society.
- Earnings come out of hard work. We will not waste it in gambling and liquor. We will become the role models for our children.
- We need to tell our children about the importance of education as learning gives knowledge and knowledge makes the children succeed.

- We need to jointly protect our forests and prevent pollution.
- We will plant at least five trees/saplings.

Inspiring Poetic Quotes

Beautiful hands are those that do
Work that is earnest and brave and true
Moment by moment
The long day through.
(*Wings of Fire*, p. 73)

If you want to leave your footprints
On the sands of time
Do not drag your feet.
(*Ibid.*, p. 76)

Do not look at Agni
as an entity directed upward
to deter the ominous
or exhibit your might.
It is fire
in the heart of an Indian.
Do not even give it
the form of a missile
as it clings to the
burning pride of this nation
and this is bright.
(*Ibid.*, p. 152)

(Wrote in his diary at the launching of Agni on May 22, 1989.)

Prayer

"Almighty, create thoughts and actions in the minds of the people of my nation so that they live united.

Help all religious leaders of my country, give strength to the people to combat the forces of division.

Embed the thought 'Nation is bigger than the individual' in the minds of the leaders and people.

O God bless my people to work and transform the country into a prosperous, nation soon". (*Ignited Minds*, p. 195)

8

B.R. Ambedkar[1]

Few Indians in the 20th Century had deliberately chosen to get educated in an open society like the USA. One among these was Dr. B.R. Ambedkar and the other prominent figure was Jayaprakash Narayan. Though both the leaders differ in their struggles and outlook, but there was a common bondage that could put them together. It was their strong belief in democracy. United States of America at that time was trumpeted as the symbol of liberty and therefore, democracy. There was also a reason for this. One of the prominent advocates of democracy and a great pragmatist was teaching in Columbia University and spreading the message of democracy through his disciples. It was John Dewey a great educationist and a democrat. This has perhaps, attracted the attention of Ambedkar and he chose to study in Columbia University. In fact, the formative years of Ambedkar were shaped by the academic atmosphere in Columbia and particularly the lectures of John Dewey. We will find in the writings of Ambedkar quoting regularly John Dewey in support of his arguments. Ambedkar got his P.G and Ph.D degrees from Columbia which is even today considered to be one of the liberal campuses in the USA.

PROMOTER OF EDUCATION

Scholars have written elaborately about the contributions of Ambedkar to Philosophy, Sociology, Religion among other fields. But there are very few attempts by scholars to project him as a great educationist. In fact, more than half of his life was spent in educational institutions. Even while he was in the thick of politics he took interest in the educational programmes of dalits. Out of 65 years of his personal life, he spent around 40 years as student, scholar, teacher and promoter of education. Therefore, it is necessary to understand and alanyse his contributions to the development of education in India in general and to the educational upliftment of weaker sections in particular. In the formulation of special provisions for scheduled castes and other backward classes in the Constitution, Ambedkar seems to have consciously chosen the concept of "educationally and socially backward classes". He knew that those who were considered as backward or

1. Prof. K.S. Chalam, Former Vice-chancellor, Dravidian University, A.P.

uncivilized at that time were the ones who were denied education. Therefore, Ambedkar had been assiduously fighting for the educational rights not only of dalits, but for the illiterate and ignorant masses of the country. It is unfortunate that experts in education in India seldom recognize his contributions.

EDUCATIONAL PHILOSOPHY

As far as the educational philosophy of Ambedkar is concerned, it was totally influenced by John Dewey, who was a great pragmatist and a signatory to the Humanist Manifesto. Dewey was arguing that education was not a preparation for life, it was life itself. He has popularized the democratic concept of education both in theory and padagozical practice. His educational philosophy was also adopted in communist Russia at that time. Naturally, Ambedkar turned out to become a great pragmatist and wanted that the dalits should get opportunities of education in practical fields that bring them a vocation. He thought that an untouchable could reach or would become a part of civil society only through education. As the dalits were poor and landless, there was no alternative except to enter into an organized public sector to sustain. Therefore, he has encouraged dalits to get formal education. In fact, he had created special scholarships for dalits to go abroad and study during his tenure as member of the Governor General's Council.

Ambedkar was a popular teacher. We can find his teaching notes printed as part of his writings by the Government of Maharashtra. The notes are prepared in such a meticulous way that any student can understand the English constitution by reading this without going to the originals. It seems students of other disciplines used to attend his classes to hear his eloquent lectures at Sydenham College and Government Law College, Bombay. Ambedkar worked as a professor of political economy at Sydenham College of Commerce and Economics and also at the Government Law College, Bombay. It was in Govt. Law College, he was made Principal of the College. His productive life in academics and politics started from Government Law College. He has developed his skills and abilities of presentation and eloquence as a teacher that have influenced his debates in the Constituent Assembly which were considered as vociferous and well articulated. He started the People's Education Society in 1944 and within 2 years he has established the Siddharth College of Arts and Science. The title of his educational society amply proves that he has ushered in a Peoples' education movement for the first time in India. The establishment of the Milind College at Aurangabad has resulted in the development of several other educational institutions in the backward region of Marthwada. He brought Dr.Rajendra Prasad, the President of India to lay the foundation stone for the College.

ROLE IN POLICY FORMULATION ON EDUCATION

Even from the beginning of his political career, he was interested in education. In the Bombay Presidency debates of 1927 and 1928 he has raised several issues relating to education which became important for policy formulations on education. In his memorandum to the Simon Commission on "concerning the State of Education of the Depressed Classes in Bombay Presidency" submitted on behalf of the *Bahish Krita Hita Karini Sabha*, he gave numerical data to bring out the miserable condition of the untouchables in the education sector. He has pointed out that enrolment of the dalits constitute 0.87% of the total primary education and 0.14% in Secondary and zero in higher education. Therefore, he wanted protection for the dalits through education guarantee by making the education of the depressed classes as the first charge on the State Revenue. He has also brought out the practice of untouchability in municipal schools of Bombay where separate lotas were given to dalit boys. This he said, made them to drop out from schools. This is a great economic wastage. He is perhaps one of the first economists in the world who had realized the economic importance of education. In his debates in the Assembly and Parliament, one can find the tenor of his argument in favour of subsidies for education in general and for the weaker sections in particular. He was arguing in the Bombay Presidency Legislative debates in 1927 as follows "We should at least spend on education the same amount that we take from the people in the form of excise revenue. The amount of expenditure that we incur per individual in this Presidency on education is only 14 annas, but the amount of money that we recover in the form of excise revenue is Rs.2-2-9 (Rs.2.17). I think it is only fair that our educational expenditure should be so adjusted that we should spend on the education of the People as much as we taken from them in the form of excise". He has also calculated the fees income at different levels and argued that it financed 36% of expenditure in collegiate education, 31% high school and 26% middle school education. Higher education should be made cheaper so that lower classes (not necessarily low castes) can enter higher education and benefit from the opportunities it creates. He had lamented that educational institutes were running on commercial lines during the British Raj. His words are prophetic that today higher education became a business that does not recognize 'merit', but only money power.

He was also emphatic in his arguments about the devolution of functions between college and university. He was not at all favourable for professorial positions who did not bother to teach and benefit under graduates. He gave written evidence before the University Reforms Committee wherein he had elaborately discussed the objects of higher education which are still relevant. He has also argued in favour of more powers for the University Syndicate and also delineated the functions in his debates on Bombay University in the Bombay Assembly.

PEOPLE'S EDUCATION MOVEMENT FOR THE POOR

Ambedkar was found to be a thorough academic in his approach to problems with practical insights. He has a total understanding of education starting from primary to University level. He has expressed his scholarly vision on research. He spent most of his life for the development of education and even after retirement from active political life, he took interest in the development of educational institutions. He is the first among many Indians who had initiated a Peoples' education movement for the poor in India.

9

Bal Gangadhar Tilak (1856-1920)

B.G. Tilak was one of the most prominent freedom fighters and the author of the statement '*Swaraj* is my birth right and I shall have it'. He waged a fierce struggle against the British imperialism with his 'pen', 'press' and 'platform'. However, his work in the field of education has generally been ignored. Professor V.P. Varma in his publication *Studies in the Philosophy of Education* (1964) has highlighted the contribution of B.G. Tilak in one of his articles entitled *Educational Ideas and Activities of Lokmanya Tilak.* This chapter is based on this article.

CONTRIBUTION OF TILAK TO EDUCATION

The Poona New English School

On January 2, 1880, the Poona New English School was established primarily with the efforts of Vishnu Shastri Chiploonkar (1850-82), B.G. Tilak and Agarkar.

The governing principle was to be self-abnegation, so much associated with educational institutions run by Jesuits; Tilak and Agarkar wanted to be 'Indian Jesuits'. A large number of scholars including V.S. Apte who acquired great fame as a profound Sanskrit scholar joined the school and left an example in self-abnegation by not accepting any salary from the school in the first year of its establishment.

As a teacher, Tilak inspired awe and admiration. The student had confidence in his erudition.

The Poona New English School became very popular in Maharashtra. Dr. Hunter, the President of the Education Commission (1882), popularly known as Hunter Commission, wrote about the school: "Throughout the whole of India, I have not witnessed a single institution which can be compared with this establishment. This institution can rival and compete with success not only with government high schools in the country, but may favourably compare with schools of other countries also.

The most important factor of success of the school was that a band of scholarly and enthusiastic young men were ready to undergo personal sacrifice for the sake of realising this noble mission of spreading education amongst their countrymen.

Philosophy of the School

The New English School was inspired by a new philosophy which was different from the professions and practices of the important educational institutions of the day. Tilak's ideal was two-fold. Along with Chiploonkar and Agarkar, he thought it essential that education had to be cheapened and teachers had to recover some of that old idealism which had been prevalent in the ancient history of this country. The great teachers and preceptors of the *Vedic* and *Upanishadic* periods were renowned not for opulence and mundane prosperity but for scholarship, integrity and devotion to duty. The re-incorporation of that old ideal in modern educational institutions was essential for the regeneration of the motherland. Tilak's second ideal was to spread education—"Education for the masses".

Value of English Education

Tilak recognised that English education had to make contribution to the growth of the Indian body politics. Even during the Home Rule Movement (1916-1918), when he toured the country as the mighty prophet of *Swaraj*, he was candid enough to confess that English system of education had been a factor for political enlightenment in the country. In 1884, Gopal Krishna Gokhale joined the Poona New English School.

For about a decade, since the beginning of his public career, Tilak worked as a school teacher and a college professor.

The Deccan Education Society and the Fergusson College: Tilak as a Professor

Tilak played a leading role in the foundation of the Deccan Education Society which was formally established in 1884.

Gopal Krishna Gokhale whom Gandhiji regarded as his political *guru* also became a member of the Deccan Education Society.

The Deccan Education Society placed before its members ideals of noble self-sacrifice. The society managed several educational institutions but of its two most important creations are the Fergusson College at Poona and Willington College at Sangli.

Tilak taught mathematics at the Fergusson College. Like Swami Ram Tiratha, he had the reputation, since his student days, of being able to solve mathematical problems which would prove difficult even for the professors. Occasionally, Tilak also used to teach Sanskrit at the Fergusson College.

National Education During the Swadeshi Period

During 1907-1908, Tilak advocated the vitalising of the educational programme by incorporating into it sentiments of strength, political rights, nationalist fervour and industrial training. Under the guidance and patronage of Tilak, *Shri Samarth Vidyalaya* was established at Talegaon (Maharashtra). The *Vidyalaya* under the name of the great preceptor of

Shivaji—the hero-saint Shri Samarth Ramdas did pioneer work in the field of national education. But in 1910, it was suppressed by the Government. Tilak did not want the students to give up their educational institutions but he insisted that because the holy work of national emancipation had been set on foot, hence it was necessary that the enthusiasm of youth should also be consecrated to the service of the motherland.

Tilak delivered several speeches on national education in different parts of Maharashtra.

Tilak condemned the existing system of English education because it sadly neglected religious education. He wrote, "After twenty years rotting in this system, one has to look elsewhere for religious study. Men who develop the idea that religion is a farce all along their educational course are afterwards found to be wanting in any conception of Duty". He has further observed, "Secular education only is not enough to build up character. Religious education is necessary because the study of high principles keep us away from evil pursuits. Religion reveals us the form of Almighty. Says our religion that a man by virtue of his action can even become a God. When we can become gods, even by virtue of our action, why we may not become wise and active by means of our action like the Europeans? Some say religion begets quarrel. But I ask, where is it written in religion to pick up quarrels?"

10

Bertrand Russell (1872-1970)

Bertrand Russell of the U.K., was one of the most creative minds of the 20th century. His researches and insights have made valuable contribution not only to the fields of mathematical logic, epistemology, history, political philosophy but also the realm of education. He wrote two important books and several papers and articles on educational theory. He ran in cooperation with his wife a coeducational school for five years.

Russell lost his parents at the age of 3 and was brought up by his grand parents. He was educated at Trinity College, Cambridge and later on worked as Professor in this institution. He published his first book *Principles of Mathematics* in 1903.

In recognition of his scholarship and outstanding works, he was awarded Nobel Prize for literature in 1950.

Publications

Russell's important works are as under:

1. *Principles of Mathematics* (1903)
2. *Principles of Social Reconstruction* (1916)
3. *Introduction to Mathematical Philosophy* (1920)
4. *The ABC of Atoms* (1923)
5. *The ABC of Relatively* (1925)
6. *The Analysis of Matter* (1926)
7. *On Education* (1926)
8. *The Outlines of Philosophy* (1928)
9. *Sceptical Essays* (1928)
10. *Marriage and Morales* (1929)
11. *The Conquest of Happiness* (1930)
12. *The Scientific Outlook* (1931)
13. *Education and the Social Order* (1932)
14. *Freedom and Organisation 1814 to 1914* (1934)
15. *Power: A New Social Analysis* (1939)
16. *An Enquiry into Meaning of Truth* (1940)
17. *A History of Western Philosophy* (1946)
18. *Human Knowledge, Its Scope and Limits* (1948)
19. *Authority and Individual* (1949)

20. *New Hopes for a Changing World* (1951)
21. *The Impact of Science on Society* (1952)

Basic Ideas of the Philosophy of Russell

1. He emphasised the creative aspect of man.
2. He was of the view that the creative instinct of man, if properly developed can bring about the desired satisfaction.
3. He believed in reasoning and wanted to test all existing beliefs on the basis of logic.
4. He was against atomic weapons. He raised his voice against war during First World War (1914-1919) for which he was imprisoned for six months.
5. He was an ardent supporter of human welfare.

Logical Atomism

Russell's philosophy has been called 'Logical Atomism'.

Russell observed, "The reason I call my doctrine logical atomism is because the atoms that I wish to arrive at as the sort of last residue in analysis are logical atoms and not physical atoms". From educational point of view this philosophy of logical atomism is not quite helpful in planning and implementing instructional programmes.

Russell was an eminent mathematician and he developed his theory as a consequence of his deep and penetrating studies in the philosophy of mathematics. In logical analysis, the objects of analysis are concepts and propositions whereas in psychological analysis, we analyse memories, thoughts, emotions and other psychological processes. The main object of logical analysis is to discover the fundamental elements of the universe and from this it follows that logical atomist philosophy postulates the reality of the universe.

Views on Education

1. *Meaning of Education*: In *Education and Social Order*, Russell wrote, "Education is the process of the perfection of the human being". In *Mysticism and Logic*, he observed, "Education is not only the process of the transmission of external information but it aims at the broad cultivation of the mind leading to an awareness of man's place and destiny in the society and the universe".

2. *Aims of Education.* Russell has pointed out the following aims of education:

(1) Education should aid in the acquisition of skills necessary for the provision of the techniques, goods and services which help in making life comfortable.

(2) Science is mainly utilitarian in aim but education has to transcend a merely utilitarian conception. It has to provide for the wise use of

leisure by proper cultural growth. Science can be also an element in culture.

(3) Education should aim not only at individual growth but also at the cultivation of the sense of citizenship.

(4) The sense of citizenship should not remain confined merely to the bonds of social coherence in the nation-state but must also teach loyalty to the world government.

3. *Education of the Citizen*: Russell writes, "The education of the individual is to my mind a finer thing than the education of the citizen; but considered politically in relation to the needs of the time, the education of the citizen must ... take the first place".

4. *Psychological Foundations of Education*: Russell insists that only an education in consonance with the conclusions of modern psychology can eliminate anti-social element. Such an education will produce a generation of children who have been trained in the atmosphere of fearless freedom. Education, properly given, can produce a population free from disease and stupidity.

According to Russell, human desires are the product of three factors: (i) Native disposition, (ii) Present circumstances and (iii) Education. It is possible by means of education to change the desires of men so that they may, in future begin to act spontaneously for the realisation of social good.

5. *Character building*: This means the inculcation of the following qualities:

(i) *Vitality*: Vitality increases happiness and develops the capacity of hard work. It depends on physical and mental health. So the school should provide all opportunities for the development of vitality.

(ii) *Courage*: A courageous person does not run away from fearful situations. Of course, in normal situation, as well as fearful situation, he applies his intelligence and resourcefulness. So the teacher must develop elements of courage in his students through education.

(iii) *Sensitiveness*: It is in the nature of children that they take particular interest in praise and hate contempt. Sympathy makes the outlook of the children wider and helps in developing desirable qualities. The teachers should develop this quality.

(iv) *Intelligence*: Intelligence according to Russell is a power which is developed on account of the instinct of curiosity. Thus education should promote curiosity in the children.

Russell points out that training in character should begin even in the first year of the child. A policy of delicate balance between neglect and indulgence should be followed with regard to the infant.

According to Russell, if conducted on right lines, training in character should be complete by the age of six.

6. *Intellectual Virtues*: The techniques of obtaining knowledge are called by Russell 'Intellectual Virtues'. These intellectual virtues include curiosity and open-mindedness which act as antidotes to dogmatism and orthodoxy which stifle the quest for knowledge. He has also emphasised that without patience and industry no intellectual victory can be achieved. Hence these are also included in intellectual virtues. Exactness or the sense of accuracy is also desirable. According to Russell, there are four forms of accuracy—muscular, factual, aesthetic and logical. The sixth intellectual virtue is concentration.

Thus Russell pointed out the following six intellectual virtues:

(i) Curiosity
(ii) Open-mindedness
(iii) Patience
(iv) Industry
(v) Exactness
(vi) Concentration

7. *Principles of Teaching-Learning*: Russell laid stress on the following principles of teaching-learning:

(i) Principle of satisfaction of the curiosity of the child.
(ii) Principle of enquiry.
(iii) Principle of freedom.
(iv) Principle of knowing the child.
(v) Principle of patience.

8. *Concept of Discipline and Freedom*: Russell explained the case for the greatest freedom in a school in *Education and Social Order* as "I found one day in school a boy of medium size ill-treating a small boy". I expostulated (reasoned) but he replied, "The bigs hit me, so I hit the babies". That's fair".

He further wrote, "Children who are forced to eat acquire a loathing for food and children who are forced to learn acquire a loathing for knowledge".

Russell strongly advocates freedom for the child. He states, "The fundamental idea is simple, that the right discipline consists not in external compulsion, but in habits of mind which lead spontaneously to desirable rather than undesirable activities".

Bertrand Russell has explained the harmful consequences of restrictions on children in these words, "The man whose tongue is constricted by laws or taboos against free speech, whose laws are constricted by an ethic which considers jealousy a better thing than affection, whose childhood has been imprisoned in a code of manners, and whose youth has been drilled in cruel orthodoxy, will feel against the world that hampers him with the same rage that is felt by an infant whose arms and legs are held motionless. In this rage he will turn to destruction becoming a revolutionary militarist or persecuting moralist according to temperament and opportunity".

In the words of Russell: "Punishment has a certain very minor place in education, but I doubt whether it need ever be severe".

"When a child persistently interferes with other children or spoils their pleasures, the obvious penalty is banishment".

9. *Love for Children*: Russell has aptly remarked, "Knowledge wielded by love is what the educator needs and what his pupils should require".

Again Russell emphasises love, "The way is clear. Do we love our children enough to take it? Or shall we let them suffer as we have suffered? Shall we let them be twisted and stunted and terrified in youth to be killed afterwards in futile wars which their intelligence was too cowed to prevent? A thousand fears obstruct the road to happiness and freedom. But love can conquer fear, and if we love our children nothing can make us withhold the great gift which it is in our power to bestow".

10. *Three Divisions of Specialisation*: Russell has made the following three broad divisions for specialisation in school.

a. Classics
b. Mathematics and Science
c. Modern Humanities which include modern language, history and literature.

11. *Reconciliation of Individuality and Citizenship*: Russell has challenged the preventions of the organised state in the name of the individual dignity. He is emphatic in pointing out the inadequacies of citizenship as the ideal for education. Russell has pointed out the defects of the educational practices of Japan, of the English and American public schools for their lauding the ideal of citizenship and exalting patriotic fervour. Russell pleads for the reconciliation of the idea of national and world citizenship. In fact he pleaded for a world government for the elimination of wars.

12. *Criticism of Public Schools*: Russell was fundamentally hostile to aristocracy and as such he criticised British Public Schools because they had a very strong oligarchical and aristocratic bias. Russell was also critical as these public schools acted as the production-factories for agents and managers of colonial imperialism.

13. *Education and Religion*: Russell regards church as an infamous thing. He asserted that church was opposed to the extension of literacy because it flourished upon ignorance. Russell regarded religion as a conservative force. Russell opposed religious education as it was not in conformity with scientific knowledge. Religious education tended to instill hypocrisy.

14. *No control of Education by the State*: Russell is opposed to state control of education because one of the purposes of the state, in education, is to produce citizens "who will be convenient" for the state. Russell criticised the system of education in Soviet Russia as it was not oriented to

pure intellectual academicism. Knowledge was not the basic goal of the Soviet System of Education.

15. *Role of the Teacher*: Russell states, "It should be the business of the teachers to stand outside the strife of parties and endeavour to instill into the young the habit of impartial enquiry, leading them to judge issue on their merits and to be on their guard against accepting '*ex-parte*' statements at their face value". According to Russell, "The teacher should not be expected to flatter or prejudice either of the mob or of the officials".

16. *Genuine Culture*: Russell writes, "Genuine culture consists in being a citizen of the universe, not only of one or two arbitrary fragments of space and time. It helps men to understand human society as a whole, to estimate wisely the ends that communities should pursue, and to see the present in its relation to past and future. Genuine culture is of great value to those who are to wield power".

Beacon Hill School

It was largely as a result of studying the problems of educating their own children that the Russell decided to start a school on novel and very 'modern' lines. The school was opened at Beacon Hill, near Petersfield, in 1927, with Bertrand Russell as headmaster, Dora Russell as headmistress and about twenty boys and girls between 4 and 11, including their children, as pupils.

The children at Beacon Hill were taught games, but not football, cricket or hockey. All questions they chose to ask were freely and frankly answered. Russell disapproved of punishment, and opposed corporal punishment under any circumstances. "Every time a child is slapped, a complicated turmoil of conflicting passions is aroused". The children were allowed to be rude if they wished, to go where they liked and read what they liked.

But Bertrand Russell has never believed that young children should be left entirely uncontrolled; on the contrary, he considers that they should be encouraged early to realise that they have duties to others and to society, and that learning what is necessary to enable them to play their part in the world is one of these duties. "Some departure from complete liberty is unavoidable if children are to be taught anything". Hence lessons were compulsory at Beacon Hill and so were certain other observances such as cleanliness, punctuality, respect for other people's property, and enough daily routine to give a child a feeling of security.

Russell's Scheme of Education

Stages of Education and Instruction at Each Stage

1.	Nursery Stage/Nursery School	–	Below 5 years of age
2.	Elementary Stage	–	Between 6 to 14 years of age

3. Secondary/Senior Secondary Stage – Between 14 to 18 years of age
4. University Stage – Above 18 years of age

(a) *Nursery School*: Russell strongly advocated nursery education for the children of rich as well as poor families, city and village.

According to Russell, the main function of nursery education is to develop healthy habits in children. The teacher should have a knowledge of psychology and medical science.

(b) *Education at the Elementary Stage (6 to 14 years of age)*: Important suggestions given by Russell are:

One. General education for 8 years.

Two. Reading, writing, dancing, singing, dancing and painting during the first 5 years.

Three. Subjects requiring mental powers to be taught after the age of 7 years.

Four. Science and mathematics to be taught after the age of 12.

Five. Classical language to be taught between 12 and 14 years of age.

(c) *Education at the Secondary and Senior Secondary Stage*: Russell considered education at this stage as a sort of specialisation. He advocates that this stage of education should be for the intelligent children only. He divides curriculum into three groups: (1) Classical Languages, (2) Mathematics and Science, (3) Modern Humanities.

Russell advocates a pleasing environment, full of activities so that children remain active participants in the teaching-learning environment.

(d) *University Education*: Russell wanted to restrict university for those who are really talented and have keen desire to pursue higher education. He advocated admission tests for entrance into higher education. According to Russell, University education has two aims.

1. Preparing men and women for various vocations.
2. Expanding knowledge and research.

Day Schools and Boarding Schools

Russell was an ardent supporter of day schools and boarding schools.

Contribution to Education

1. The most important contribution of Russell as an educational philosopher is his fundamental stress on freedom in education. The concept of freedom championed by Russell is the key to educational progress and advancement.

2. Russell has advocated a profound faith in the transforming power of education. Education according to him, if properly conducted can produce a generation of human beings who have health, generosity, vigour and joy. This hope and faith in the regenerative power of education is immensely satisfying.

3. The quest of Russell for a firm and robust moral character through education may be regarded as his third important contribution to educational thought.

Evaluation of Russell's Contribution to Education

Prof. V.P. Verma in his book *Studies in the Philosophy of Education* has observed that Russell "is important in the history of educational thought because he has had the boldness—although sometimes this boldness has been mistaken specially with regard to problems of religion and sex—to challenge established conventions. He has successfully played the role of a critic. He has made an active and energetic proposal from the intellectual standpoint. This is a very great service to democratic community... His life as well as his writings are inspiration to educationists".

Russell's most important contribution to the field of education has been his plea for the recognition of the rights of the individual. The process of education can benefit from his thought provoking arguments on the need for freedom in education, his concept of an ideal teacher and his emphasis on the concept that education begins from birth.

Russell's view on the concept of freedom and discipline are quite progressive. His advocacy for nursery education is quite justified. As regards higher education, he overemphasises research aspect. His views on restricted higher education based on entrance are quite pragmatic.

11

Confucius (551-479 B.C.)

Confucius was ancient China's eminent teacher, philosopher and political theorist. His practical experience and deep thinking have left their mark on educational development in China and other countries.

Confucius' father, a minor official, died when he was still a child. From a low-grade post of looking after livestock and granaries, he rose through the administrative hierarchy to the post of Minister of Security and Justice for the principality of Lu in one of China's provinces. He spent his final years in writing and teaching.

Role and Objective of Education

Confucius considered that the goal of education was to produce capable individuals whom he called gentlemen or men of quality who combined competence with virtue and whose subsequent careers in administration and government would bring about the ideal of a kingdom managed with integrity.

Education Process

The Great Learning, one of the oldest educational treatises written about 2,500 years ago is attributed to Confucius. In this, Confucius sets out the education process in these words: "The Great Learning consists in manifesting the clear character, loving the people and abiding in the highest good... Those who wished to make their wills sincere would first extend their knowledge. The extension of knowledge consists in the investigation of things. When things are investigated, knowledge is extended. When knowledge is extended, the will becomes sincere; when the will is sincere, the mind is rectified; when the mind is rectified, the personal life is cultivated; when the personal life is cultivated, the family is regulated; when the family is regulated, the state will be in order; and when the state is in order, there will be peace...".

Moral Instruction

Confucius gave a place of pride to moral instruction since what was needed were individuals of outstanding virtue who would assist the rulers in governing with integrity. His ethics, philosophy and politics were inseparable. Virtues emphasised were: filial piety, diligence, altruism, affability, kindness, frugality, tolerance, indulgence, wisdom and courage, power of distinguishing what is to be cultivated and what is to be eschewed and above all honest and righteous conduct. According to Confucius all these qualities stem from *'ren'* (humanity or benevolence)

Intellectual Development: Curriculum

Moral instruction did not mean that education should ignore intellectual development of the students. Confucius drafted six manuals for instilling in students the moral values of a feudal society, the basis of an all round culture and the capacities required to exercise official responsibilities. These manuals were:

1. Book of Odes ('*Shi*').
2. Book of History or Documents ('*Shu*').
3. The Book of Rites ('*Li*').
4. The Book of Music ('*Yue*').
5. The Book of Changes ('*Yi*').
6. The Spring of Autumn Annals ('*Chungiu*').

Besides essentially dealing with social relations and ethics, these didactic works also address a number of other subjects including culture, economics, history, philosophy and politics.

The Book of Music has been lost but the five others served for more than 2000 years as the basis of education in feudal China. These manuals were challenged in 1919 by the Violent Fourth May Movement.

Six Arts

Besides the above-mentioned six classics, curriculum also covered the following six arts:

(1) Archery, (2) Calligraphy, (3) Chariot-driving, (4) Mathematics, (5) Musicianship, (6) Rites.

Principles of Teaching

In the course of his lengthy career as a teacher, Confucius steadily put together the following laws of pedagogics.

1. Providing students with an education that matched their aptitudes.
2. Inspiring and guiding them and to lead them by stages.
3. Explaining the present in the light of the past.
4. Devoting oneself conscientiously to study and take delight in it.
5. Combining theory with practice.
6. Ensuring that personal behaviour was in conformity with the principles examined.
7. Encouraging independent thought.
8. Taking account of the age of the learners.
9. Practising self-control and analysis.

10. Setting a good example.
11. Correcting one's errors and improving oneself.
12. Curbing evil and exhaling the good.
13. Welcoming criticism.
14. Accepting correction.
15. Forgetting past affronts.

Role of Teachers

Confucius was considered as a remarkable teacher himself and was revered throughout China – a feudal society at that time. He served as a model for countless generations. He declared, "My teaching is open to everyone, without distinction. In his thirties, he accepted disciples and took nearly 3,000 in his life. The school of Confucius was unique for its age. The ethical code of education which Confucius elaborated and his own performance as a teacher are still considered as his finest and greatest contributions to the cause of learning.

Confucius considered the following qualities as essential for teachers:

1. *Commitment*: A teacher should first and foremost be conscientiously and passionately committed to his work.
2. *Breadth of Knowledge*: His own knowledge must be broad in scope and he should have mastery over it.
3. *Love for Pupils*: For eliciting good results, a teacher must love his pupils.
4. *Understanding of Pupils*: The teacher must know and understand his pupils thoroughly.
5. *Psychological Understanding*: The teacher should understand the psychological peculiarities.
6. *Effective Methodology*: The teacher should develop sound methodology of instruction.
7. *Political Convictions*: The teacher should hold firm political positions.
8. *Human Relations*: The teacher should be modest and discrete in his relations with others.
9. *Expression*: He should convey his knowledge in a disinterested fashion, keeping nothing to himself. He should express elegantly and in a lively fashion.
10. *Moral*: He should cultivate his own personal morality.
11. *Personal Deeds*: He should match his deeds with his words.

Impact of Confucius on Education

The impact of Confucius has been highlighted by Prof. Yang Huang as: "Today, Confucius still has an important place in the education system of countries of the region — Japan, Singapore, the Republic of Korea and

Southern Vietnam (before the unification of the country) remained particularly faithful to his thought, especially in the domain of education".

"Although, during his lifetime, Confucius was unable to attain his goals as a teacher, his posthumous contribution to the history of culture and of teaching in China and in other countries throughout the world has won for him not only the reputation of 'Supreme Sage' and 'Teacher of Ten Thousand Generations' in Chinese feudal society, but also what amounts to universal esteem. Since ancient times, many countries have compared their leading scholars, educators and thinkers to Confucius: the distinguished teacher Ch'oe Ch'ung, who opened the first private school in the Kingdom of Koryo, was styled 'the Confucius East of the Sea'; the Enlightenment philosopher Quesnay 'the European Confucius'; the great German poet Goethe 'the Confucius of Weimar'. As a token of the respect and admiration which he inspired, the Italian Jesuit Matteo Ricci, who established parallels between Western and Chinese civilisations, was known as 'the Christian Confucius'.

In China before 1949, his birthday was celebrated as a holiday; this is still the case today in Taiwan, in Vietnam and among the Asian communities of the United States – an occasion marked by commemorative events and ceremonies to honour especially meritorious teachers, and to encourage others to draw inspiration from the virtues of the great educator". (*Prospects*, Vol. 1, 23 (1/2), 1993)

12

Emile Durkheim (1858-1917)

Durkheim, a French Social Scientist, is usually considered as the 'Father of Educational Sociology'. The young Durkheim sensed that he had a role to play in the progress of society and that by choosing to be a teacher he could contribute to that progress through education. For a few years, he taught philosophy in secondary schools. In 1887, he became lecturer in Social Science and Pedagogy. In 1902, he took a chair in the Science of Education, later renamed Science of Education and Sociology at Sorbonne in Paris – a post he held until his death in 1917.

Major Works

Durkheim wrote in French but today all his works have been translated into several languages of the world.
The following four books were published during his lifetime.

1. *The Division of Labour in Society.*
2. *The Rules of Sociological Method.*
3. *Suicide.*
4. *The Elementary Forms of Religious Life.*

After his death, his following books were published:

5. *Education and Sociology.*
6. *Sociology and Philosophy.*
7. *The Education Morale.*
8. *Pragmatism and Sociology.*

The Function and Meaning of Education

According to Durkheim, "Education is the action exercised by the adult generations over those who are not yet ready for social life. Its purpose is to arouse and develop in the child a certain number of physical, intellectual and moral states which are demanded of him both by the political society as a whole and by the specific environment for which he is particularly destined. Education consists of a methodical socialisation of the young generation":

Components of the School System

Durkheim describes the components of the school system in these words: "Any school system is made up of two kinds of components. On the one hand, there are a whole series of fixed stable arrangements and established methods, in a word, institutions; but at the same time, within the machine thus constituted, there are underlying ideas at work, urging it to change. Seen from the outside, secondary education appears to us as a series of establishments whose physical and moral organisation is fixed; but, seen from another angle, that same organisation harbours aspirations seeking fulfillment. Underlying this fixed, consolidated existence there is a life on the move which, though less visible, is by no means insignificant".

In his series of lectures, Durkheim clearly stated that educational reforms reflect the general context and the way in which the school takes care of emerging needs.

Moral Education

Durkheim attempted to establish that there might very well be a rational basis for a 'moral' and not only 'intellectual' education which derived its authority neither from religion nor from pure ideologies. He was convinced that a rationalist faith and an individual-oriented scheme for action were not separable and that children should therefore be taught to submit voluntarily to the rules of a society that placed the cult of the individual at the heart of its values. Durkheim explained this as: "Moral discipline is not only useful for moral life as such; its action extends beyond that. It plays a significant role in the shaping of character and of the personality in general. Indeed, what is most essential in character is the aptitude to exercise self-control, the faculty of restraint, or, as they say, inhibition that enables us to contain our passions and desires and to call them to order... Discipline is useful, therefore, not only in the interest of society and as an indispensable means without which there would be no regular cooperation, but in the interest of the individual himself. Especially in democratic societies like ours children must be taught this healthy moderation. This is because the conventional barriers, which forcibly curbed desires and ambitions in societies organised differently, have partly fallen away and so only moral discipline is left to exercise this regulatory function".

The Teacher-Pupil Relationship

Durkheim was very emphatic that the outcome of the process of education depends basically on the attitudes of the teacher in relation to pupils. He stressed that to perform his functions effectively, the teacher must have a 'deep sense of his mission' so as to command a specific form of 'respect' from his pupils. He observed: "It is 'through words and gestures' that the 'great moral ideas of his time and of his country', of which he is the exponent, can be transmitted from his own consciousness to that of the child; those words and those gestures must therefore be conceived by the teacher having regard to that very purpose".

Conception of a Class

Durkheim outlined the conception of a class as a teacher-pupil group. He wrote in this regard: "There is a special form of psychology that is of particular importance to the teacher, namely group psychology. A class is in fact a miniature society and must not be conducted as though it were merely a conglomeration of individuals independent from each other. Children in class think, feel and act differently from when they are apart. In a class there will be phenomena of contagion, demoralisation, mutual excitement and healthy effervescence and these must be discerned so that they can be either prevented, countered or used, as the case may be".

Durkheim further wrote: "The teacher must be on the lookout for everything that he may cause all the children in the same class to sense their unity in a common enterprise".

The better the teacher is able to keep the classroom group alive, the more the school will open up to society as a whole, and the more forces there will be to counteract the risk of despotism, a risk proportionality greater the younger the pupils.

School Curriculum

Durkheim's interest in achieving the objective of 'socialisation of the pupil' led him to concern himself with the teaching of these subjects in primary and secondary schools: Literature and arts, mathematics and the natural sciences. He observed, "Our aim must be to make each of our pupils not a complete scientist but a complete reasoning being. We must train rationalists, in other words people who are intent on clear thinking".

Training of Teachers

Durkheim repeatedly insisted that side-by-side and including a 'psychological culture', the subject of sociology must become an integral part of teacher training programme. This subject according to him should help teachers to have a clear idea of their place within the educational system. A grounding in sociology as part of teacher training programme would encourage the teachers to engage in reflection both as individuals and as a group so as to better grasp the meaning of pedagogical practices. They would also go beyond routine and legacy of the past and become aware of social dynamics. Durkheim maintained that this would guide the teachers how to conduct the classroom group, control their own authoritarian attitudes and understand their pupils.

One of the direct consequences of Durkheim's views on pedagogy and teacher training was the introduction of a course in sociology in the curricula of primary-school teacher training colleges in 1920s.

Essence of Educational Thought of Durkheim

In the words of Prof. Jean-Claude Filloux, "The fact that Durkheim in effect inaugurated, under the name 'Sociology of Education', a 'scientific' approach to educational facts as social functions gave rise to an extensive body of literature in several countries dealing with the study of the relations between school and society". (*Source*: 'Emile Durkheim', Jean-Claude Filloux in 'Prospects', Vol. I, 23 (1/2), 1993)

13

Erasmus Desiderius (1467-1536)

A Dutch educator and humanist, Erasmus is popularly known for his masterpiece *Praise of Folly*. He is also known as 'Prince of Humanism'. Thomas More, the author of *Utopia,* who was Lord Chancellor of England, was his best friend.

He was ordained as a priest in 1492. After 1495, he lived an independent life, gave lessons to the sons of rich bourgeois and aristocratic English and German families.

Erasmus wrote textbooks which later became teaching manuals and remained in use for centuries in schools such as St. Paul's School and Eton College in England.

Erasmus established a reputation as an 'orator' and poet in humanist circles. He taught for many years at Cambridge University before finally settling in Switzerland. Erasmus ridiculed religious superstitions but did not support the more direct attacks of men like Martin Luther on the Church.

Publications on Education

1. *On the Right Method of Instruction.*
2. *On the Liberal Education of Boys from the Beginning.*
3. *Education of the Christian Man.*
4. *The Education of the Christian Prince.*
5. *On a Liberal Education for Children.*
6. *Literacy and Educational Writings*. (Ed. J. Kelley Swards), Toronto, Toronto University Press, 1985)

Erasmus wrote several works for his own pupils. Such works included:

- *The Twofold Abundance of Words and Things* dealing with rhetoric, grammar and syntax, style and Latin elegance.
- *On Letter Writing* an absorbing manual or the art of writing.
- *On the Correct Pronunciation of Latin and Greek.*
- *Comparisons and Similarities.*
- *On the Civility of Children's Behaviour.*
- Children should be given a liberal education from a very early age.

Philosophy of Education

Erasmus's philosophy has two noteworthy characteristics: The individual implications of education and the social implications of education.

He pointed out three elements which were important.

a. Nature (innate capacity of the individual).
b. Training – skilled application of instruction and guidance.
c. Free exercise of the activity and behaviour implanted by nature and training.

About the social implications of education, Erasmus observed that education is a matter as much of social concern as of individual concern.

Erasmus laid importance of beginning a child's education from the earliest years. He pointed out that the parents and the state are obliged to educate a child in the interest of the State. He wrote: "It is a public obligation in no way inferior to the ordering of the army".

Educational Ideals

Erasmus turned to the past for the ideals of social regeneration. He looked to the secular institutions of ancient Greece and Rome. Erasmus was satisfied with the establishment of a small aristocracy of intellect.

Education of Children at Home

Erasmus preferred education at home under the guidance of a tutor carefully chosen by the parents.

Liberal Education

Jean Claude Margolin explains the concept of liberal education as interpreted by Erasmus in these words,

"For Erasmus, to educate young people was to educate adults, inasmuch as—and this he deeply believed—the future of individuals and the quality of their lives depended, in large measure, on the education they had received in their youth. "A man is not born a man, but becomes one" is the vigorous assertion of one of the sayings in the *De pueris* whereby Erasmus distinguishes man from all other creatures—"A dog remains a dog and an oak an oak, because they are no more than that with which nature has endowed them, once and for always. But human beings, thanks to the reason with which God endowed them when He created them, can improve their primitive nature; education will achieve this on condition that it is 'liberal', which means based on free will (which even children possess), and that the tutor has the wisdom and skill to use persuasion and gentleness, rather than brutally imposing precepts and dogmas".

Emphasis on Classical Literature

Erasmus took no interest in the vernacular literature. His sources of deriving the substance of knowledge were the Greek and Latin languages. His conviction was that the classical works contained all essential knowledge.

Place of Grammar

Regarding the place of grammar in the teaching of literature Erasmus said: "It is not by learning rules that we acquire the power of speaking a language but by daily intercourse with those accustomed to express themselves with exactness and refinement and by the copious reading of the best authors". He insisted that grammar should be kept strictly subordinate to the content. He considered formal grammar necessary but stated that it should be preceded by an informal acquaintance with the language through conversation on all kinds of subjects and on all facets of life.

Methods of Teaching and Learning

The methods advocated by Erasmus are surprisingly modern in their historical context. The methods are a complete departure with the scholastic methods of Middle Ages which were based on learning by rote. Competition was encouraged among children. There was no place for the traditional corporal punishment.

Education of Women

Erasmus shared the views of all his contemporaries that girls had no need of advanced intellectual education since their lot was either to marry, have children and keep house or to enter a convent.

Summing up: The works of Erasmus are so wide-ranging and varied in both content and form that he is sometimes called the 'Tutor of Europe'. His contribution has been summed up by Margolin as "A teacher and educational adviser to the schoolmasters of his time, Erasmus became, by vocation and also because circumstances required it of him, the theoretician at one and the same time of a political philosophy based on peace and the protection of the people by their prince, of a code of religious ethics concerning the status of women, and of a renovated theology based on scrupulous interpretation of the Gospels and on rhetoric, which is used by the preacher in the exercise of his function".

In Erasmus, the humanist outweighed the reformer.

14

Frederich August Froebel (1782-1852)

The Play-Way Method

Froebel, the founder of the Kindergarten was born on April 21, 1782 in Oberweiback, a village in South Germany. He lost his mother when he was just nine months old. His father remarried when Froebel was only four years of age. His father was indifferent towards him and his step mother's treatment was very unfair. Thus he was deprived of parental affection, love and care. At the age of eleven he was adopted by his uncle who was associated with a church near his village. In school, he was considered as a dunce.

At the age of fourteen, he became an apprentice to a forester. It was here that he developed a deep love for nature and acquired the habits of observation and concentration which characterised him throughout his life.

At seventeen, he joined the University of Jena where he was profoundly influenced by the idealistic philosophy of Fitche and Schelling. On account of financial difficulty, he discontinued his studies.

For four years, he remained a 'career-wanderer'. He wandered from place to place, picking up professions of different nature and failing miserably in them, one after the other.

Interest in Education

A turning point came in the life of Froebel when he began to study architecture at Frankfurt. There he came in contact with Dr. Grunner who was the Director of a model school. Dr. Grunner discovered that Froebel had the potential to become an excellent teacher and persuaded him to join his school. This marked a turning point in his life. Froebel was greatly satisfied and he found his 'long missed life element' and was 'inexpressibly happy'. He declared, for the first time "I found something I had always longed for, but always missed, as if my life had at last discovered its native element; I felt as happy as a fish in the water or a bird in the air".

After spending three years at Frankfurt, Froebel paid a visit to Pestalozzi's institute at Yverdun. There Froebel learnt in detail the principles and method of Pestalozzi. Froebel's contact with Pestalozzi prepared him for carrying out his own experiments which led to the founding of his own school.

In 1816, Froebel established a small school at Griesheim which later on was shifted to Keilhau. In this school, Froebel developed his own principles and methods of instruction. After passing through several vicissitudes, this school became a successful institution in a period of ten years. 'Play' and 'art work' were the chief features of this school.

Publication of *The Education of Man*

In 1826, Froebel published his famous book *The Education of Man*. In this he says: "The true method of education consists in considering the mind of the child as a whole in which all the parts work together to produce harmonious unity". After this he started many schools in Germany. The Government suspected the revolutionary ideas of Froebel and an enquiry was conducted. The inspector gave a favourable report: "I found here a closely united family of some sixty members held together in mutual confidence and every member seeking the good of the whole—The aim of institution is by no means knowledge and science merely, but free self-active development of the mind from within".

Froebel's Work

On account of financial difficulties, Froebel shifted his work to Switzerland in 1830. The Swiss Government appreciated his work and sent for training under him. He then moved to Burgdorf. There he became a superintendent of an orphanage. He continued his work of training teachers. There he realised that due to non-availability of education in the pre-school age, the school suffered and did not get good raw material—the educand.

Froebel returned to Germany in 1836 and founded his first kindergarten in 1849 in the village of Blankendurg. He married his kindergartener in 1849. He spent his whole time in the founding and devising his apparatus for kindergartens.

His views were not accepted by the German Government and forbade him from establishing any school. This was a great shock and he could not long survive it. Froebel died in 1852, in poverty, misery and agony. His grave is marked by a slab with a cube, a cylinder and a sphere on it.

Main Features of Educational Philosophy and Principles

1. *Object of Education*: In Froebel's own words, "The object of education is the realisation of the faithful, pure, inviolable and hence holy life. The divine essence of man should be unfolded, brought out, lifted into consciousness, and man himself raised into free, conscious, obedience to the divine principle that lives in him and to a free representation of this principle in his life. Education should lead and guide man to clearness concerning himself and in himself, to face with nature, and to unity with God".

Froebel maintains that the aim of education is not to make the mind of the child a jumble of words. He writes: "The essential business of school is not so much to communicate a variety and multiplicity of facts as to give prominence to the ever living unity that is in all things". Again he writes: "Human education requires the knowledge and appreciation of religion, nature and language in their intimate living reciprocity and mutual interaction. Without the knowledge and appreciation of the intimate unity of the three, the school and we ourselves are lost in the fallacies of bottomless, self-provoking diversity." So the aim of education is to enable the child to realise the unity in diversity.

2. *Principle of Development*: Froebel asserts: "Each individual must develop from within, self-active and free, in accordance with the internal law".

3. *Mind of the Child as a Living Whole*: According to Froebel, "The true method of education consists in considering the mind of the child as a living whole in which all the parts work together to produce harmonious unity".

4. *Creativeness of Childhood*: Froebel proposed a new concept of childhood. He stressed that childhood is not merely a preparation for adulthood. Childhood is a value in itself and possesses its own creation. An adult has no right to feel superior and to interfere with the nature of children. Rather the adult must first understand the child and then guide him accordingly.

5. *Inner Relatedness of all Education*: This means that that educator ought to lead the child through such situations as will help to relate his experiences organically one with another. Only then can the child realise his own personal unity and the unity inherent in the diversity of life.

6. *Totality of Educational Endeavour*: In order to realise the driving character of the universe and his part in it, man needs his senses and emotions as well as reasons. They all are windows of the soul. Hence Froebel emphasised the totality of educational endeavour.

7. *Play and Activity*: According to Froebel, "Play is the purest, most important activity of man at this stage. It gives, therefore, joy, freedom, contentment, inner rest and peace with the world. It holds the source of all that is good". Froebel recognised that play needs to be organised and controlled on definite materials so that it may not degenerate into aimless play "instead of preparing for those tasks of life for which it is destined".

8. *Freedom to the Child*: The child should be educated in free atmosphere. Freedom means obedience to self-imposed law.

9. *Social Aspect*: Froebel stressed the social aspect of education also. He believed that all social institutions like the home, the school, the church and the State, etc. are the agencies of development of the individual wherein he is to realise the unity in diversity.

10. *Importance of Songs*: He devised songs, gestures and construction as the chief means of stimulating the imagination of the child.

11. *Role of the Teacher*: The teacher is like a gardener who carefully nurses and protects children in order to secure their full and free development along most desirable lines. The educator by his efforts assists the educand who is developing according to the law of his nature to attain levels that would be denied to him.

Kindergarten: Meaning, Objective and Environment

Meaning of the Kindergarten: Kindergarten is a German word which means a children's garden. Froebel conceived the school as a garden, the teacher as the gardener and the students as tender plants. The teacher, like the gardener, looks after the little human plants and waters them to grow to beauty and perfection. Froebel discovered great similarity between a child and a plant. He believed that the process of growth and development of the plant and the child is the same. The plant grows from within according to the seed that is within. In the same way the child grows from within. He unfolds his tendencies and impulses from within.

Objective of the Kindergarten: In the words of Froebel, "The objective of a kindergarten is to give the children employment in agreement with their whole nature, to strengthen their bodies, to exercise their senses, to engage their awakening mind and through their senses to make them acquainted with nature and their fellow creatures. It is specially to guide the heart and the affections, and to lead them to the original ground of all life, to unity with themselves".

Environment of the Kindergarten: The environment of the kindergarten is to be that of freedom, play and joy – an environment which fosters self-expression. There are to be no books or fixed intellectual tasks for children, but training in expression is to be given in three ways – songs, movements and construction. These three are to go together. Though the means are separate yet the process is connected as a whole, e.g., when a story is told or read, it is expressed in song, dramatised in movement and gesture, and illustrated by construction from blocks, paper, clay or drawing. Thus the child's imagination and thought are encouraged and stimulated by concerted means. His hands and limbs, his eyes and other senses are trained by making him do certain things.

Chief Characteristics of Kindergarten

1. *Free Self-Activity*: Froebel regarded self-activity as a process by which the individual realises his own nature and builds up his own world and then unites and harmonises the two. An inspector reported about this self-activity: "Self-activity of the mind is the first law of this institution, the kind of instruction given here does not make the young mind a strong box into which, as early as possible kinds of coins of the most different values and coinage, such as are now current in the world that are stuffed, but slowly, continuously, gradually and always inwardly that is according to a connection found in nature of the human mind, the instruction steadily goes

on without any ticks, from the simple to the complex, from the concrete to the abstract, so well-adapted to the child and his needs that he goes as easily to his learning as to his play".

The following points should be noted regarding activity:

(i) It should not be vague.
(ii) It should be a sublimated or controlled activity.
(iii) Social atmosphere is essential in order to secure meaningful activities.
(iv) Self-activity may take the form either of work or of play.

2. *Play*: According to Froebel, "Play is the purest, most spiritual activity of man at this stage. ... It gives, therefore, joy, freedom, contentment, inner rest and peace with the world. It holds the source of all that is good". Froebel recognised that play needs to be organised and controlled on definite materials so that it may not degenerate into aimless play instead of preparing for those tasks of life for which it is destined". There should be rational conscious guidance. Consequently, Froebel has given seven gifts to children to play with.

3. *Songs, gestures and construction*: Froebel saw an organic relationship between songs, gestures and construction. He regarded these as three coordinate forms of expression in the child. What is to be learnt by the pupil is first expressed in a song, then it is dramatised or expressed in gesture or movement and lastly illustrated through some constructive work such as paper or clay. Thus, a balanced development of the mind, the speech organs and the hand is aimed at. These three activities provide exercise to the senses, limbs and muscles of the child.

4. *Gifts and occupations*: For providing appropriate activities, Froebel devised suitable materials known as gifts. The gifts suggest some form of activity and occupations are the activities suggested by gifts. These have been carefully graded. They possess all the novelty of play things. The order of the gift is devised in such a way as it leads the child from the activities and thought of one stage to another.

5. *Role of the Teacher*: The teacher is not a spectator and a passive person. He is expected to suggest suitable occupations when gifts are given to children. He demonstrates certain activities to them. He also sings a song with a view to help the child to form appropriate ideas.

A teacher has important responsibilities to perform. He has to inculcate sympathetically values like love, sympathy, humility, cooperation and obedience to elders.

6. *Positive Discipline*: The teacher has to avoid external restraint and bodily punishment. The child should be made to realise that discipline depends upon his love for order, goodwill and mutual understanding. Froebel stressed that women should be trained for training children at this stage.

7. *Curriculum*: It is in term of activities. The divisions of the curriculum are:

(i) Manual work.
(ii) Religion and religious instruction.
(iii) Natural science and mathematics.
(iv) Language.
(v) Arts and objects of art.

Froebel's Gifts

For the complete education and training of child, Froebel devised a series of gifts. The gifts comprise carefully graduated series of materials which possess all the novelty of playthings, and form the basis of his educational method. They are to train the senses of sight and touch, to give the child an idea of size and surface, and to present him a correct idea of number. The activities suggested by these gifts are called occupations. The gifts are given to the child in a certain order. The gradation and order elements of gifts are determined by the principle of development. The gifts are twenty in number although only the first seven are now usually called by this name.

Gift I

It consists of six coloured woollen balls, three in primary colours, red, yellow and blue, and three secondary colours, orange, green and purple. The occupation consists in rolling them about in play. Thus they develop in the children the idea of colour and material, form, motion, direction and muscular sensibility.

Gift II

It consists of a sphere, cube and cylinder made of hardwood. In playing with these gifts, the child notices the difference between the stability of the cube, and the mobility of the sphere. He observes that the cylinder is both stable and movable, and that it harmonises both the qualities in one.

Gift III

It is a large cube divided into eight smaller equal cubes. From these the child can build up a number of useful artistic forms such as benches, steps, doors, bridges, etc. and for this reason the third gift is often called the *first building box*. The child can also gain elementary ideas of addition and subtraction through these cubes.

Gift IV

It consists of the large cubes divided into eight oblong prisms in each of which the length is twice the breadth and the breadth is twice the thickness. This helps the child to construct different kinds of buildings and patterns when combined with the third gift.

Gift V

It is every much like the third gift. It consists of a large cube divided into twenty-seven small cubes, three of which are again divided diagonally into halves and three into quarters. The child can construct many beautiful forms and patterns by combining the third, fourth and fifth gifts. Form and number can very well be taught by the use of this gift.

Gift VI

It is again similar to gift four. In it there is a large cube divided into eighteen whole and nine small oblong blocks. Still further designs in forms and construction may be made by the child. It is also useful in teaching numbers.

Gift VII

It is also a set of square and triangular tablets made of fine wood in two colours. It provides material for several exercises in geometrical forms and mosaic work.

Other gifts consist of materials such as stick-laying, perforating, paper-cutting, threading of beads, mat-making, embroidery, basket-making, wire work, drawing and modelling.

Play-Way Method

Froebel used play for the development and growth of the child in the kindergarten established by him. This method came to be known as the play-way method in teaching-learning.

Play-Way is thus a method which envisages that all work should be done in the spirit of play. Play-Way is quite different from the normal meaning of the word play which is considered as a form of physical activity. Play-Way, on the other hand, is a means for the cognitive, and affective development of the child, *i.e.,* development of intellect, skills and feelings.

Principles of Play-Way Method

1. Principle of growth and development of the child through play.
2. Principle of self-development under teacher's guidance.
3. Principle of self-activity.
4. Principle of self-expression through play.
5. Principle of spontaneity.
6. Principle of freedom.
7. Principle of happiness and joy in play activities.
8. Principle of unity.
9. Principle of aesthetic appreciation.
10. Principle of creativeness.
11. Principle of drawing out.
12. Principle of discipline through love.
13. Principle of sense training.
14. Principle of concrete to abstract.

Gifts, Occupations, Songs, Gestures and Construction in the Play-Way

We have already stressed the place of activity and play. To provide activities, Froebel devised suitable materials known as gifts. The gifts suggest some form of activity and occupations are the activities suggested by gifts. These have been carefully graded. They possess all the novelty of play things. The order of the gift is devised in such a way as it leads the child from the activities and thought of one stage to another. Froebel saw an organic relationship between play, songs, gestures and construction.

Play-Way Activities Connected with Songs

Selection of Songs. Froebel has given songs in his book *Mother and Nursery Songs*. There are fifty play songs. The idea of the introduction of songs is to enable the child to use his senses, limbs and muscles and also to familiarise him with the surroundings. The child begins to use language through these songs. Each song is accompanied by a game such as 'Hide and Seek'. The selection of the song is determined by the teacher in accordance with the development of the child. There are three parts in a song.

1. A motto for the guidance of mother or teacher.
2. A verse accompanied by music.
3. A picture illustrating the song.

The song for drill is:

Let us have a drill to-day,
March along grand array,
And whoever steps the best,
Shall be captain over the rest,
And lead us on our way.

Play-Way Activities Based on Gifts and Educational Objectives

Some Examples:

	Educational Objective	*Components of the Gift*	*Activity*
1.	Enabling the child to learn the concept of colour, form, motion, direction, and muscular sensitivity.	Six coloured balls of different colours.	Children are required to roll these balls in play-way attitude of mind.
2.	Enabling the students to learn the concept of stability and mobility and to differentiate between these two.	One sphere. One cube. One cylinder – made of hard wood.	Children are required to observe the stability and mobility of each article while playing.
3.	Enabling the students to learn the concepts of addition and subtraction.	One large cube divided into eight smaller equal cubes contained in a box.	Children are required to build a number of forms, e.g., benches, doors, etc.

	Educational Objective	*Components of the Gift*	*Activity*
4.	Enabling children to develop concepts of designs or patterns.	A large cube divided into eight oblong prisms. Each has a length twice its breadth and breadth twice its thickness.	Children are occupied in the building of a variety of patterns by using these prisms.
5.	Enabling the children to develop the concepts of form and number through gifts 3, 4 and 5.	Gift 5 consists of a large cube divided into 27 small cubes. Three of these are sub-divided diagonally into haves; three further sub-divided into haves; three further subdivided into quarters.	Children are occupied in developing a variety of forms using gifts 3, 4 and 5.
6.	Enabling the children to develop the concept of numbers.	Large cubes divided into eighteen wholes and nine small oblong bricks (Like gift 4).	Children are directed to develop designs using the material of the gift.
7.	Enabling the children to acquire the concept of mosaic and geometrical forms.	A set of triangular and square tablets of fine wood in two different colours.	Children are directed to prepare geometrical forms and mosaic work.

Role of the Teacher

The teacher plays the role of a gardener who looks after the tender plants. He provides an environment of life and freedom. He plans his work very carefully and demonstrates the play-way activity. He always keeps in mind the chief objectives which the gifts and songs should serve.

Merits of Play-Way Method

1. It stresses the importance of play in early education.
2. The gifts and occupations of the Kindergarten give a new approach to method of teaching.
3. The inclusion of creative work in the school makes children creative workers.
4. There is sufficient scope for activity in a Kindergarten.
5. Various gifts provide sensory training.
6. The inclusion of nature study in the curriculum helps to develop love for nature and the world in the mind of the students.

Limitations of Play-Way Method

1. In the Kindergarten, too much stress is laid on the development from within.

2. Songs as given by Froebel are out of date. These cannot be used in every school.
3. The gifts of Froebel are formal in nature.
4. The order of presentation of gifts is arbitrary.
5. They do not serve much purpose of sense training.
6. There is little of correlation in the teaching of various subjects.
7. It is not possible to accept his excessive emphasis on play in education as it is likely to detract the child from serious learning.
8. Philosophy on which Froebel based his method is very complicated. It is very difficult for children to understand his symbolism.

Contribution to Educational Thought and Principles

Froebel has made a very valuable contribution to educational theory and practice. Froebel's Play-Way finds place in the teaching-learning process at all stages of education and in all subjects. Following are the important elements which are emphasised by modern educators and thinkers:

1. *Respect for the Child's Individuality*: Froebel lived for children, worked for children and died for children. He had profound love and sympathy for children.

2. *Emphasis on the Study of the Child*: Froebel stressed the need for the study of the nature of the child, his instincts and impulses. Modern educator is very careful to see that adequate scope is provided for the free play of the impulses and instincts of children.

3. *Education Through Play*: Froebel believed that play is the highest phase of self-development. He introduced Play-Way in the activities of the school. Today we find that the principle of Play-Way has been accepted by every educator. We teach children through songs, movements, gestures, dramatisation, hand-work, etc.

4. *Activity in Education*: Froebel was the first educator to make self-activity as the basis of education. 'Learning by doing' is the slogan of the day.

5. *Sense Training*: Froebel introduced gifts for the training of the senses of children. With the help of these gifts, he wanted to give the idea of shape, form, colour, size and number. Audio-visual aids form an integral part of the present system of education.

6. *Nature Study in Education*: For Froebel, nature study was a means of bringing the child nearer God. He advocated nature study to enable the child to understand the world in which he lives and to develop habits of careful observation. This idea has become so popular that we do not regard any school worthy of name if it does not provide for nature study.

7. *Women Teachers at the Nursery Stage*: It will not be wrong to say that it is due to the influence of Froebel that we find a trend to entrust the education at the pre-primary or pre-basic stage to women teachers who are considered to be more suited for this task of instruction at this stage.

8. *Stress on Nursery or Pre-Primary Education:* The present educator fully recognises the importance of the education in the early years. Today we find a large number of schools catering to the needs of such children. Froebel often said, "Until the education of nursery years was reformed nothing solid and worthy could be achieved."

9 *New Conception of School:* His kindergarten school was a little world where responsibility was shared, by all, individual-rights respected by all, brotherly sympathy developed and voluntary co-operation practised. His school was an ideal society in miniature.

Froebel's Eternal Message

'Come! Let us live for Children".

15

Gijubhai Badheka (1885-1939)

Gijubhai, a pioneer of pre-primary education in India was born on 15th November, 1885 in Gujarat. He became a pleader in the district court. He left this profession and joined Dakshin Murti Vidyarthi Bhavan as a rector and later became the headmaster of the '*Vinay Mandir*' (High School). During this time, he observed students and teachers closely but it was the world of little children that was beginning to intrigue and allure him. He finally resigned from the High School to start Bal Mandirs.

Gijubhai's experiment in the area of child education was influenced by the writings of Madame Montessori who was working in the same field, about the same time. However Gijubhai had to discover his own idiom. Gijubhai finally managed to convince a few parents to send their children to him. In those days, when children would be kept at home till they were seven or eight, it seemed a mad idea to imagine a school for three-year-olds.

Bases of Philosophy: Concept of the Learner: World of Children

Gijubhai had an intense love for children. His philosophy is based on the following observations made by him.

1. Heaven is in the happiness of the child
2. Heaven is in the health of the child.
3. Heaven is in the pleasure of the child.
4. Heaven is in the playful innocence of the child.
5. Heaven is in the songs and humming of the child.

Gijubhai further said: "A child is a complete person who has intellect, emotions, mind and understanding, has strengths and weaknesses—and has likes and dislikes ... let us understand the emotions of the child".

Essence of Bal Mandir

The word *Mandir* has specific connotation of child worship.

Gijubhai coined the Slogan *Baladev Bhava* meaning worship of the child.

Educational Principles: Child-Centred Education

1. Education should be child/learner-centred.
2. Child's sanctity should be kept intact.

3. Healthy environment should be provided to the learner.
4. There should be maximum involvement of the child in the teaching-learning process.
5. Child should learn in an environment which is full of love and understanding of the child.
6. Child should learn by 'living'.
7. Child should learn by 'doing'.

Environment of the Bal Mandir (Children's School or Children's Temple or Children's World)

Bal Mandir in the real sense provided an environment which was very healthful and playful. It was full of happiness for the child. It provided interesting songs. It gave maximum freedom to the child to develop his potential. The teachers showed real concern for the development of the child.

Following were the chief characteristics of the Bal Mandir of Dakshinamurti School of Bhavnagar in Gujarat. Other schools established by him and his associates also made all possible efforts to follow this.

1. *Mutual Understanding and Cooperation*: Here in the school a 'world' is created where children learn from each other. Older children help the smaller ones to climb up the stairs; fill their own cups with water; find their rickshaws while remembering lines of songs and answers or riddles. Children also spend nights here—so that they can together see and understand the sunset and rise, the moon and stars in the sky and also peel potatoes for the collective dinner. The overnight stay of tiny tots might cause anxiety to parents who drop in to see their children, but the latter are happy to be on their own.

2. *Locally made Inexpensive Learning Material*. Initially, he implemented the use of tools and methods envisaged by Montessori, but later moved away into thinking of ways that were inexpensive and he used material which was easily available locally.

3. *Sharing Activity with Children*. As he was a man who could play with toys, children could overcome their fear of a strange adult and play with him. He could also tell stories, not only of kings and queens, but of animals, plants and naughty children—and the stories invariably ended in small plays, in which he also acted. *Mian Tuski* and a *King* in the *Rat's Tale* are roles which his contemporaries recollect with glee and amusement.

4. *Understanding Teacher*. To be a good teacher one must listen carefully to what a child has to say—and observe him (her) attentively—but without intruding on the child's effort to do things all by herself (himself).

5. *Observing Nature*. There was also emphasis on observing nature and walks and outings were a regular feature of the school. Here emphasis was not on tools and techniques of teaching the alphabets or numbers, but on giving the children an atmosphere where they would feel free to express themselves.

6. *Use of the Word Mandir for School: School a sacred place.* Evidently, this approach excludes examinations and gradation in the conventional sense. Children have to pass one phase of development before the other. The very fact that labels like 'primary', 'middle' and 'high school' are not used speaks of the attitude of the founders. Instead words like 'Bal Mandir', 'Kishore Mandir' and 'Vinay Mandir' have been preferred; 'Mandir' having specific connotations of worship of the child.

7. *Freedom Without Fear.* There was no place for punishment to the child. The child was not insulted or jeered. His personality received the utmost respect and care.

Teaching of Language

Gijubhai wrote a book on teaching language at the primary stage. In this book Gijubhai discusses the method of the teaching different aspects of language to children. The salient features of the method are as under:

1. Reading should precede writing.
2. Writing should start with drawing lines.
3. Children should be taught how to use the pen in writing — how to hold it, how to turn it, how to control it and how to shape the letter through drawing absurd shapes.
4. The purpose of dictation is to help the child acquire speed and accuracy of writing after learning.
5. Folk songs should be made the media of teaching.
6. The poems should be based on stories. They should be simple and descriptive.
7. Thrill and joy aspects of the poem should be stressed.
8. Play should be used to teach grammar. Grammar should not be taught separately.

Teaching of Social Studies and Other Subjects

1. History should be taught through stories.
2. Globe should be used to teach geography.
3. Didactic type of apparatus should be used to teach mathematics.
4. Drawing should be taught by asking the students to draw the shape of guava, mango, table, etc.

Games

Gijubhai stressed the usefulness of games for providing joy and pleasures to students. He was not in favour of competitions.

Publications

Gijubhai wrote more than 200 books – 180 books for children and 20 for parents and teachers.

His important publications for teachers and parents are:

1. *Prathmik school mein shiksha* (Education in Primary School)

2. *Mata-Pita se prashna* (Questions to Parents)
3. *Divaswapna* (Day-dreams)

Divaswapana (Day-dreams) is an Educator's Reverie. It was first published in Gujarati in 1931. It established Gijubhai as a luminary in the field of education. It was translated in English in 1989.

Divaswapana is the imaginary story of a teacher who rejects the orthodox concept of the teaching-learning process. The teacher conducted several experiments in a primary school against heavy odds—cynical teachers, naughty students, indifferent parents. He was able to get the approval of the Department of Education to conduct experiments. He neglected the traditions of teaching from prescribed books. The teacher with untiring patience was successful.

Prof. Krishna Kumar describes the richness of the experiments contained in *Divaswapana* in these words: "As a reader of '*Divaswapana*', one is blown off in gust of joy and curiosity, leaving behind the sadness borne out of one's knowledge of India's colourless, dust-wrapped primary schools. One starts to paint the picture of the future in which the talent imprisoned in the nation's schools will break forth and children will enjoy the pleasure of taking stock of the world round the classroom with their teacher".

Gijubhai is considered as one of the most important writers of children's literature in Gujarati. He wrote books for children keeping in view their aptitudes, feelings and interests. He discarded the traditional approach of writing stories and poems which gave moral sermons. He was keen to give ethical message to children indirectly. He was convinced that children's work should be so forceful that it spontaneously attracts children. They should get joy and pleasure. Ethical message should come to them indirectly.

His books have been translated into several Indian languages. Following are the important books translated and published in Hindi.

1. *Nani Ke Ghar Jane De*
2. *Tad Tad Tadak*
3. *Bhut Ka Bhai*
4. *Nayee Aur Poonch Kata Bagh*
5. *Kani Gauraya*
6. *Budhia*
7. *Mendak Ki Shadi*
8. *Billi Ke Gale Mein Haddia*
9. *Unt Ke Pair Sade*
10. *Moorkh Brahman*

In his magazine entitled *Sikshan Patrika*, Gijubhai highlighted the 'World of Children' by writing about the nature of the children and teaching-learning of children.

Contribution

Bal Mandir of Dakshinamurti School of Bhavnagar, established in 1920, is a great tribute to its founder—a man who dreamt of a school for children where there would be no fear of the cane; a place to which they would go willingly and not be dragged or bribed by parents.

He established several Bal Mandirs in different parts of Gujarat and especially in the tribal areas. He also established teacher training institutions.

The work of Shri Gijubhai inspired many persons in Gujarat, Maharashtra and other states. He also greatly influenced ladies like Smt. Tarabai Modak who was also working for the promotion of Montessori System in India. Gijubhai will be remembered for years to come on account of unique contribution to pre-primary and nursery education.

To Sum up: As already observed perhaps Gijubhai is the only educator in India who paid so much attention to pre-primary education. He was a successful practitioner in the field. Indeed, he was a man who dreamt of a school for children where there would be no fear for them and a place where they would go happily, cheerfully and willingly. His dream was turned into a reality in his Bal Mandir—a heaven for children and place of worship. Gijubhai has become a great source of inspiration for those engaged in nursery education.

16

Gopal Krishan Gokhale (1866-1915)

Gokhale as Champion of Compulsory Education: Gopal Krishan Gokhale (1866-1915) besides being a statesman, social reformer and educator, was a great champion of compulsory primary education in India. He was a Professor and Principal of Poona Ferguson College for a number of years, President of the Indian National Congress (1905), founder of the Servants of India Society and Member of Imperial Legislature. Between 1910 and 1913 Gokhale made heroic efforts to make the government accept the principle of compulsory education. The demand for compulsory education was strengthened by the fact that the Gaekwar of Baroda had introduced compulsory education throughout his State in 1906. Gokhale moved the resolution for compulsory education in 1910 in the Imperial Council.

I beg to place the following resolution before the Council for its consideration:

"That this Council recommends that a beginning should be made in the direction of making elementary education free and compulsory throughout the country, and that a mixed Commission of officials and non-officials be appointed at an early date to frame definite proposals." (*Extracts*)

My Lord, there is much truth in the homely adage that where there is a will there is a way. I think that this question of compulsory and free primary education is now in this country the question of questions. The well-being of millions upon millions of children who are waiting to be brought under the humanizing influence of education depends upon it. The increased efficiency of the individual, the higher general level of intelligence, the stiffening of the moral backbone of large sections of the community, none of these things can come without such education. In fact, the whole of our future as a nation is inextricably bound up with it. My Lord, however this resolution may be disposed of here today. I feel that in this matter we are bound to win. (*Extracts from the Speech*)

Important Suggestions Contained in the Resolution

Important suggestions contained in his resolution, moved in the Legislative Council, were as follows:

1. That in the area where 35% boys were receiving education, elementary education should be made free and compulsory. This provision should apply to the age group of 6 to 10 years.

2. The cost of primary education should be shared by the Provincial Government and Local Bodies. The Local Bodies and the Government Bodies should bear the expenditure in the ratio of 1:2.
3. A secretary should be appointed to organise, supervise and look after the primary education.
4. There should be a separate Department in the Central Government to draw up scheme for the expansion of primary education; and in the budget statement there should be a portion describing the progress of primary education.

On the assurance of the Government of India, that the whole question should be examined, Gokhale withdrew the Bill.

Gokhale's Second Attempt (March 18, 1912)

On March 16, 1911, Gokhale brought in a bill to make better provision in the extension of compulsory education. On March 18, he moved the Resolution that his Bill be examined by a Select Committee of 15 members of the Viceroy's Council.

Main suggestions contained in the Bill are given below:

a. He suggested that compulsory primary education should be introduced in the areas where a certain percentage was fixed by the Governor-General in Council.
b. After securing the sanction of Government, the local body shall enforce the rule. Local Bodies at their end were to have the right to introduce compulsion in the whole or part of the area under their jurisdiction.
c. Local bodies were also given the right to levy cess to meet the cost of free and compulsory primary education.
d. Expenditure on education was to be spared by the Local Bodies and the Provincial Government in the ratio of 1:2.
e. It was also suggested by Gokhale that primary education should be made compulsory for the boys of the age group of 6 to 10, and the defaulting guardians should be penalised for non-compliance of the provisions of sending their wards to recognised primary schools.
f. It was also recommended that the primary education shall also be made compulsory for girls.
g. Guardians whose monthly income is less than Rs.10/- should not be asked to pay any fee.

While rejecting Gokhale's Bill, the Government promised to extend recurring and non-recurring grants to primary education. The Government could not entirely ignore the growing popular demand for the spread of mass education. The seeds sown by Gokhale came up quickly for harvest. Gokhale's Bill created a flutter in the British Parliament also. In the course of the discussion on the Indian budget, the Under-Secretary of State for India admitted the need for paying more attention to Indian education. As a result, the Government of India passed the Resolution on Educational Policy on February 21, 1913.

Gokhale's efforts bore fruit gradually. His work was taken up by Vithalbhai Patel. In 1917, he moved in the Bombay Legislative Council, a Bill for the introduction of compulsory/primary education in the Municipal limits of Bombay. The Bill was passed with some modifications and became the first Law on compulsory education in India. It is known as the Patel Act of 1918.

Gokhale's Elementary Education Bill, 1911 (Extracts)

This, my Lord, is briefly the whole of my Bill. It is a small and humble attempt to suggest the first steps of a journey, which is bound to prove long and tedious, but which must be performed, if the mass of our people are to emerge from their present conditions. My Lord, this question of a universal diffusion of education in India depends, almost more than any other questions, on the hearty and sympathetic cooperation of the government and the leaders of the people. The government must, in the first instance, adopt definitely the policy of such diffusion as its own, and it must, secondly, not grudge to find the bulk of the money, which will be required for it, as governments in most other civilised countries are doing. And this is what we are entitled to ask at the hands of the government in the name of justice, for the honour of the government itself, and in the highest interests of popular well-being. The leaders of the people, on their side, must bring to this task high enthusiasm, which will not be chilled by difficulties, courage, which will not shrink from encountering unpopularity if need be, and readiness to make sacrifices, whether of money or time or energy, which the cause may require.

If a beginning is made without further delay, if both the government and the people persevere with the task in the right spirit, the whole problem may be solved before another generation rises to take our place. If this happens the next generation will enter upon its own security of success. As for us, it will be enough to have laboured for such an end—laboured with not only profound humility but also profound wisdom in the faith which says:

"I do not ask to see the distant scene;
One step enough for me."

Gokhale's Speech in 1912 in the Council (Extracts)

My Lord, I know that my Bill will be thrown out before the day closes, I make no complaint, I shall not even feel depressed. I know too well the story of the preliminary efforts that were required even in England, before the Act of 1870 was passed. Moreover, I have always felt and have often said that we, of the present generation in India, can only hope to serve our country by our failures. The men and women who will be privileged to serve her by their successes will come later. We must be content to accept cheerfully the place that has been allotted to us in our onward march. The Bill thrown out today, will come back again and again, till on the stepping-stones of its dead selves, a measure will ultimately rise which will spread the light of knowledge throughout the land. It may be that this anticipation will not come true. It may be that our efforts may not conduce even indirectly to the promotion of the great cause which we all have at heart and that they may turn out after all to be nothing better than the mere ploughing of the sands of the seashore. But, my Lord, whatever fate awaits our labours, one thing is clear. We shall be entitled to feel that we have done our duty, and, where the call of duty is clear, it is better even to labour and fail than not to labour at all. (*Rejection of the Bill*: The Bill was rejected by 38 votes to 13.)

Government Resolution on Educational Policy, 1913 (Extracts)

The proposition that illiteracy must be broken down and that primary education has, in the present circumstances of India, a predominant claim upon the public funds, represents accepted policy no longer open to discussion. For financial and administrative reasons of decisive weight the Government of India have refused to recognise principle of compulsory education; but they desire the widest possible extension of primary education on a voluntary basis. As regards free elementary education, the time has not yet arrived when it is practicable to dispense wholly with fees without injustice to the many villages which are waiting for the provision of schools. The fees derived from those pupils who can pay them are now devoted to the maintenance and expansion of primary education, and a total remission of fees would involve to a certain extent a more prolonged postponement of a provision of schools in villages without them. In some provinces elementary education is already free and in the majority of provinces liberal provision is already made for giving free elementary instruction to those boys whose parents cannot afford to pay fees. Local Governments have been requested to extend the application of the principle of free elementary education amongst the poorer and more backward sections of the population. Further than this, it is not possible at present to go…

It is the desire and hope of the Government of India to see in the not distant future some 91,000 primary public schools added to the 100,000 which already exist for boys and to double the 4½ millions of the pupils who now receive instruction in them.

17

Herbert Spencer (1820-1903)

Herbert Spencer was an English philosopher. He was born in Derby. His father was a learned teacher of chemistry and physics. He made suitable arrangement for the education of his child at home. Spencer's natural inclination was towards original thinking. He showed a keen interest in performing experiments in natural sciences and mathematics. He acquired a good deal of knowledge in all subjects while he was just seventeen. His first interest was biology, but he turned to engineering. From 1837 to 1846, he worked as an engineer for the London and Birmingham Railway. Later he served as editor of the Economist. Spencer left the *Economist* in 1853 to pursue his philosophical career. He gained a wide reputation as a philosopher.

Herbert Spencer is known for scientific trend in education.

Publications

1. *The Principles of Psychology* (1855)
2. *Education* (1861)
3. *First Principles* (1862)
4. *The Principles of Biology* (1864-1867)
5. *The Principles of Ethics* (1892-93)
6. *The Principle of Sociology* (1896)

Contribution to Education

Spencer held that the aim of education was 'to prepare us for complete living'. For complete living one must know how to develop one's body and mind, how to manage one's affairs.

How to manage one's affairs implies:

(i) To bring up a family.
(ii) To behave like a good citizen.
(iii) To utilise leisure profitably.
(iv) To utilise one's whole capacity for one's own and social welfare.

Maxims of Teaching

Spencer has given us the following maxims of teaching:

1. From simple to complex.
2. From known to unknown.

3. From indefinite to definite.
4. From concrete to abstract.
5. From empirical to rational.

Scientific Humanism in Education

Spencer is considered as one of the most important propounders of scientific humanism in education.

Main Features of Scientific Humanism

Scientific humanism has the following characteristics:

1. Scientific humanism rejects all supernatural powers.
2. Scientific humanism opposes all fatalist theories.
3. Scientific humanism gives reasoning the primary importance.
4. Scientific humanism believes in change.
5. Matter and energy exist independently. They do not owe their existence to mind.
6. Humanism believes that man has the immense potential to solve his own problems on the basis of reasoning and analytical power.
7. According to humanism, within certain objective limits, man is the master of his own destiny.
8. Scientific humanism believes in ethics as the moving spirit behind earthly human relations and experiences.
9. Scientific humanism believes in raising the material standard of living of all people.
10. Scientific humanism stands for the welfare of the society.
11. Scientific humanism emphasises democratic values.
12. Scientific humanism believes in the international economic order.

Curriculum

Spencer gave first priority to subjects like physiology, hygiene, physics and chemistry and placed history, politics and economics at the other end of the curriculum.

According to Spencer, science is the key which opens the locks of the knowledge of other subjects. He said, "History cannot be utilised properly without the knowledge of science".

Spencer observed that science introduced the element of utility. There was no work and vocation which could be learnt without the help of science. Spencer was of the view that the knowledge of science was essential for preparing us for life.

Moral Training

Spencer laid stress on the moral behaviour of the parents for moral training of the children. He believed in the 'theory of natural consequences' as emphasised by Rousseau.

18

Immanuel Kant (1724-1804)

Kant was an idealist philosopher. He belonged to the family of Pietists, a sect of German Puritans. He studied physics, astronomy, logic and psychology. He dipped into the abstractions of metaphysics, and the realities of algebra, geometry and physics at the University of Konigsberg.

Publications

1. *The Critique of Pure Reason.*
2. *The Critique of Practical Reason.*
3. *The Critique of Judgment.*
4. *On Physical Education.*
5. *On Practical Education.*

The Critique of Pure Reason: Kant maintains that our knowledge does not entirely come through our senses which are but imperfect measures of reality. The real world is beyond our sensory comprehension but not beyond our intellectual comprehension. He said, "The eye without the mind is blind and impotent".

The Critique of Practical Reason: It is a refutation of his previous views. He based his religion not on pure reason but on morals. Ethical obligation is a reality.

The Critique of Judgement: In this book, Kant finds God in the beautiful design of nature based on "patterns laid up in the heavens. The layman feels the presence of God in the two great mysteries 'the starry heavens above and the law within'.

Importance of Education

He wrote, "Man can become only through education".

Aim of Education

Kant wrote, "Children should be educated not with reference to present condition of things, but rather with regard to a possibly improved state of the human race—that is according to the ideal of humanity and its entire destiny and perfection which consist in absolute moral worth".

Guidelines for Moral Education

Prof. Marlow Ediger has summarised Kant's guidelines in stressing morality as under:

1. Morality should stress universals in space and time. Moral guidelines are not specific but flexible such as the Golden Rule. Flexibility in implementing the Golden Rule makes moral generalisations applicable to any place or region on the face of the earth, as well as applicable in any period of time. The time of application could be in the past, present, or future.
2. Morality in its manifestations may not bring happiness necessarily to the personal self. It could be painful to apply the Golden Rule. Certainly, just acts and deeds may not always bring contentment to the doer.
3. It is a duty to treat others as ends and not as means to an end. Duty is different from desire or wish.
4. Each person has the freedom to choose. Hopefully, ethical rather than unethical values will be chosen. Each person then possesses free will.
5. Individuals are entirely responsible for their choices whether they be moral or immoral.
6. Human beings are born as being good individuals. However, wrong decisions can be made pertaining to the unethical and the immoral.
7. Students must be taught to be thinking, reasoning individuals. The goal in education is to develop the moral being.
8. Self-discipline is necessary to curb the undesirable choices and decisions in life.
9. Human nature is improved through education and schooling.
10. Cultivation of the mind or intellect is a major goal of education. The intellect must develop into a being who is able to think critically, as well as analyse information.
11. Individuals need to emphasise the concept of wisdom when developing the rational powers.
12. Predictions in science do not interfere in the decision making arena. Cause and effect then is not involved in reasoning and in thinking.
13. Kant's *Critique of Practical Reason* states that the individual makes choices and decisions in the ethical domain. In his *Critique of Pure Reason*, Kant emphasises that nature stresses causes and effects.

19

Isaacs Susan (1895-1948)

Susan was a pioneer in the area of child education. As a keen and perceptive observer she studied a group of children in school at the Malting House in England. She came to the conclusion that learning should be linked with experience.

As Head of the Child Development at the Institute of Education, University of London, she was involved in various observational studies.

Susan was greatly influenced by the psycho-analysis movement. She observed in this regard, "My own personal study of young children has served only to increase my deep admiration and gratitude for the genius of Freud in being able to penetrate so deeply and so surely to the actual mind of the little child, through the study of the minds of the adults".

Publications

1. *The Nursery Years.*
2. *Social Development in Young Children.*
3. *Children and Parents.*
4. *The Children We Teach.*

In *The Nursery years*, she deals with the daily problems of the children, *viz.*, fear, fantasy, jealousy and rivalry. Other problems dealt with are: companionship, development of skills, value of play in education, thumb sucking, playing kitchen, value of movement etc. She discusses the child's development relationships with the world which surrounds him and suggests guidelines for their solutions.

In *Social Development in Young Children*, she deals with ego-centric attitude among young children, guilt and shame, love and hate, hostility and aggression, social relations and sexuality.

In *Children and Parents*, Susan Isaacs deals with the problems and difficulties of nursery teachers and parents.

20

Jan Amos Comenius (1592-1670)

Jan Amos Komensky is generally known as Comenius—Latinised form of his name (Jean Piaget in *Prospects*, Vol. X & III, No. 1-12, 1993). He was born on March 28, 1592 in Moravia, now part of the Czech Republic.

Comenius was of a piercing nature from his early childhood. He did not like the prevailing system of education. He had an open mind and did not hesitate to receive education from any kind and from any place. He travelled extensively and established contact with the scholars of his time through correspondence.

He was educated at Heidelberg University in Germany. Subsequently, he became a clergyman. Upon his return to his native place, he served as a school teacher and later as the Church Pastor at Fulnek. The start of the Thirty Years' War was the beginning of his misfortunes and he was forced to flee his homeland. In 1628 Comenius settled in Leszno, Poland, where he wrote his books calling for the reform of the educational system. His publications earned him reputation in other countries and he was invited first to England, and then to Sweden and Hungary to reform school systems.

Major Publications

1. *The Great Didactic*
2. *The School of Infancy*
3. *The Gate to Languages Unlocked*
4. *Visible World in Pictures*

Views on Various Dimensions of Education

Concept of Education. Comenius believed that education is not limited to the action of the school and family but is part of general social life.

Nature of the Child and the Role of the Teacher. Comenius was of the firm view that the teachers should understand how a child's mind develops and learns.

Books for Children. Comenius was the first to use an illustrated book for children—*Visible World in Pictures* (1658).

Teaching Techniques. Comenius is best known for his contribution to teaching techniques. He tends to mention the following principles to reform techniques of teaching:

1. Whatever is taught, its objective should be made clear.
2. Learning material should have practical utility.
3. General rules should be explained before hand.
4. All topics should be taught in a sequential manner.
5. The matter should not be left unless the child understands it clearly.
6. All topics as far as possible should be taught in a correlated manner.
7. Thinking on the part of the child should be encouraged.
8. Whatever is to be taught to the child should be taught in direct and in clear words.
9. Education should not be made a complex affair.

Discipline as a Great Motive Power

Comenius explains the importance of discipline in the life of a school in *The Great Didactic*: "There is a proverb in Bohemia, 'A school without discipline is like a mill without water', and this is very true. For example, if you withdraw the water from a mill, it stops and in the same way, if you deprive a school of discipline, you take away from it its motive power. A field also, if it is never ploughed, produces nothing but weeds, and trees if not continually pruned, revert to their wild state and bear no fruit. It must not be thought, however, that we wish our schools to resound with shrieks and blows. What we demand is vigilance and attention on the part of the master and of the pupils for discipline is nothing but an unfailing method by which we may make our scholars in reality".

Discipline to be Always Watchful

He goes to explain the concept of discipline as,"Our enemy, Satan, is on the watch not only while we are asleep but also while we are awake and as we sow good seeds in the minds of our pupils, he continues to plant his own weeds there as well and sometimes a corrupt nature brings forth weeds of its own accord, so that these evil dispositions must be kept in check by force. We must, therefore, strike against them by means of discipline, that is to say, using blame and punishment which should always be administered on the spot, that the vice may be checked as soon as it shows itself, or may be, as far as possible, torn up by the roots. Discipline, therefore, should be ever watchful, not with the view of enforcing application to study (for learning is always attractive to the minds, if it be treated with the right method) but to ensure clearly morals".

'Why', 'When' and 'How' of Discipline

Comenius considers punishment "like a bitter draught presented for them (for children) by the doctor". He explains the 'Why', 'When' and 'When' of punishment as "Punishment should be employed towards those who err. But it is not because they have erred that they should be punished (for what has been done cannot be undone), but in order that they may not err again in the future. Discipline, therefore, should be free from personal elements, such as anger or dislike and should be exercised with such frankness and sincerity of purpose, that even the pupils may feel that the action taken is for their good, and that those sit over them are but exercising paternal authority. They will thus regard it in the same light as a bitter draught prescribed for them by the doctor".

Setting a Work on Scientific Principle

Comenius advised to learn a lesson from nature. "The very sun in the heaven gives us a lesson on this point. In early spring, when plants are young and tender, it does not scorch them but warms and invigorates with slow degrees not putting forth its full heat until they are full-grown and bring forth fruit and seeds. The gardener proceeds on the same principle, and does not apply the pruning-knife to plants that are immature. In the same way, a musician does not strike his lyre a blow with his fist or with a stick, nor does he throw it against the wall because it produces discordant sound, but setting a work on scientific principle, he tunes it and gets it into order".

Contribution

Addressing the winners of the Comenius Medal at a solemn ceremony in October, 1988, in Paris, the Director-General of UNESCO, Mr. Federico Mayor said that 'among the eminent educators of the past, Comenius is one of those who incarnates in the best possible way the image one may have of a UNESCO precursor. His philosophy that encouraged political unity, religious reconciliation and international cooperation in the field of education… has lost nothing of its actuality'.

To use the words of Jean Piaget, "Comenius was the first to conceive the full-scale science of education". His educational objective can be summed up in the axiom on the title page of *The Great Didactic*, 'Teaching Thoroughly All Things To All Men'. He is also considered to be the first educator to have put forward the concept of international education. His ideas on education for everyone and for all peoples, and on the international organisation of public education make him a fore-runner of many modern institutions and trends of thought. Comenius' efforts on behalf of universal education earned him the title of 'Teacher of Nations'.

(*Source*: '*Educational Innovation*' No. 98. March 1999, IBE-Geneva)

21

Jawaharlal Nehru (1889-1964)

Jawaharlal Nehru, one of the foremost freedom fighters and the first Prime Minister of India was a many faceted personality. He was a prolific writer in English. From age fifteen to twenty-three he studied in England at Harrow Public School, then at Cambridge and later at Inner Temple and became Barrister-at-law. From 1925 to 1945, he had one leg in jail and the other outside. For him prison was the best of universities where he had time to write his famous books. Under his presidentship in 1929, the Congress declared 'Complete Independence' as its goal. He authored about 60 books on different subjects.

Here some extracts from his writings on various dimensions of education are presented.

Social Relevance of Education

The ideal of education has long been the improvement of the individual. The ideal must invariably hold, for without individual advancement there can be no social progress. But even that care of the individual must today be considered in terms of the mass of the people or else the enlightened individual will be submerged in the unenlightened mass. And, in any event, is it right or just that a group of individual should have opportunities of advancement and growth which are denied to the many.

… All education must have a definite social outlook and must train our youth for the kind of society we wish to have. Politicians may strive for political and economic changes in order to bring that society into existence, but the real basis of that society must be laid in the teaching of our schools and colleges.

If this is the accepted ideal of our future society then all our education must be fashioned to that end and must not pay homage to anything that is against this conception of the social order. That education will always have to think in terms of the hundreds of millions of our people, and not sacrifice their interests for any group or class. The teacher will then be not just a follower of a profession which gives him a livelihood, but one who has chosen his vocation in the ardent spirit of a missionary in a sacred cause which fills his being (*Address at the All India Educational Conference, Dehradun, December* 29, 1939)

Process of Education

In the final analysis, no subject is of greater importance than that of education. It is the men and women in a country that make and build a nation and it is education that is supposed to build those men and women.

The process of education, therefore, must help to build men and women suited to the age and the tasks they have to perform. It should presumably deal with certain basic factors in the development of boys and girls to give them strength of character and the right outlook on life. I do not mean by this that that they should be conditioned only in one particular way, but rather that they should develop, apart from the essentials of character, a trained receptive and tolerant mind which is capable of considering problems in their entirety and trying to arrive at solutions. They should in effect develop into integrated human beings. Integration means not only a process within themselves, which of course is highly important, but also a measure of integration with the environment.

The part of training that deals with the environment will necessarily vary with the age and the kind of work that these people may be called upon to do. We live, as is well known, in an intensely transitional age. We cannot go back upon it and we can only try to understand it and look forward to the changes that are likely to come. (*Message to the Hindustani Talimi Sangh*, November 8, 1957)

Education: Real and Superficial

I suppose everyone is concerned in every country because more and more it is realised that it is through education that you can ultimately influence people's minds and thereby events. I think in the Preamble of the Constitution of UNESCO it is stated that wars begin in the minds of men. Well, if wars begin in the minds of men as they surely do, then one has to influence the minds of men and women. That seems obvious enough and therefore, whether we look at it from the narrower point of view of imparting education say, in the scientific or technological fields which is so essential or other fields, the basic thing that should be necessary is to direct people towards thinking in terms of let us say, peace and cooperation and understanding and not in terms of the type of international life that we lead today.

But we find that the most highly educated nations and peoples in the world, who have all the advantages of technical education, advantages of education in humanities and who have succeeded in a large measure in getting rid of some of the ancient evils from which humanity has suffered like poverty, etc., in another context not only do not get on with each other but are full of violent hostility towards each other.

Now, is that the result of different types of education or lack of education? Does education lead to greater hostility in spite of greater understanding? It is a problem which, I will submit to you, deserves consideration. I am quite sure that education is essential and I am not decrying education but the fact is education or, if I may say so, that the type of education that we have had has not led to that peaceful and cooperative international approach which has become so essential to the world's growth or even to the world's survival. That troubles me.

And in thinking about our own educational problems in this country—as we do very often, even a layman like me—we may argue as to greater stress sometimes on scientific training, technological training or may stress about humanities, the importance of the humanities...

It does surprise me that while education is obviously desirable, inevitable and essential, I do not find the educated person always so desirable. He is often, in spite of his education, rather narrow-minded and throws his weight about on others whom he considers inferior to him, whether he does it as an individual, as a group or as a nation, but he does it. And in some ways he has got, in spite of his education, rather a closed mind. He does not look into other people's minds, peep into it and understand it because he starts with the presumption that he has got all that he wants to have in his mind and does not open it to others' impressions. That surely cannot be a good result of education. Education should open the mind and enable a person to understand other human beings and be understood by them...

Big revolutionary changes are taking place in the minds of the people. Education, I think, is the most revolutionary factor in India and is changing the face of India. It is not so suddenly obvious but any person who goes and sees the changes taking place is tremendously impressed by it.

Basic Education

What it is

...Basic education laid stress on various factors of importance, notably the coordination of the mind with manual work. That is an essential feature which we have to encourage...

Basic education, started at Wardha in 1937, was designed to develop the basic abilities of the child and therefore gave a primary place to manual training in the child's education. With the mother tongue as the medium of instruction, it was to be free and compulsory, and of seven-year duration at the school level. It was believed that such education apart from stimulating the intellect, "would be a kind of insurance against unemployment". (*Inaugural Address to the W.C.O.T.P. Conference*, New Delhi, December, 1956)

Physical Education

The type of education which concerns itself only with the reading of books is, from the human point of view, from any point of view, incomplete. You may become a high-class mathematician or something else as an individual, but you will find that you will be a better mathematician if your body functioned adequately and properly. It has, therefore, become necessary in our country to lay greater stress on physical fitness. I do not like any person going about with a bent back. I want them to be straight like a ram-rod. I want them to be quick in their walking, not sauntering as many of us do. It has thus become a matter of extreme importance, this stress on two things-physical culture and physical fitness and ability of the hands to do something. You can take it from me that if your hands can do something, your mind will work much more satisfactorily. I have no doubt in it. (*Speech proposing the Resolution on Education at the Avadi Session of the Congress*, January, 1955)

Higher Education: A Place of Culture

I take it that a university is essentially a place of culture, whatever 'culture' might mean... There is a great deal of culture all over the place and I, normally, find that those people who talk most loudly of culture, according to my judgement, possess no culture at all. Culture, first of all, is not loud; it is quiet, it is restrained, it is tolerant. You may judge the culture of a person by his silence, by a gesture, by a phrase or, more especially, by his life generally. The peculiar, narrow idea of culture that is spreading is that culture depends on the kind of headgear you wear or the kind of food you eat or on similar superficial things which, I do not deny, have a certain importance but which are very secondary in the larger context of life.

Each country has certain special cultural characteristics which have been developed through the ages. Similarly, each age has a culture and a certain way of its own. The cultural characteristics of a country are important and are certainly retained, unless, of course, they do not fit in with the spirit of the age. So, by all means, adhere to the special culture of your nation. But there is something that is deeper than national culture and that is human culture. If you do not have that human culture, that basic culture, then even that national culture of which you may be so proud has no real roots and will not do you much good. Today more especially, it has become essential for us to develop, in addition to such national culture as we may have, something that can only be called a world culture. There is much talk of One World and I believe that, at some time or other, that talk must bear fruit or else this world will go to pieces. It may be that we will not see that One World in our generation but if you want to prepare for that One World you must at least think about it. You have at least a culture to sustain you; and there is no reason why you should live your lives in narrow grooves, trying to think yourselves superior to the rest of the world. (*Convocation Address at University of Ceylon, Colombo*, January 12, 1950)

Role of Universities

A University stands for humanism, for tolerance, for reason, for progress, for the adventure of ideas and for the search for truth. It stands for the onward march of the human race towards even higher objectives. If the universities discharge their duty adequately, then it is well with the nation and the people. But if the temple of learning itself becomes a home of narrow bigotry and petty objectives, how then will the nation prosper or a people grow in stature?

A vast responsibility, therefore, rests on our universities and educational institutions and those who guide their destinies. They have to keep their lights burning and must not stray from the right path even when passion convulses the multitude and blinds many amongst those whose duty it is to set an example to others.

A nation cannot progress if it merely imitates its ancestors; what builds a nation is creative, inventive and vital activity. I seek the creative mind. How do creative minds come to be? In many ways, I suppose. I know that... what the University can do is to provide an environment in which creativeness and vitality of mind and body have a place and can prosper. (*An Address at Allahabad University*, December 13, 1947)

Reforms in University Education

...The whole question of university education has recently been considered by the Universities Commission of which Dr. Radhakrishnan was Chairman... This Commission was composed of very eminent educationists from India, the United States and England. They have done a remarkably good piece of work in a short time... They have pointed out the evils of tying up our examination system with government appointments. These examinations of ours and the education that lies behind them are looked upon just as stepping-stones to employments by government. Nothing could be worse for education. Our universities turn out tens of thousands of graduates who do not know what to do and appear to be incapable of doing anything except in some office. Our education has been described, perhaps a little uncharitably, as a training for unemployment. That may be an exaggeration. But there is a great deal of truth in it. So it is suggested that university examinations should be completely divorced from official appointments for which there should be separate tests.

One other matter to which I attach great importance, and about which I think I have previously written to you, is the necessity of some kind of manual labour for each student. I think it should be a good thing if every graduate, before he got his degree, was expected to put in a full year's labour in a factory or field or some other place. It might be some kind of social work. This is not a novel idea, as something like this has been tried with success in other countries. Many countries go in for conscription for military service. Why should we not have conscription for social service and labour? That would include, of course, some kind of elementary military training without arms. That discipline is badly needed in this country. (*Letter to Chief Ministers*, September 2, 1949)

University Administration

I have often noticed that the appointment of vice-chancellors to universities is considered almost entirely from the administrative point of view. Administration is important, but essentially a university is a body of persons devoted to academic pursuits, and this must always be kept in view so that a proper academic atmosphere is maintained and encouraged. If the vice-chancellor, who is the executive head of the university, is merely an administrator, then he cannot enter into that academic life which is so important, nor is he likely to be respected greatly by the large body of students. I think it is essential, therefore, that our vice-chancellors should be men of learning and high academic standards. (*Circular*, July 3, 1961)

Universities and Research Institutes

...Among the many disappointments that we have had, there is at least one achievement for which we can take credit and that is the advance of scientific research in this country. Our new laboratories are magnificent institutions of which any country can be proud. In this connection, I should like to draw your attention to a certain tendency which is doing harm to science. This is a tendency towards separation of research from teaching. This is accentuated in India by the separation of most research institutes from the universities. Even from the point of view of governmental organisation, they are separate. It seems to me essential that there should be the closest coordination between research institutes and universities. Also that we should encourage research work in universities. After all, our major research institutes must be fed from the universities and if the universities dry up, then the research institutes cannot survive for long. (*Letter to Chief Ministers*, April 15, 1950)

Girls Education

There is one thing that struck me as illustrating is the great need for girls' education. You will find that in the past, wherever girls' education was encouraged in India, there was progress. I suppose Punjab is one of the places where girls' education had an earlier beginning than elsewhere. In many respects, Punjab is one of our progressive States. I suppose that might be true of some other places, too. So girls' education is not an end in itself but is intimately connected with the social fabric and with advance along other lines, too.

A great French writer once remarked, "If you want me to tell you what a nation is like or what a social organisation is like, tell me the position of women in that nation". The status and social place of women will indicate the country's character more than anything else. That applies equally to the educational, social, economic and other fields. (*Speech at Mahila Vidyapith*, Allahabad, July 12, 1934)

22

Jean Jacques Rousseau (1712-1778)

Rousseau was a Swiss educational reformer and thinker. Opportunistic, unreliable, unscrupulous, at times a gigolo, at other times a liar, a thief and the unacknowledged father of several illegitimate children by his own confession. He had the flash of a genius that seemed to attract followers and friends despite his shortcomings. His writings have exercised such an influence on educational theory and practice that they are widely quoted even today. There is no doubt that he is considered one of the great leaders of the world.

Early Childhood

Rousseau lost his mother at an early age. His father who was a poor watch-maker could not provide him regular schooling. Rousseau left school at the age of 12. He tried unsuccessfully all sorts of occupations—apprentice to a rotary and then to an engraver etc. He became a music critic for sometime at Paris. From the age of twelve to twenty nine years, he remained a vagabond and during his wanderings he met different types of people, learnt to sympathise with the poor. He developed love for nature. He also defied the conventional rules of society.

Interest in Education

His experiences at different places awoke in him a keen interest in the problem of education. At about the age of about 25, he studied Hobbes, Locke, Montaigne, Pascal, Voltaire Malebranche, Leibnitz and Desccartes.

Rousseau's Suicide

Rousseau revolted against the established (canons) of society and advocated the doctrine of "Back to nature". He wrote, "Man is born free and every where he is in chains". His ideas were vehemently opposed by the establishment. His books were burnt. He incurred the displeasure of the French authorities and had to live in exile for many years. He was so much disgusted and disappointed that he committed suicide in 1778. However, his greatness was recognised later and his views had tremendous influence on the outbreak of the French Revolution in 1789.

Publications and Essence of His Writings

After wandering for a number of years, he settled down in Paris (France). In 1750, at the age of 38, Rousseau wrote his first book *The Progress of the Art and the Science*. This was followed by *The Origin of Inequality Among Men* (1753), *The New Heloise—a romance* (1759); *Social Contract* (1762), and *Emile* or *Concerning Education* (1762).

In his publications, he criticised the existing institutions. He attributed the existing oppression and corruption of the society to the advancement of civilisation, which according to him was the main cause of the differences and inequalities among men. Regarding the absolute powers of the sovereign, Rousseau wrote, "He cannot impose upon his subjects fetters that are useless to the community".

Educational Philosophy

'Return to nature' was the theme of his two educational publications (novels): *The New Heloise* (1761) and *Emile* (1762). These books, were among the most widely read of the popular writing of the century.

Rousseau was an arch enemy of child neglect. His *Emile* made Europe child conscious. It is still widely quoted in almost all books on educational philosophy, principles and practices.

Sources of Education

According to Rousseau following are the three main sources of education:

1. *Education of Nature*: "The constitutional exertion of our organs and faculties is the education of nature".

(Discussed Separately)

2. *Education given by Men*: "The uses we are taught to make of that exertion, constitute the education given to us by men".

3. *Education from Circumstances*: "And in the acquisition made by our own experience, on the objects that surround us, consists our education from circumstances".

By education from nature he meant development according to the child's endowments and capacities. By education from men, he emphasised the importance of social environment, teaching how to make use of that development. By education from things, he understood physical environment, helping to gain experience by ourselves. He says that harmonious development of these three factors constitutes an ideal scheme of education.

Such harmony in education is possible by subordinating the education of men and things to that of nature because we have no control over nature. We, must, therefore, direct the other two, to ensure cooperation of these factors for imparting ideal education.

Theory of Negative Education

Rousseau believed that everything is good as it comes from nature and it generates in the hands of man, so he advocated that the education of the child should be purely negative. The child should not be taught the principles of truth and virtue but guarded against evil. He wrote, "I call a positive education one that tends to form the mind prematurely and to instruct the child in the duties that belong to him. I call negative education one that tends to perfect the organs that are the instruments of knowledge and endeavours to process the way for reasons, by the proper exercises of senses".

Aims of Education

Rousseau's aim of education was the attainment of fullest natural growth of the individual, leading to balanced, harmonious useful and natural life. The real aim of education is to help the child to live his life. He says, "To live is not merely to breathe. It is to act, to make use of our organs, senses, our faculties and of all those parts of ourselves, which give us the feeling of our existence".

This general aim of education was split up by Rousseau according to the nature at different stages of human development.

(i) *Infancy, i.e.*, from birth to the age of five years, the aim of education is to develop a well-regulated freedom.

(ii) *In childhood, i.e.*, between the age of five and twelve, the main aim of education is to provide the child with the strength which he needs for the attainment of well-regulated freedom.

(iii) *In boyhood or pre-adolescent period, i.e.*, from twelve years to fifteen years the aim of education is "to acquire such knowledge which may satisfy the wants of the child and must be functionally useful". This is the period for intellectual education—the period of instruction, labour and study.

(iv) *In adolescent period, i.e.*, from 15 to 20 years, the aim of education is the training of heart, to make the child loving and tender-hearted so that he may live peacefully in social relationship. In this period, religious, moral and social education is recommended. In the previous periods, the child has already developed physically and intellectually. He must now grow emotionally, aesthetically, socially and morally. The sex instinct, which is sufficiently developed by this time, is to be sublimated by re-directing it to the love of some noble idea and by keeping the young occupied in work and activity.

Curriculum

Rousseau recommends curriculum in accordance with the nature of each stage of the child.

Curriculum at the First Stage: Curriculum at the first stage (from one to 5 years) would be such as it develops physical strength. The child should be allowed to wander freely in the countryside. His play-things should be very simple such as branches with fruits and flowers and no expensive toys. 'Let him not be pampered! Let him not be subdued'.

Curriculum at the Second Stage: Curriculum at the second stage (between 5 to 12 years) should lead to the development of senses. Rousseau thinks that if senses are not trained properly, independent reasoning and judgement are impossible. Emile (the hero of the novel *Emile)* is to be given the greatest freedom of physical movement, simple diet and light clothing. There will be no verbal lessons for him. He will not be instructed in language, history and geography. Emile is to learn from his own experience. No moral instruction is to be given. "Exercise the body, the organs, the senses and powers but keep the soul lying fallow as long as you can. Training for senses means learning to judge, foresee and reason through them. It is more than the mere use of them. All learning must come by play-way. There is no need for the child to learn anything by heart. For Emile there is no curriculum. He has to learn by activity and experience.

Curriculum at the Third Stage: Curriculum at the third stage of pre-adolescence (12 to 15 years) should be built around curiosity which should create an urge for knowledge. Rousseau states that this is the period for developing intellect. Emile is introduced to studies that reveal nature, astronomy, science and the arts and crafts. Rousseau emphasises the learning of manual and industrial arts partly to make Emile independent and partly to overcome the prejudice held against the manual work. Rousseau wanted that the boy must be taken from one workshop to another and he must try his hand at every trade. In this way Rousseau wanted to teach him industrial exchange, banking and transportation. Rousseau does not recommend the study of books. The only book he recommends is *Robinson Crusoe*, a study of life according to nature.

Curriculum at the Fourth Stage: In the fourth stage of the adolescence period (15 to 20 years of age), training of heart should receive attention. In the earlier stages, the boy was an individual working for self-perfection and self-development. Now he has to be social and adapt himself to the conduct and interest of others. The study of society, politics, economics, history and religion are the appropriate studies for the youth to understand complex social relationships. Emile must be provided opportunities for training in moral education about his relations with his fellow men and moral qualities such as benevolence, kindness, service and sympathy. Rousseau recommends that moral education should be given through activities and occupations and not through lectures on ethics. History will be utilised as a means of moral instruction. Travel is recommended for knowing the world and the institutions of the neighbouring countries. At this stage the youth undergoes a new birth on account of the appearance of sex impulse. Sex instruction is to consist of direct moral exhortation on chastity and an explanation of the mysteries of creation in the world of plants, animals and men in a dispassionate manner.

Education of Women: Rousseau maintained that women were the makers of men. They were, "the chaste guardians of our morals, and the sweet security of our place". Their education was to be different from men. Rousseau believed that "Woman is made specially to please man". She has, therefore, to be taught to be soft and sweet and learn to suffer and bear the wrongs of her husband without complaint". The duty of women towards man is "to train him in childhood, to tend him in manhood, and to counsel him throughout his life". Rousseau, therefore, advocated that her studies, should be practical. Intellectual interests, he believed, destroyed her nature. He stated, "I would a hundred times prefer a simple girl, rudely brought up to a girl of learning".

He remarked, "A woman of literacy education (culture) is the plague of her husband; her children, her family her servants—everybody". Sophie, therefore, is to learn embroidery, lace making, the art of house decorating and house keeping, sewing etc.

Methods of Teaching

Observation of the Nature of the Child: Rousseau wrote, "I wish some discreet person would give us a treatise on the art of observing children—an art which would be of immense value to us but of which parents and schoolmasters have not yet learnt the very first rudiment".

Art of Teaching: Rousseau further said, "To know how to suggest is the art of teaching".

Rousseau emphasised, "The highest function of the teacher consists not much in imparting knowledge as in stimulating the pupil in its love and pursuit".

He was against the harsh and unsympathetic methods of education which repressed the natural inclinations and tendencies of the child. He advocated simple and direct methods of instruction and urged "experience before expression" and "objects before words". He said, "Give your scholar no verbal lesson. He should be taught by experience alone. Teach by doing whenever you can and only fall back upon words when doing is out of question. Book knowledge should be as little as possible". Emphasising "object teaching", he remarked, "let the senses always be the guides. Let there be no books but the world and no other instruction than facts. The child who reads, does not think, he merely reads. He is not receiving instruction but learning words".

Methods of teaching advocated by Rousseau are summed up as under:

1. Do not teach books. "I hate books. They only teach us to talk about things that we know nothing about. To conceal their deficiencies teachers choose the dead languages—words, words, words".
2. Provide opportunities to children from their own experience and not from books.

   "Let him (the child) not be taught science, let him discover it".

3. Provide sense training.
4. Never substitute the symbol for the thing unless it is impossible to show the thing itself.

Role of the Teacher

Rousseau assigns a minor place to the teacher in the educative process. He is not called an instructor but only a guide. His main responsibility is to motivate the child to learn. This he can achieve by exploiting the innate tendencies of the child. He must possess a profound understanding of the child's nature and be able to control his emotional reactions. He is not to impose any rules of control upon the child. He is to allow him perfect freedom and guide him properly.

Rousseau wrote, "The highest function of the teacher consists not so much in imparting knowledge as on stimulating the pupil in its love and pursuit". Further he advises, "To know how to suggest is the art of teaching". Rousseau placed stress on developing the reasoning power of the child. He observed, "If ever you (teacher) substitute authority in the place of argument, he (child) will reason no longer, he will ever afterwards be handed like a shuttle cork between the opinion of others".

Freedom of the Child—Discipline by Natural Consequences

He believes in freedom of the child. It is only in a free atmosphere that the child will be able to develop his inborn and innate capacities. He does not believe in punishing the child so as to correct his future behaviour. The reason behind this assumption according to Rousseau is very simple-the child is not able to link up the punishment administered and the mischief done by him. Children, therefore, should be left alone to experience the consequences of the mischief done by them. Nature, according to Rousseau, is a great teacher. If children commit mistakes and violate the principles of nature, they naturally invite the retribution of nature. This conception in the field of education is known as "Discipline by natural consequences".

Secondly, in the field of education, Rousseau starts with the assumption that the nature of child is essentially good, hence he should have freedom in his actions. Firstly, he believes that the child will not commit any immoral act, and secondly, even if he commits any, he will learn morality by the natural consequences of the action done.

Rousseau's concept of freedom and discipline are summed up as:

1. Discipline by natural consequences.
2. No punishments.
3. Full freedom to the child.

'*Emile*': An Important Treatise on Education

'*Emile*' is a treatise on education cast in the form of a novel in which there are three characters; Emile, who may be regarded as 'Rousseau' while a boy, and his tutor, who is obviously Rousseau, as a man, Sophie, who is destined to be the mate of Emile.

'*Emile*' consists of five books or parts on training and education.

Book I deals with the infant; Book II with childhood; Book III with the pre–adolescent between the ages of twelve and fifteen; Book IV with adolescence; and Book V with the education of girls.

(Curriculum given in Emile has been detailed above)

Lord Morley has described the value of '*Emile*' in these words: "It touched the deeper things of character. It filled parents with a sense of the dignity of their task. It cleared away the accumulation of clogging prejudices and obscure inveterate usage, which made education one of the dark formalistic arts. It admitted floods of light and air into the tightly closed nurseries and school rooms. It effected the substitution of growth for mechanism… It was the charter of youthful deliverance".

On the other hand, the Parliament of Paris criticised '*Emile*' very severely. It was ordered to be burnt publicly. Orders for the arrest of Rousseau were issued and he had to run away from France to Switzerland. The reading of *Emile* was forbidden by the Archbishop of Paris. The book was condemned on account of 'Containing an abominable doctrine, ready to subvert natural law and to destroy the foundations of the Christian religion… tending to trouble the peace of States, to cause subjects to revolt against their sovereigns; as containing a large number of prepositions false, scandalous, full of hate against the Church, derogatory to the respect of holy scriptures …. erroneous, impious, blasphemous and heretical".

Rousseau's Naturalism and His Theory of Negative Education

The term negative education denotes Rousseau's hatred for the formal educational system prevailing in the society. He considered it unnatural and against the nature of child. He vehemently criticised it and advocated to replace it. Since the formal system was considered as the positive system of education, he termed his own system of education as negative. It will be seen from the following characteristics of the negative education, that they are at variance with that of the positive system of education.

Chief Characteristics of Negative Education

The following are the chief characteristics of his theory of Negative Education:

1. *Direct Experience of the Child*: Rousseau would like Emile to learn from his own experiences and not from books. Knowledge acquired from books is second-hand and easily forgotten. Personal knowledge directly acquired, from various learning situations, is something permanent, which the child will not forget. This will constitute the permanent nature of his character.

2. *The Heuristic Method*: Rousseau also advocates the heuristic method of teaching. He would like to place the child in the position of an original

discoverer. The child will learn science with self-made and self-invented apparatus. The same method is to be applied to other subjects of the curriculum.

3. *No Time Saving in Childhood*: According to Rousseau, in childhood no time should be saved. It should rather be lost. Let the child run, jump and play all day long. In all these activities he will have a continuous reconstruction of experience which is nothing but education, pure and simple. Time lost on play and recreational activities in childhood, is not lost but profitably gained; childhood is not the time for intellectual pursuits.

4. *No Book Learning:* Rousseau says, "I hate books because they are a curse to children. They teach us to talk only that which we do not know. Instead of making the child stick to his books, I keep him busy in the workshop; his hands will work to the profit of his mind".

5. *No Habit Formation*: In his own words, "The only habit which the child should be allowed to form is to contract no habit at all". Young children should not be made slaves of rigid habits. They should be left free in all their activities. If any habits are to be formed in childhood, let them form natural habits.

6. *No Direct Moral Education*: Rousseau is not in favour of teaching of morals. Let the child be left free to act and learn what is right and wrong, by the consequences of his own actions. He says, "Much more harm than good is done by your ceaseless preaching and moralising". He further says, "Inflict on the child no sort of punishment and never make him ask your pardon. As there is no moral quality in his actions, he can do nothing wrong".

7. *No Formal Discipline*: *Discipline by Natural Consequences.* Rousseau is in favour of free and positive discipline for children. Let the children suffer natural consequences of their own actions without the intervention of human beings to protect or punish and in this way they will set themselves right. If a child breaks a window pane, let him sit in the cold wind that gushes in as a result of his folly. If he climbs a tree, let him fall down and learn not to do so again.

8. *No Sticking to Traditional Procedure of Education*: Rousseau was greatly disgusted with the prevailing social, political, economic, religious and educational conditions in his country. So he said, "Follow the reverse of the current practice and you will almost do right". He challenged the traditional procedure of education saying, "Give me a child of twelve who knows nothing at all. At fifteen I will restore him to you, knowing as much as those who have been under instruction from infancy, with the difference that your scholar only knows things by heart, while mine knows how to use his knowledge".

9. *Individual Instruction*: Rousseau emphasised the due importance of individual instruction. He believed that the individuality of the child should be recognised by the educator and duly respected by him. He was right when he said that children are children before they become men.

10. *The Principle of Learning by Doing*: He lays stress on the principle of learning by doing. He says, teach by doing whenever you can and only fall back on words when doing is out of question. He believes that the child should take part in various activities and learn in a natural way. When the child wants to do something with his own hands his urge to creative activity must be satisfied.

11. *Example is Better than Precept*: For imparting moral education Rousseau believes in the principle that example is better than precept. There is no use lecturing on morality to him; he should have an example of moral behaviour and opportunities may be provided to him to practise virtue.

12. *Social Knowledge by Social Participation*: The child in his period of adolescence will get knowledge about social relations by actually visiting places and coming in contact with the members of the community.

Limitations of Rousseau's Naturalism in Education

1. Physical nature alone is not sufficient for providing education.
2. Naturalism in its extreme form neglects books and other media.
3. Naturalism ignores the higher ends in the education process.
4. It is very difficult to find naturalistic surroundings for locating educational institutions.
5. Naturalism assigns very little importance to teacher in the educative process.
6. Absolute freedom to child is a myth. It cannot exist. Child cannot be allowed the freedom to hang himself.
7. Naturalism does not offer definite aims of education.
8. Rousseau never tried to put into practice his theory and principles of education. Rousseau's naturalism seems to be a utopian concept.
9. Rousseau's views on women education are not in accordance with their nature. Rather they are outmoded in the present context.

Contribution to Education

Notwithstanding some limitations of Rousseau's views in the present context, his contribution to educational theory and principles is very valuable. He ushered in a new era for child education. His major contribution are as under:

1. Rousseau propounded the new gospel of faith in the nature of the child in place of the old ones.
2. His emphasis on the 'discovery' and 'recognition' of childhood traits has brought about a revolutionary change in the thinking of educators.
3. His stress on the 'concrete' led to 'Learning by Doing'.
4. Rousseau anticipated the modern heuristic Method when he declared the child as a 'discoverer'.
5. Rousseau showed the way to the teacher that he must study the child thoroughly.

6. It is due to Rousseau that the need for sense training and physical activities in the earlier development of the child has been recognised in the modern system of education.
7. His concepts of freedom, growth, interest and activity are noteworthy in educational theory and practice.
8. Rousseau showed the value of motivation and of creating problems and of utilising the senses and activities of the child.
9. Present day emphasis on vocational education finds its root in Rousseau.
10. The concept of discipline in naturalism is very desirable. Punishment is based on the consequences of wrong deeds. Children share freedom as well as responsibility.
11. Naturalism in education draws our attention to the aesthetic aspect of surroundings. This also implies that schools should be located in natural surroundings. Education can be imparted in the open.

Robert Rusk describes the work of Rousseau in these words, "Rousseau nevertheless stands to modern education as Plato to ancient education".

According to Charles W. Coulter and Richard S. Rimanoczy, the impact of Rousseau may be stated as "Rousseau made Europe more child-conscious and the formal European educational system more self-conscious'.

P.P. Graves observes in *A Student's History of Education*: "Disregarding the weak and offensive personality of the author, and forgetting the inconsistencies and the contradictions of the work itself, the '*Emile*' has always been accounted a work of great richness, power and underlying wisdom, and each of its defects is more than balanced by a corresponding merit".

Essence of Rousseau's Naturalism

Rousseau is the most prominent naturalist. As a matter of fact Rousseau and naturalism are inseparable. We cannot think of naturalism without Rousseau.

The key-note of Rousseau's philosophy is to have a 'State of Nature', 'Natural Man' and 'Natural Civilisation'.

'Return to nature' was his slogan. He observed, "Everything is good as it comes from the hands of nature but everything degenerates in the hands of man". Again he wrote, "Civilised man is born, lives and dies in the state of slavery. Leave him alone".

According to Rousseau, the state of nature in which man lived long ago was a blissful state. Modern civilisation is the main cause of the misery of mankind. The alternative before mankind is back to nature. The customary procedures of the civilised society should be done away with and the natural state may be accepted again.

Regarding the state of children in the prevailing state of affairs of society, Rousseau wrote, "The age of cheerfulness and gaiety is spent in the midst of tears, punishments, threats and slavery. We torment the poor creatures, for their future good: and perceive not that death is at hand, and ready to seize them amidst all this sorrowful preparation for life. Who can tell how many children have fallen victims to the extravagant sagacity of their parents and guardians? Happy to escape such cruelty, the only advantage the poor suffers reaped from the evils they endured, being to die without regretting a life of misery.

"Man, be humane! It is the first, the chief of moral duties, to exercise humanity to everything, of whatever age or condition, that is relative to man. What! Is wisdom void of humanity? Have a tender regard for children".

Rousseau contends that all the ills and miseries of civilisation are on account of a departure from a 'State of Nature'.

23

Jiddu Krishnamurti (1895-1986)

Jiddu Krishnamurti, the eighth child of his parents was born on May 11, 1895 in a well to-do family in the small hill town of Madanapalli about 240 km. north of Madras (Chennai). The Jiddu family was Telugu speaking Brahmin. Krishnamurti's father, though an orthodox Brahmin was a member of the Theosophical Society.

Krishnamurti's bouts of fever and his father's frequent transfers interrupted his schooling. Moreover he hated book learning. Nevertheless he was a keen observer and when his interest was aroused, he would stand for long stretches at a time watching trees and clouds or squat on the ground gazing at plants and insects. About his school, he wrote in his memoir: "I cannot say I was particularly happy at school, for the teachers were not very kind and gave me lessons that were too hard for me. I enjoyed games as long as they were not rough, as I had very delicate health."

At the age of 15, Krishnamurti accompanied Mrs. Annie Besant, the moving spirit of the Theosophical Society, to England in 1911. While in London, Krishnamurti enjoyed most the theatres he was taken to. He saw the *Prison of Zenda, The Julius Caesar, Macbeth* etc. The Oxford Cambridge, Eton and Harrow cricket matches were also enjoyed very much. Krishnamurti made three unsuccessful attempts to pass Matriculation, an entrance examination to the London University.

Krishnamurti made his first speech in London in 1911. In 1912, he wrote a book entitled *Education as Service* in which he described the life of an ideal school where love rules and inspires, where the students grow into noble adolescents under the fostering case of teachers who feel the greatness of their vocation. Krishnamurti's first poem *Hymn of the Initiate Triumphant* was published in the *Herald* in January 1923.

At the age of 14, in 1909, Krishnamurti was hailed as the 'World Teacher' or 'Lord Maltraya' by Charles Webster, one of the most mystic seers of the Theosophical Society. Mrs. Annie Besant, the President of the Society also endorsed this view and she more or less adopted Krishnamurti as her younger brother. In August 1922, Krishnamurti is said to have had an unusual spiritual experience that became a turning point in his life and he became a world spiritual leader.

Krishnamurti gave discourses to large gatherings in Australia, England, Holland and North and South America. With the generous offerings of his followers, Krishnamurti established several centres for philosophical studies in various countries.

Major Works

1. *Kingdom of Happiness* (1927)
2. *Path* (1930)
3. *Search* (1931)
4. *Commentaries from the Unknown* (1950)
5. *Commentaries on Living: II Series* (1951)
6. *Commentaries on Living: III Series* (1952)
7. *First and Last Freedom* (1954)
8. *Education and the Significance of Life* (1955)
9. *Life Ahead* (1963)
10. *Talks in Europe* (1967)

Philosophy of Life

Krishnamurti summed all disciplines and rejected all mentors and preceptors. He initiated no new faith or dogma. He claimed no authority, no religion and initiated no programme of social reform. He postulated nothing more than a total transformation of the individual self as a cure for conflict and suffering in the world. He advised his audience to think for themselves, to feel passionately, to shed the burdens of the past or future and to free their minds from fear.

Krishnamurti used to say: "I desire those who seek to understand me, to be free, not to follow me, not to make me a cage which will become a religion, a sect."

His message to mankind was: "First understand the purpose of your life—the purpose of this individual existence. Understand what is it towards which you are thriving. Then utilize every emotion, every thought to strengthen you."

Krishnamurti also observed: "It is necessary to encourage the development of a good mind that is capable of dealing with the many issues of life as a whole and which does not try to escape from them and so become contradictory, frustrated, bitter or cynical. And it is essential that it should be aware of its own conditioning, its motives and purposes. Knowledge then is essential only as a means of cultivating the mind and not an end in itself."

"The self is made up of a series of defensive and expansive reactions, and its fulfillment is always in its own projections and gratifying identifications. As long as we translate experience in terms of the self, of the "me" and the "mine," as long as the "I", the ego, maintains itself through its reactions, experience cannot be freed from conflict, confusion and pain. Freedom comes only when one understands the ways of the self, the experience. It is only when the self, with its accumulated reactions, is not the experiencer, that experience takes on an entirely different significance and becomes creation."

What is essential for man, whether young or old, is to live fully, integrally, and that is why our major problem is the cultivation of that intelligence which brings integration. Undue emphasis on any part of our total make-up gives a partial and therefore distorted view of life, and it is this distortion which is causing most of our difficulties. Any partial development of our whole temperament is bound to be disastrous both for ourselves and for society, and so it is really very important that we approach our human problems with an integrated point of view.

To be an integrated human being is to understand the entire process of one's own consciousness, both the hidden and the open. This is not possible if we give undue emphasis to the intellect. We attach great importance to the cultivation of the mind, but inwardly we are insufficient, poor and confused. This living in the intellect is the way of disintegration; for ideas, like beliefs, can never bring people together except in conflicting groups."

Krishnamurti's philosophy may be summed up in 2 F's, *i.e.*, FREEDOM OF MIND AND FEARLESSNESS

Shortcomings of the Prevailing System of Education

Krishnamurti pointed out the following shortcomings of the Indian education.

1. Conventional education makes independent thinking extremely difficult.
2. Conventional education puts an end to spontaneity.
3. Conventional education leads to dullness of mind and heart.
4. Conventional education develops fear in our mind and makes us afraid to be different from established standards.
5. Conventional education makes us field uncomprehensively to environment.
6. Conventional education merely prepares us to get a better job or enables us to gain professional efficiency.
7. Conventional education fails to enable us to understand the higher and wider significance of life.
8. Conventional education does not develop deep integration of thought and feeling.
9. Conventional education is lopsided. It ignores the many-sided development of an individual.
10. Conventional education trains us only to seek personal gain and security and fight for ourselves.
11. Conventional education is merely a training of the mind.

12. Conventional education has made examinations and degrees the criterion of intelligence and have developed cunning minds that avoid vital human issues.
13. The present system of education is making us subservient, mechanical and deeply thoughtless.
14. The present system of education, though awakens us intellectually, inwardly it leaves us incomplete, stultified and uncreative.

J. Krishnamurti denounces the present technique as "Present-day education is a complete failure because it has over-emphasized technique. In over-emphasizing technique we destroy man. To cultivate capacity and efficiency without understanding life, without having a comprehensive perception of the ways of thought and desire, will only make us increasingly ruthless, which is to engender wars and jeopardize our physical security. The exclusive cultivation of techniques has produced scientists, mathematicians, bridge builders, space conquerors; but do they understand the total process of life? Can any specialist experience life as a whole? Only when he ceases to be a specialist."

He further criticises the exclusive emphasis on technical education in these words: "Technical knowledge, however necessary, will in no way resolve our inner, psychological pressures and conflicts; and it is because we have acquired technical knowledge without understanding the total process of life that technology has become a means of destroying ourselves. The man who knows how to split the atom but has no love in his heart becomes a monster."

"Our technical progress is fantastic, but it has only increased our powers of destroying one another, and there is starvation and misery in every land. We are not peaceful and happy people."

"Education as it is at present in no way encourages the understanding of the inherited tendencies and environmental influences which condition the mind and heart and sustain fear, and therefore it does not help us to break through these conditionings and bring about an integrated human being. Any form of education that concerns itself with a part and not with the whole of man inevitably leads to increasing conflict and suffering."

Development of mere Theories only: "Modern education, in developing the intellect, offers more and more theories and facts, without bringing about the understanding of the total process of human existence. We are highly intellectual; we have developed cunning minds, and are caught up in explanations. The intellect is satisfied with theories and explanations, but intelligence is not; and for the understanding of the total process of existence, there must be an integration of the mind and heart in action. Intelligence is not separate from love."

Function of Education: Integral Education and Creation of Integrated Individuals

In the words of J. Krishnamurti: "Without an integrated understanding of life, our individual and collective problems will only deepen and extend.

The purpose of education is not to produce mere scholars, technicians, and job hunters, but integrated men and women who are free of fear; for only between such human beings can there be enduring peace." To understand life is to understand ourselves and that is both the beginning and the end of education.

"Education is not merely acquiring knowledge, gathering and correlating facts; it is to see the significance of life as a whole. The function of education is to create human beings who are integrated and therefore intelligent. We may take degrees and be mechanically efficient without being intelligent. Intelligence is not mere information; it is not derived from books, nor does it consist of clever self-defensive responses and aggressive assertions. One who has not studied may be more intelligent than the learned. Intelligence is the capacity to perceive the essential, the *what* is; and to awaken this capacity, in oneself and in others, is education.

"Education helps us to discover lasting values so that we do not merely cling to formulas or repeat slogans; it should help us to break down our national and social barriers, instead of emphasizing them, for they breed antagonism between man and man."

Integral education implies the following characteristics:

1. *Development of the Capacity to Face Challenges:* If the individual is to grapple with life from moment to moment, if he is to face its intricacies, its miseries and sudden demands, he must be infinitely pliable and therefore free of theories and particular patterns of thought.

2. *Development of Self-Knowledge:* Education should not encourage the individual to conform to society or to be negatively harmonious with it, but help him to discover the true values which come with unbiased investigation and self-awareness. When there is no self-knowledge, self-expression becomes self-assertion, with all its aggressive and ambitious conflicts. Education should awaken the capacity to be self-aware and not merely indulge in gratifying self-expression. The individual is of first importance, not the system; and as long as the individual does not understand the total process of himself, no system, whether of the left or of the right, can bring order and peace to the world.

Understanding comes only through self-knowledge, which is awareness of one's total psychological process. Thus, education, in the true sense, is the understanding of oneself, for it is within each one of us that the whole of existence is gathered.

3. *Helping to have Integrated Experience*: J. Krishnamurti points out in this regard: "The right kind of education, while encouraging the learning of a technique, should accomplish something which is of far greater importance; it should help man to experience the integrated process of life. It is this experiencing that will put capacity and technique in their right place. If one really has something to say, the very saying of it creates its

own style; but learning a style without inward experiencing can only lead to superficiality."

4. *Freedom from Ready-made Ideals:* According to J. Krishnamurti, "Ideals have no place in education for they prevent the comprehension of the present. Surely, we can be aware of *what is* only when we do not escape into the future. To look to the future, to strain after an ideal, indicates sluggishness of mind and a desire to avoid the present."

"Is not the pursuit of a ready-made Utopia a denial of the freedom and integration of the individual? When one follows an ideal, a pattern, when one has a formula for what should be, does one not live a very superficial, automatic life! We need, not idealists or entities with mechanical minds, but integrated human beings who are intelligent and free."

5. *Development of Maturity to be Free:* The right kind of education is not concerned with any ideology, however much it may promise a future Utopia; it is not based on any system, however carefully thought out; nor is it a means of conditioning the individual in some special manner. Education in the true sense is helping the individual to be mature and free, to flower greatly in love and goodness. That is what we should be interested in, and not in shaping the child according to some idealistic pattern.

6. *Re-education:* Right education comes with the transformation of ourselves. We must re-educate ourselves not to kill one another for any cause, however righteous, for any ideology, however promising it may appear to be for the future happiness of the world. We must learn to be compassionate, to be content with little, and to seek the Supreme, for only then can there be the true salvation of mankind.

7. *Development of Consideration for Others:* The right kind of education will encourage thoughtfulness and consideration for others without enticements or threats of any kind.

8. *Development of Right Understanding of Environment:* What we must realise is that we are not only conditioned by environment, but that we *are* the environment—we are not something apart from it. Our thoughts and responses are conditioned by the values which society, of which we are a part, has imposed upon us.

We never see that we are the total environment because there are several entities in us, all revolving around the "me", the self. The self is made up of these entities, which are merely desires in various forms. From this conglomeration of desires arises the central figure, the thinker, the will of the "me" and the "mine"; and a division is thus established between the self and the not-self, between the "me" and the environment or society. This separation is the beginning of conflict, inward and outward.

9. *Development of Wisdom and Not Acquiring Knowledge:* In our search for knowledge, in our acquisitive desires, we are losing love, we are blunting the feeling for beauty, the sensitivity to cruelty; we are becoming more and more specialized and less and less integrated. Wisdom cannot be

replaced by knowledge, and no amount of explanation, no accumulation of facts, will free man from suffering. Knowledge is necessary, science has its place; but if the mind and heart are suffocated by knowledge, and if the cause of suffering is explained away, life becomes vain and meaningless. And is this not what is happening to most of us? Our education is making us more and more shallow; it is not helping us to uncover the deeper layers of our being, and our lives are increasingly disharmonious and empty.

Information, the knowledge of facts, though ever increasing, is by its very nature limited. Wisdom is infinite, it includes knowledge and the way of action; but we take hold of a branch and think it is the whole tree. Through the knowledge of the part, we can never realize the joy of the whole. Intellect can never lead to the whole, for it is only a segment, a part.

10. *Development of Attitude of Love Towards Others:* Only love and right thinking will bring about true revolution, the revolution within ourselves. But how are we to have love? Not through the pursuit of the ideal of love, but only when there is no hatred, when there is no greed, when the sense of self, which is the cause of antagonism, comes to an end. A man who is caught up in the pursuits of exploitation, of greed, of envy, can never love.

11. *Development of Right Relationship:* The purpose of education is to cultivate right relationship, not only between individuals, but also between the individual and society; and that is why it is essential that education should, above all, help the individual to understand his own psychological process. Intelligence lies in understanding oneself and going above and beyond oneself.

12. *Development of Simplicity:* To educate a child is to help him to understand freedom and integration. To have freedom there must be order, which virtue alone can give; and integration can take place only when there is great simplicity. From innumerable complexities we must grow to simplicity; we must become simple in our inward life and in our outward needs.

13. *Development of Creative Intelligence:* It is constant inquiry, true dissatisfaction, that brings creative intelligence; but to keep inquiry and discontent awake is extremely arduous, and most people do no want their children to have this kind of intelligence, for it is very uncomfortable to live with someone who is constantly questioning accepted values.

14. *Freedom from Ideology:* This conditioning of the child's mind to fit a particular ideology, whether political or religious, breeds enmity between man and man. In a competitive society we cannot have brotherhood, and no reform, no dictatorship, educational method can bring it about.

15. *Development of International Understanding:* As long as you remain a New Zealander and I a Hindu, it is absurd to talk about the unity of man. How can we get together as human beings if you in your country, and I in mine, retain our respective religious prejudices and economic ways? How

can there be brotherhood as long as patriotism is separating man from man, and millions are restricted by depressed economic conditions while others are well off? How can there be human unity when beliefs divide us, when there is domination of one group by another, when the rich are powerful and the poor are seeking that same power, when there is maldistribution of land, when some are well fed and multitudes are starving?

If we are to change radically our present human relationship, which has brought untold misery to the world, our only and immediate task is to transform ourselves through self-knowledge. So we come back to the central point, which is oneself; but we dodge that point and shift the responsibility on to governments, religions and ideologies. The government is what *we* are, religions and ideologies are but a projection of ourselves; and until *we* change fundamentally there can be neither right education nor a peaceful world.

16. *Freedom and Discipline:* It is only in individual freedom that love and goodness can flower; and the right kind of education alone can offer this freedom. Neither conformity to the present society nor the promise of a future Utopia can ever give to the individual that insight without which he is constantly creating problems.

The right kind of educator, seeing the inward nature of freedom, helps each individual student to observe and understand his own self-projected values and impositions; he helps him to become aware of the conditioning influences about him, and of his own desires, both of which limit his mind and breed fear; he helps him, as he grows to manhood, to observe and understand himself in relation to all things, for it is the craving for self-fulfillment that brings endless conflict and sorrow.

One of the dangers of discipline is that the system becomes more important than the human beings who are enclosed in it. Discipline then becomes a substitute for love, and it is because our hearts are empty that we cling to discipline. Freedom can never come through discipline, through resistance; freedom is not a goal, an end to be achieved. Freedom is at the beginning, not at the end; it is not to be found in some distant ideal.

Freedom does not mean the opportunity for self-gratification or the setting aside of consideration for others. The teacher who is sincere will protect the children and help them in every possible way to grow towards the right kind of freedom; but it will be impossible for him to do this if he himself is addicted to an ideology, if he is in any way dogmatic or self-seeking.

17. *Rewards and Punishments:* Sensitivity can never-be awakened through compulsion. One may compel a child to be outwardly quiet, but one has not come face to face with that which is making him obstinate, impudent, and so on. Compulsion breeds antagonism and fear. Reward and punishment in any form only make the mind subservient and dull; and if this is what we desire, then education through compulsion is an excellent way to proceed.

Discipline is an easyway to control a child, but it does not help him to understand the problems involved in living. Some form of compulsion, the discipline of punishment and reward, may be necessary to maintain order and seeming quietness among a large number of students herded together in a classroom; but with the right kind of educator and a small number of students, would any repression, politely called discipline, be required? If the classes are small and the teacher can give his full attention to each child, observing and helping him, then compulsion or domination in any form is obviously unnecessary. If, in such a group, a student persists in disorderliness or is unreasonably mischievous, the educator must inquire into the cause of his misbehaviour, which may be wrong diet, lack of rest, family wrangles, or some hidden fear.

18. *Spiritual Training and Not Religious Education:* Dogmas, mysteries and rituals are not conducive to a spiritual life. Religious education in the true sense is to encourage the child to understand his own relationship to people, to things and to nature. There is no existence without relationship; and without self-knowledge, all relationship, with the one and with the many, brings conflict and sorrow. Of course, to explain this fully to a child is impossible; but if the educator and the parents deeply grasp the full significance of relationship, then by their attitude, conduct and speech they will surely be able to convey to the child, without too many words and explanations, the meaning of a spiritual life.

True religious education is to help the child to be intelligently aware, to discern for himself the temporary and the real, and to have a disinterested approach to life; and would it not have more meaning to begin each day at home or at school with a serious thought, or with a reading that has depth and significance, rather than mumble some oft-repeated words or phrases?

Past generations, with their ambitions, traditions and ideals, have brought misery and destruction to the world; perhaps the coming generations, with the right kind of education, can put an end to this chaos and build a happier social order. If those who are young have the spirit of inquiry, if they are constantly searching out the truth of all things, political and religious, personal and environmental, then youth will have great significance and there is hope for a better world.

Methods of Teaching

1. We should not teach the child 'what' to think but 'how' to think.
2. Each student should have the freedom to think for himself.
3. Each student should be studied thoroughly and methods of teaching employed accordingly.
4. The student should be treated as an equal partner.
5. Repetition encourages the mind to be sluggish. A 'shock' is needed to awaken it, which we then call a 'problem'.

6. Teachers should not try to solve the problem according to their 'well-worn' explanations, justifications and condemnations.

J. Krishnamurti sums up the right kind of teaching in these words: "Without the right kind of teaching, illusion is taken for reality, and then the individual is ever in conflict within himself, and therefore there is conflict in his relationship with others, which is society. One teaches because one sees that self-knowledge alone, and not the dogmas and rituals of organized religion, can bring about a tranquil mind; and that creation, truth, God, comes into being only when the "me" and the "mine" are transcended."

Role of the Teacher

(a) *Understanding the Child and Not Thrusting His Ideals:* J. Krishnamurti wrote: "The right kind of education consists in understanding the child as he is without imposing upon him an ideal of what we think he should be. To enclose him in the framework of an ideal is to encourage him to conform, which breeds fear and produces in him a constant conflict between what he is and what he should be; and all inward conflicts have their outward manifestations in society. Ideals are an actual hindrance to our understanding of the child and to the child's understanding of himself.

"If the teacher is of the right kind, he will not depend on a method, but will study each individual pupil. In our relationship with children and young people, we are not dealing with mechanical devices that can be quickly repaired, but with living beings who are impressionable, volatile, sensitive, afraid, affectionate; and to deal with them, we have to have great understanding, the strength of patience and love. When we lack these, we look to quick and easy remedies and hope for marvellous and automatic results. If we are unaware, mechanical in our attitudes and actions, we fight shy of any demand upon us that is disturbing and that cannot be met by an automatic response, and this is one of our major difficulties in education."

(b) *Observing the Child:* To understand a child we have to watch him at play, study him in his different moods; we cannot project upon him our own prejudices, hopes and fears, or mould him to fit the pattern of our desires. If we are constantly judging the child according to our personal likes and dislikes, we are bound to create barriers and hindrances in our relationship with him and in his relationships with the world. Unfortunately, most of us desire to shape the child in a way that is gratifying to our own vanities and idiosyncrasies; we find varying degrees of comfort and satisfaction in exclusive ownership and domination.

(c) *Integration of the Educator Himself:* Human beings must be integrated if they are to come out of any crisis, and especially the present world crisis, without being broken; therefore, to parents- and teachers who are really interested in education, the main problem is how to develop an integrated individual. To do this, the educator himself must obviously be integrated; so the right kind of education is of the highest importance, not only for the young, but also for the older generation if they are willing to leam and are not too set in their ways. What we are in ourselves is much more important than the traditional question of what to teach the child, and if we love our children we will see to it that they have the right kind of educators.

A True Teacher: J. Krishnamurti sums up the pen picture of a true scholars: "An educator is not merely a giver of information; he is one who points the way to wisdom, to truth. Truth is far more important than the teacher. The search for truth is religion, and truth is of no country, of no creed, it is not to be found in any temple, church or mosque. Without the search for truth, society soon decays. To create a new society, each one of us has to be a true teacher, which means that we have to be both the pupil and the master; we have to educate ourselves.

"If a new social order is to be established, those who teach merely to earn a salary can obviously have no place as teachers. To regard education as a means of livelihood is to exploit the children for one's own advantage. In an enlightened society, teachers will have no concern for their own welfare, and the community will provide for their needs.

"The true teacher is not he who has built up an impressive educational organization, nor he who is an instrument of the politicians, nor he who is bound to an ideal, a belief or a country. The true teacher is inwardly rich and therefore asks nothing for himself; he is not ambitious and seeks no power in any form; he does not use teaching as a means of acquiring position or authority, and therefore he is free from the compulsion of society and the control of governments. Such teachers have the primary place in an enlightened civilization, for true culture is founded, not on the engineers and technicians, but on the educators." (Adapted from *Education and the Significance of Life)*

Picture of a School as Visualised by Krishnamurti

Following points reflect the thinking of J. Krishnamurti on the concept of an ideal school:

An integrated personality can only be developed in a school having a limited number of students. Mass instruction is suicidal to the integrated development of the individuality of the students.

Teachers must be alert, dedicated and thoughtful.

A careful study and understanding of the child's capacities, difficulties and limitations should be made.

A small school can be maintained through the spirit of self-sacrifice.

School's functioning should be without the influence of any ideology.

The head should not assume all the responsibility. On the contrary each teacher should feel responsible for the whole.

In a group of true educators, the problem of authority does not arise.

There should be unstained cooperation among all the teachers.

No teacher should be afraid of the head master, nor should the head feel intimidated.

There should be feeling of equality and cooperation.

Equal distribution of work gives leisure to all.

The spirit of individual freedom should pervade the whole school at all times.

A student council should be formed to discuss all matters relating to the well being of the whole group.

The school should enable the student to discover what he is most interested in.

The school must gain the confidence and cooperation of the parents.

Provision for proper guidance should exist in a school.

Highlights of the Philosophy and Educational Thought and Practices—A Summary

Integral Education for Integrated Life

Krishnamurti emphasized integral education which implies that education should encourage self-observation and the experience of life as a whole, not "me" and "mine" but to go above and beyond to discover the real. Integration takes place by understanding the whole process of existence. He stressed that human beings must be integrated if they are to survive. An integrated individual is one who is capable of dealing with life as a whole.

According to Krishnamuni, conservative (prevailing) education was just like having a right arm highly developed, strong and vital while the rest of the body withered and became weak.

Education according to him is not to transmit the existing values in the minds of the children but to enable them to think critically and rationally. Intelligent understanding on their part is very important.

In the words of J. Krishnamurti: "Education in the true sense is helping the individual to be mature and free, to flower greatly in love and goodness. That is what we should be interested in, and not in shaping the child according to some idealistic pattern. The idealist like the specialist, is not concerned with the whole, but with a part. There can be no integration as long as one is pursuing an ideal pattern of action, and most teachers who are idealists put away love; they have dry minds and hard hearts. To study child, one has to be alert, watchful, self-aware, and this demands for greater intelligence and affection than to encourage him to follow an ideal."

Role of the Teacher

Krishnamurti held that only a teacher who himself is a properly integrated human being could deliver the goods. The teacher must help each pupil to discover his inner psychological resources, realize his weaknesses and develop his own individual strengths.

For this the teacher has to provide/create the right environment. He must be affectionate as well as patient. Dedication and vitality are needed in the teachers.

The teacher has to encourage creative intelligence of the students. He should discourage students from merely accepting statements and quotes from books. Questioning and critical thinking need to be made a part of the instructional process in the class-room. Students should be encouraged to be considerate to their classmates.

The teacher should not regard himself merely as an instrument for imparting knowledge but a person who is concerned with the task of leading students to a way of life according to their resources. He, however, must not impose his beliefs, manners and ideologies on them. Let them form their own judgements. The job of the teacher is not to teach 'what to think' but to teach 'how to think and act'.

Role of the School

The function of the school is to produce integrated individuals. This is possible only when the number of students in a school is limited and classes are small. Such a school needs organisers and teachers who possess a spirit of self-sacrifice.

The head of the school must associate his teachers in the functioning of the school. He should allow freedom to them to discuss educational matters.

Delegation of many kinds of responsibilities to students should form an important part of the educative process.

Pupils' abilities, aptitudes, interests and problems should be discussed with their parents and necessary strategies worked out to create an enlightened community.

Contribution of J. Krishnamurti

Education had always been closer to Krishnamurti's heart. He established nearly a dozen co-educational schools in India and abroad to translate his ideas into practice. Ten per cent of the seats in these schools were reserved for non-paying pupils. Krishnamurti used to visit them every year for discussion with students and teachers.

Although the ordinary curriculum was followed in these schools, his main object in starting these schools was to provide children adequate opportunities and freedom to grow up without any of the national, racial, class and cultural prejudices that build barriers between one human being and another and give rise to violence.

Krishnamurti's conception of methods of teaching, school organisation and the role of a teacher is truly progressive in nature and based on sound philosophy of education. His emphasis on the development of an integrated personality through integral approach to education is highly commended by almost all thinkers.

24

John Dewey (1857-1950)

John Dewey, one of the most distinguished educators, philosophers, practitioners and thinkers, was born in October 1859 at Burlington in America. After graduating from the University of Vermont in 1879, he started his career as a school teacher. After leaving his job of a school teacher, Dewey joined John Hopkins University and obtained his Ph.D. Degree in Philosophy in 1884. Thereafter for several years, he worked as a Professor of Philosophy at the Universities of Minnesota, Michigan and Chicago. His last assignment was his Professorship of Education and Philosophy at the University of Columbia, New York.

Prof. Dewey delivered lectures on education and philosophy at the University of Peking for a period of two years. The Government of Turkey invited Dewey to draw up a report on the re-organisation of national schools.

Prof. Dewey's philosophy is not simply speculative but based on actual experiences in the classroom. His principles and practices grew out of his experiments in the University Laboratory School, Chicago. He founded this school in 1896, for the chief objective of testing educational theory through experiments.

Publications

Perhaps no educator has written such a standard and diverse literature on educational principles and practices as Prof. Dewey. Likewise, enormous material has been published on him and his works. His first article entitled *The Metaphysical Assumption of Materialism* appeared in *Journal of Speculative Philosophy* in April 1882. Dewey's important publications are:

1. My Pedagogic Creed (1897), 2. Psychology and Philosophic Method (1899), 3. Studies in Logical Theory (1903), 4. *Ethics* (1908), 5. *The Influence of Darwin and Other Essays* (1910), 6. *How We Think* (1910), 7. *Democracy and Education* (1916), 8. *Essays in Experimental Logic* (1916), 9. *Creative Intelligence* (1917), 10. *Lectures at Tokyo Imperial University* (1920), 11. *Reconstruction in Philosophy* (1920), 12. *Human Nature and Conduct* (1922), 13. *Experience and Nature* (1925), 14. *The Public and Its Problem* (1927), 15. *The Quest for Certainty* (1927), 16. *Art as Experience* (1934), 17. *A Common Faith* (1934), 18. *Philosophy and*

Civilisation (1934), 19. *Liberalism and Social Action* (1935), 20. *Experience in Education* (1938), 21. *Freedom and Culture* (1939), 22. *Theory of Valuation* (1939), 23. *Problems of Men* (1946), 24. *Knowing and the Known* (1949), 25. *Education Today* (1949), 26. *Interest and Effort in Education* (1953), 27. *Schools of Tomorrow* (1953), 28. *The Child and the Curriculum* (1956), 29. *The School and Society* (1900), 30. *Philosophy of Education* (1958), 31. *Moral Principles in Education* (1959)

Views on Various Aspects of Education

1. *Philosophy of Education:* Dewey's philosophy of education is given various names. 'Experimentalism', 'Functionalism', 'Instrumentalism', 'Operationalism', 'Practicalism', 'Pragmatism' and 'Progressivism'. Of course, his philosophy of education is mostly associated with the term 'Pragmatism'. All these terms indicate the dynamic, ever-changing and performing character of life. Dewey suggested the application of experimental logic. He emphasised that as all experiences cannot be educative, the business of the educator is to select an experience or experiences which would enable the individuals to live creatively, constructively, dynamically and fruitfully in the changing environment.

What is a thing for? What's its use? Action must precede knowledge. Whatever knowledge we possess has resulted from our activities, our efforts to survive. Only that which has been organised into our dispositions so as to enable us to adapt our environment to our needs and to adapt our aims and desires to the situations in which we exist is real knowledge.

2. *Meaning of Education: Education as a Psychological and Social Process:* Dewey does not believe in absolute values. According to Dewey, "Education is the process of re-construction or re-constitution of experience, giving it a more detailed value through the medium of increased social efficiency". Dewey further observed: "What nutrition and reproduction are to physiological life, education is to social life". He considered education as "the fundamental method of social progress and reform. In sum, I believe that the individual who is to be educated is a social individual and that society is an organic union of individuals. If we eliminate the social factor from the child, we are left only with an abstraction; if we eliminate the individual factor from society, we are left only with an inert and lifeless mass. Education, therefore, must begin with a psychological insight into the child's capacities, interests, and habits. It must be controlled at every point by reference to these same considerations. These powers, interests, and habits must be continually interpretted—we must know what they mean. They must be translated in terms of their social equivalents in terms of what they are capable of in the way of social service".

"I believe that all education proceeds by the participation of the individual in the social consciousness of the race. This process begins unconsciously almost at birth, and is continually shaping the individual's powers, saturating his consciousness, forming his habits, training his ideas, and arousing his feelings and emotions. Through this unconscious education the individual gradually comes to share in the intellectual and moral resources which humanity has succeeded in getting together. He becomes an inheritor of the funded capital of civilisation. The most formal and technical education in the world cannot safely depart from this general process. It can only organise it or differentiate it in some particular direction.

"I believe that the only true education comes through the stimulation of the child's powers by the demands of the social situations in which he finds himself".

3. *Concept of Social Efficiency*: Social efficiency broadly speaking includes three elements of efficient industrial development and the art of living together. A man must learn to be economically self-sufficient and at the same time acquire qualities and values of an enlightened citizen. An individual must be able to earn his livelihood. An individual who is not able to earn his livelihood is a parasite. Education must take into account economic aspect. An individual should be trained to make the best use of national resources. A school was considered as a 'society in miniature'.

Dewey was a firm believer in democratic values. He, therefore, insisted that education should provide suitable opportunities to the students to imbibe democratic values.

4. *Functions of Education*: Dewey explains the functions of education in these words: "It is a common place to say that development of character is the ultimate end of all school work. In general, character means organised capacity of social functioning. It means social interest and responsiveness". He further says: "The function of education is to help the growing of a helpless young animal into a happy, moral and efficient human being".

5. *Child's Place in the Educative Process*: Dewey observes: "Education must begin with a psychological insight into the child's capacities, interests and habits. These must be continually interpreted, we must know what they mean. They must be translated into their social equivalents—into terms of what they are capable of in the way of social service". In this regard he outlined the function of the teacher as "The more a teacher is aware of the past experience of students, of their hopes, desires, chief interests, the better will he understand the forces at work that need to be directed and utilised for the formation of reflective habits".

6. *Curriculum*. The curriculum must grow out of child's interests, experiences, impulses and needs. The curriculum must be child-centred. He stressed that the school subjects should be woven around the child's activities. Lessons should begin with social topics such as food, shelter, modes of communication, speech, reading, drawing, modelling, etc. While

laying stress on the needs of the children, Dewey also took into account the needs of the community in which the children live.

Following are the main characteristics and principles of the curriculum:

(i) Curriculum should reflect the social life and social activities. It should have utility.

(ii) It must follow the principle of progressive organisation of knowledge consisting of educative experiences and problems of the learners.

iii) The new experiences and problems should grow out of the old ones.

(iv) The experiences should be flexible and changeable in accordance with the child's interests and should be graded.

7. *Methods of Teaching*: Dewey said: "All learning must come as a by-product of actions and for its own sake". This reveals his concepts of observation, and direct experience. According to him, a child learns through participation in various activities. He advocated 'learning by doing' and 'learning by living'. He recommended the Project Method which is based on problems, activities, experiments and interests of the learners.

Dewey has explained the problem method of teaching in his books: *How We Think* and *Interest and Effort in Education* as "the processes by which the mind of the individual comes into relation with the objective world. Interest and self-activity are the characteristic features". It is a method which deals with the intellectual processes that are antecedent to induction and deduction.

Dewey briefly recommended the following methods of instruction:

a. Learning by doing.
b. Learning by integration and correlation.
c. Learning through productive and creative activities.

8. *Concept of Discipline:* Dewey held that the natural impulses of the child ought to be directed and disciplined through the cooperative activities of the school—"Out of doing things that are to produce results, and out of doing in a social and cooperative way, there is born a discipline of its own kind and type". Dewey believed that the child's activities—intellectual, social, moral and physical—are disciplinary in their effect if they are carried out in cooperation with others.

9. *On the role of the teacher*: The teacher is engaged not simply in the training of individuals, but in the formation of the proper social life. Every teacher should realise the dignity of his calling; that he is a social servant set apart for the maintenance of proper social order and the securing of the right social growth.

In this way the teacher always is the 'prophet of the true God' and the usherer in the true kingdom of God. He also said: "The teacher is a guide and director; he steers the boat, but the energy that propels it must come from those who are learning. The more a teacher is aware of the past experiences of students, of their hopes, desires, chief interests, the better will he understand the forces at work that need to be directed and utilised for the formation of reflective habits".

10. *Concept of Democracy and Democratic Values in Education*: Dewey states that democracy is the political and moral philosophy of education. "If education is equivalent to genuine living, then democracy is the moral foundation of education. The essence of education is the extension of shared areas of meaningful action and this is also the essence of democracy".

The school as the 'democratic society in miniature' should provide for the participation of the students in the activities of the school on the one hand and on the other hand it should realise the significance of the experiences, needs and interests of the child as a personality.

Democracy postulates full freedom of enquiry into social and political problems and solving them. Likewise the schools should promote a spirit of enquiry in educational thinking. Discussion should be freely permitted. The schools should become guardians of academic freedom. Intellectual or moral freedom is the basis of political freedom. These should become living examples of the practices of freedom of enquiry, experimentation and intelligent communication. Excessive heavy routines and rules are not conducive to self and social disciplines.

Dewey advocates that teacher should be provided opportunities to "participate in the formation of the controlling aims, methods and materials of the school of which he is apart".

To sum up. Dewey wants that education should reflect democratic principles and practices in matters of school organisation, selection of activities and experiences and other matters.

Functions of the School: School Related to Social Life

Dewey regarded school as the 'epitome' of life outside, as the 'miniature society' and also the 'lengthened arm of the family'. He said: "The school, now divorced from life, must be re-united with it through activities that will simplify its relations, develop its essential meaning, eliminate its unworthy and obsolescent features, and extend the individual's social environment so that he escapes from the limitations of the group into which he is born".

Dewey sets out the following functions of the school:

1. *Providing a Simplified Environment*: A complex civilisation is too complex to be assimilated in toto. It has to be broken up into portions, and assimilated in a gradual and graded way. The relationships of our present social life are so numerous and so inter-woven that even a child placed in the most favourable position could not readily share in many of the most important of them. The first function of the school, therefore, is to select those features which are fairly fundamental and capable of being responded to by the young.

2. *Eliminating 'the Unworthy Features of the Existing Environment'*: Dewey explains this point: "As a society becomes more enlightened, it realises that it is responsible not to transmit and conserve the whole of its existing achievements but only such as make for a better future society. The school is the chief agency for the accomplishment of this end".

3. *Balancing the Various Elements in the Social Environment*: It is the function of the school to coordinate within the disposition of each individual the diverse influences of the various social environments into which he enters.

That education which does not occur through forms of life, forms that are worth living for their own sake, is always a poor substitute for the genuine reality, and tends to cramp and to deaden.

The school, as an institution, should simplify existing social life; should reduce it, as it were, to an embryonic form. Existing life is so complex that the child cannot be brought into contact with it without either confusion or distraction; he is either overwhelmed by the multiplicity of activities which are going on, so that he loses his own power of orderly reaction, or he is so stimulated by these various activities that his powers are prematurely called into play and he becomes either unduly specialised or else disintegrated.

The social life of the child is the basis of concentration or correlation in all his training or growth: The social life gives the unconscious unity and the background of all his attainments. The subject-matter of the school curriculum should mark a gradual differentiation out of the primitive unconscious unity of social life.

We violate the child's nature and render difficult the best ethical results by introducing the child too abruptly to a number of special studies, of reading, writing, geography, etc. out of relation to this social life.

The true centre of correlation on the school subject is not science, nor literature, nor history, nor geography but the child's own social activities.

The studies represent the possibilities of development inherent in the child's immediate crude experience.

Laboratory School, University of Chicago

Objective: Dewey felt that the changed times demanded that the training of students for a complete living in the society should be provided in the school. For finding out the type of training to be imparted, he carried out his experiments in the school which he established in 1896.

Problems: Following were the main educational problems which Dewey wanted to solve:

1. How to bring the school into closer relation with the home and surrounding life.
2. How to introduce subject-matter in various disciplines like history, science and art to impart a positive value and real significance in child's life.

3. How can instructions in different subjects be carried on with everyday experience and occupation, as the background and be correlated with each other.
4. How individual powers and needs be catered to.

Manual Occupations as the Basis: Dewey introduced the following manual occupations related to everyday life for imparting knowledge of various subjects:

(i) Shop work with wood and tools.
(ii) Cooking work
(iii) Work with textiles (sewing and weaving).

Dewey accorded a central place to occupations and other subjects were treated incidentally as ancillary to practical activities. Dewey observed that the students think out how to make cloth and reinvent the carding frame, tool for spinning and understand the loom. They learn at the same time enough art and science. "Make the construction adequate, make it full, free and flexible, give it a social motive, something to tell and you have a work of art". Likewise, the knowledge of various subjects revolves round such occupations.

Graded Curriculum: Development of interests through occupations was to take place in a developing sequence in accordance with the mental development of the child. Elementary school life was divided into the following periods.

1. Play Period (4 to 8 years of age).
2. Period of Spontaneous Attention (8 to 12 years of age).
3. Period of Affective Attention (12 years onwards).

In the elementary school, the curriculum is based on the four-fold interest of the child.

a. Interest in conversation and communication.
b. Interest in inquiry.
c. Interest in making things or construction.
d. Interest in artistic expression.

Dewey's Instrumentalism and Experimentalism

Before discussing the various dimensions of instrumentalism, it may be stressed that instrumentalism and experimentalism are complementary and supplementary.

Dewey's instrumentalism implies that education serves as an instrument, *i.e.,* means of achieving the ends of producing a socially efficient individual by providing continuous experiences and integrating knowledge. Education is an instrument of 'catching up' the spirit of the social group to which an individual belongs. Instrumentalism is the name given to pragmatism by Dewey.

Chief Characteristics of Dewey's Instrumentalism

1. *Nature of an Idea*: According to Dewey's instrumentalism, no idea is fixed or permanent or true in itself. The goodness of an idea is tested through experiments. An idea is considered good if it becomes an instrument of controlling a situation. Otherwise it has no significance.

2. *Nature of Knowledge*: According to instrumentalism 'knowledge for the sake of knowledge has no significance'. Only that knowledge is true and useful that enables an individual to adjust himself to his environment. Knowledge is the basis for further experimentation. Knowledge is gradually modified through "continuous reorganisation and reconstruction of experiences and integration of activities".

3. *Nature of Values*: An instrumentalist considers every value relative and subjective. Values are considered useful in the context of a situation. A value may be more useful in one study and not so useful in another study.

A value has been defined by Dewey as "The value means primarily to prize, to esteem, to appraise, to estimate. It means the act of cherishing something, holding it and also the act of passing judgment upon the nature and amount of values as compared with others".

4. *Order of Values*: It is not possible to determine the order or hierarchy of values. An instrumentalist chooses values according to the task in hand.

5. *Role of the Teacher in Deciding Values*: A teacher chooses values according to particular objective to be achieved.

Major Concerns of an Instrumentalist: An instrumentalist considers that reality is within the experiment. Experiment is the basis to test the truth.

An instrumentalist also considers school as an instrument of achieving the goals of education and this is possible through experiences.

Educational Implications of Instrumentalism

Dewey as an instrumentalist considers education as a dynamic force. For him it is not merely unfolding the latent powers of the child, it is not merely preparation for remote future, but it is rather constant reorganisation or reconstruction of human experiences. Growth is a continuous unending life process and, therefore, it requires a constant reorganisation, reconstruction and integration of experiences and activities. Every human activity should lead to some sort of learning and enrichment of the learner. Every human activity must have an immediate and approximate end. It should lead to present learning or in other words an enrichment of the meaning of the present experience. But this is not enough. Activity and experience should enter into new combinations. They should increase the ability to direct further normal activities and experiences.

Experimentalism

Experimentalism is the key word in Dewey's scientific methodological procedure. According to him, "The heart of the experimental method is determination of the significance of observed things by means of deliberate instruments of modes of interaction".

Dewey is a firm believer in the universal application of the experimental method developed by modern science. Furthermore he stresses the cultivation of the scientific spirit of detachment, impartiality and objectivity.

Dewey's Experimental Philosophy: The new philosophy of education is an experimental philosophy. All experiences cannot be educative. The traditional education gave pupils experiences but not of the right type. The business of the educator is to set a kind of experience which while being agreeable promotes having desirable future experiences. The central problem of an educator based upon experience is to select the kind of present experiences that live fruitfully and creatively in subsequent experiences. The continuity of experience is the philosophy of educative experience. It is held that education is development within, by, and for experience... Education by, of, and for experience... Thus a full integrated personality exists only when successive experiences are integrated. This continuity and interaction provide the measure of the educative significance, and value of an experience.

Experience and Experimental Method: Dewey explains that where there is experience, there is a living being. In the orthodox view, experience is regarded primarily as a knowledge affair. But to eyes not looking through ancient spectacles, it assuredly appears as an affair of the intercourse of living being with its physical and social environment. To learn from experience is to make a backward and forward connection between what we do to things and what we enjoy or suffer from things in consequences.

Three Stages of Activities and Experiences

An educationally important activity passes through three stages.

In the first stage, the child starts his activity in an unregulated manner. Its meaning and significance are not understood. It begins in an impulsive form, *i.e.,* it is blind. It does not know what it is about, that is to say, what are its interactions with other activities. Its consequences are not anticipated.

In the second stage, by doing things constantly, mind gradually grasps the meaning and the activity becomes purposeful. The mind now understands. It can anticipate the consequences also. Results come by intention and not by accident.

In the third stage, activity and experience imparts to the mind the power of subsequent direction and control. The mind can, at this stage, combine old activities and experiences into new patterns to meet novel situations.

Three Types of Activities

1. An activity may be aimless and at random. One does not care what happens. One just lets oneself go and avoids connecting the consequences

of one's act. We frown upon such aimless random activity of children. But in fact such activity is due to maladjustment with surroundings.

Children do things under external influence. Children do things because they are asked to do things. They act blindly without having a purpose of their own. Our present day education is confined to this level, resulting in little learning. This state of affairs must be changed.

2. The second type of activity is the positive activity which increases skill to do a particular thing. It has only a limited educative effect. Nevertheless this has a place in Dewey's concept of education.

3. A genuinely educative activity is that which leads to new perception of connections and consequences. Educative experiences are those which help us to meet new situations. So we should keep an eye not only on results but on processes.

"*Every continuous experience or activity is educative and all education resides in having such experiences*".

True education should, therefore, help reconstruction and reorganisation of experience for future work. It should be both retrospective and prospective. This reconstruction of experience may be both personal and social. The immature child has to "catch up" the spirit of the social group to which he belongs.

The experiences of the young should be shaped according to their future needs. True education is not content with mere production of habits but rather with forming better habits so that the future society is an improvement upon the present one. Unworthy features of our civilisation are to be eliminated by conscious efforts. Education should build up a better and happier world and it is possible only if the process of re-construction and reorganisation of human knowledge on the past experience and activity is constantly carried on.

Basic Elements of Experimentation

1. The problem must be clearly defined.
2. Attempts may be made to review the literature related to the problem.
3. Hypothesis should be formed.
4. Instruments should be clearly selected.
5. All relevant factors which can influence the result should be carefully considered.
6. Data should be collected systematically.
7. Data should be analysed objectively.
8. Conclusions should be reported in clear-cut language.

Role of the Schools: Educational Implications

What should the schools do?

1. The schools should provide greater scope for a rich variety of activities and experiences.

2. The activities should not be merely unrelated and unconscious ones.
3. These activities should be made purposeful.
4. The interest of the learner must be aroused and constant consciousness of the transfer of knowledge to newer situations be maintained.
5. Projects should be organised.
6. Socially useful productive activities should be organised on a large scale.

Essence of John Dewey's Work: Contribution to Education

1. Dewey fused both the psychological and sociological aspects of education.
2. Dewey emphasised democratic values in all dimensions of education.
3. Dewey laid stress on providing rich and varied activities and experiences to students.
4. Dewey's approach to methodology of teaching led to the emergence of the Project Method in education.
5. Dewey advocated that the programmes of the school should be linked with the life of the society. In this regard, he pointed out that the activities should be simplified and that unworthy activities should be discarded.
6. Dewey wanted that the natural interests of the child should be given due attention.
7. Dewey believed in social discipline that could develop through useful activities.
8. Dewey's watchword was social efficiency coupled with individual efficiency.

Evaluation of Dewey's Work

Following points of criticism are usually made:

1. Dewey does not suggest any definite aim of education.
2. Dewey attaches more importance to materialism.
3. Dewey does not accept any truth as something permanent.
4. Dewey puts excessive emphasis on individual differences.
5. Dewey lays too much emphasis on experiences.

Prof. V.P. Verma in *Studies in the Philosophy of Education* (1964) has given the following merits and demerits of Dewey's theory of education.

Merits: (a) It is a 'social' theory of education as opposed to the stress on the isolated self of the individual.

(b) It is a passionate plea for a wide application of the 'experimental' method in education.

(c) It provides the conception of 'democracy' as a social psychological theory of the progressive extension of shared experiences.

Demerits: (a) Dewey's attempt to trace the roots of the dualist approach (two opposed groups of antagonistic interests)—two-fold division of society is a mistake.

(b) Scientific objectivity and veracity may be difficult for being reconciled with democracy, which in practice, means numerical majority.

(c) The neglect of religious education may result in the destruction of the roots of humanistic values and social ethics.

Fredrik Mayor in his '*American Ideas in Education*' has summed up the contribution of John Dewey in these words: "In Dewey the voice of the pioneer, the stirring energies of the reformer, the patient method of the scientist and the faith of the teacher are united in a search for a new education through which man can survive in a chaotic age".

According to Rusk, "In education we cannot but be grateful to Dewey for his great services in challenging the old 'static cold storage ideal of knowledge' and in bringing education more into accord with the activities of present day life".

Regarding the work of Dewey, Irwin Edman (Ed.) in *John Dewey: His Contribution to American Tradition* (1955) has observed: "The breakdown of the violation of school from society, of book learning from vital experience, of the individual from his environment—the extent to which schools and colleges have removed these separations is a measure of the direct impact of refreshing reconstruction of Dewey's thinking".

Prof. Ulich in *History of Educational Thought* has summed up the contribution of John Dewey in these words: "Dewey's work encourages an experimental and scientific attitude. It shows what men can achieve if they rely on their reason and courage instead of clinging to their prejudice".

25

John Henrich Pestalozzi (1746-1827)

Pestalozzi, a great Swiss educator was born at Zurich in 1746. His father, a physician, passed away when he was just five years old. He was brought up by his mother who encouraged his sensitivity. He hated the Latin school at Zurich as it lacked realism. He, however, enjoyed his college years at the *Collegium Humanitatis* and *Collegium Carolinum*.

Pestalozzi tried several professions including law and politics but was not successful. He took up agriculture and developed a farm at Neuh. During his work at the farm, he began his first experiments in education. He started to educate his own child, Jacobi, in the manner of Emile but soon made some modifications. He wrote, "To have a knowledge of words with no distinct idea of the things they represent enormously increases the difficulty of getting at the truth... Teach him nothing by words that you can teach him by things themselves. Nature teaches him better than men. Remember that if restraint robs you of your pupil's confidence, all your labour is lost".

Pestalozzi turned his farmhouse into a refuge for destitute children. He thought that their natural need to be active and inborn powers would lead to self-support at an early age. He, therefore, combined education, moral regeneration and practical training in agriculture and handicrafts. He taught the children by means of conversation on all kinds of topics. This farm and consequently school at the farm had to be closed on account of financial difficulties.

Pestalozzi's work at Neuh and Stanz where he was in charge of poor children convinced him that a new approach to education was needed.

Pestalozzi set up a school at Burgdorf and a boarding school at yerdun where he conducted his educational experiments. The school with its natural and relaxed environment ran harmoniously and attracted attention of educators. His method of instruction was greatly appreciated.

A letter of appreciation from the school examiners/inspectors reflects his work: "All that you hoped from your method of teaching has been realised. You have shown that what powers already exist in even the youngest child, in what way are these powers to be developed, and how each talent must be sought out and exercised in such a way as to bring it to maturity. The astonishing progress made by your young pupils in spite of their many differences of character and disposition, clearly shows that every child is good for something, when the master knows how to find out his talents, and cultivate them in a truly psychological manner. Your teaching has brought to light the foundations on which all instructions must be based, if it is ever to be of any real use; it also shows that from the tender age, and in a very short time, a child's mind can attain a wonderful breadth of development which must make its influence felt, not only during his few years of study, but throughout his whole life".

Publications

Pestalozzi's views on education are contained in his following publications:

1. *Evening Hours of a Hermit*
2. *Leonard and Gertrude*
3. *How Gertrude Teaches Her Children*
4. *The Swan Song*
5. *Letters on Early Education*

In his *Evening Hours of Hermit*, Pestalozzi has explained his ideas in three ways—as a practical educational reformer, through his philosophical and sociological thought.

Like Rousseau's *Emile*, Pestalozzi's *Leonard and Gertrude* is written in the style of a novel. However, the difference between them is striking. While Rousseau dreamt of social isolation, Pestalozzi presented his story in a Swiss Village, with complete absorption in the life and grief of poor fellow men. Gertrude represents the living symbol of the 'road of nature'. He wrote, "Nature, herself, bids a man to look to his own interests and those of his family".

In *How Gertrude Teaches Her Children*, Pestalozzi provides a systematic psychological theory of his educational method. He says, "The mechanism of physical human nature is essentially subject to the same laws by which physical nature generally unfolds her powers. According to these laws, all instruction should graft the most essential parts of its subjects firmly into the very being of the human mind; then join the same essential parts of its subjects firmly into the very being of the human mind; then join the less essential gradually but uninterruptedly to the most essential, and maintain all the parts of the subject, even to the outermost, in one living, proportionate whole".

Gertrude, the pious mother of the children of the village where Leonard lived, brought about the regeneration of the village, primarily through education. The method of instruction was very simple. She gave them instruction in the rudiments of arithmetic with daily exercises. She taught them to count the number of steps from one end of the room to the other. Two of the rows of five panels each, in one of the windows gave her an opportunity to unfold the decimal relations of numbers. She also made them count their threads while spinning. She taught how to observe the forces of nature carefully and intelligently.

How Gertrude Teaches Her Children is a sort of manual to the mothers. It contains exercises for children. It also provides a systematic theory of his methods.

Pestalozzi also wrote 'Fables' with a Moral

Luella Cole in *A History of Education – Socrates to Montessori* has given an account of Pestalozzi's work with pre-school children. In the course of his work, it occurred to him that the task of educating a child inevitably began with the mother who could use the pre-school years to better purpose than was often the case, so that children might arrive at school age already in possession of simple facts and skills. The time thus saved would permit teachers to give a more advanced education during the school years than was possible when the children had no training before entrance in the lowest class. In his book he set forth a number of exercises some of which are certainly too hard for pre-school children".

Main Educational Ideas and Practices Propounded

1. *Meaning of education*: "Education is the natural progressive and harmonious development of all the powers and capacities of human beings".

In *Swan Song* Pestalozzi wrote, "The education of all three sides of our nature procedes on common lines in equal measure".

2. *Direct method of acquiring knowledge*: Pestalozzi named his direct method of acquiring knowledge an *Anschauung*. This means that the child acquires knowledge by his own experience. He observed, "I wish to psychologise education".

The function of instruction is to remove the confusion of the first impression. This implies:

(i) Separating the objects from one another to make them distinct.

(ii) Putting together in imagination those which are related to each other to make them all clear to children.

(iii) Putting across in children clear ideas through proper explanation.

3. *Model of the School*: Pestalozzi stressed that the school should follow the model of the home. Let the teacher act like a father. He should set an example in all activities. Just as cooperation and mutual understanding govern a good house, so these ideals should be applied to the school.

4. *Sense perception*: He was a believer in the value of sense impressions for learning. He said, "Man's knowledge must be founded on sense impression".

5. *Medium of play*: Pestalozzi believed that children express their natural drives through play.

6. *Discipline*: According to Pestalozzi, the children's trust in their teachers, their love and gratitude for them should take the place of rules and discipline.

7. *Vocational education*: Pestalozzi emphasised the necessity of vocational education.

8. *Three well-marked stages in the development of mind*:
   (i) The mind first begins with impressions. Gradually impressions become distinct and take individual forms as units of experience.
   (ii) At the next stage, sense impressions become clear. The form and other qualities of things are imagined by the mind.
   (iii) At the last stage, the clear images of things are transformed into ideas by which things can be understood clearly.

9. *Curriculum*: Activities at Yverdun schools included drawing, writing, singing, physical exercises, group recitations, model making, collecting map making and field trips.

Lower Class			**Upper Class**		
Sl. No.	*Curriculum*	*Hrs.*	*Sl. No.*	*Curriculum*	*Hrs.*
1.	Nature Study	2	1.	Natural history	2
2.	Description of products of art	2	2.	Technical work	2
3.	Geography	2	3.	Arithmetic	6
4.	Knowledge of the country (walking)	2	4.	Geometry and Drawing	4
5.	Mental arithmetic	6	5.	Language	4
6.	Drawing	4	6.	Singing	3
7.	Reading and language	6	7.	Religion	9
8.	Singing	3			
9.	Religion	6			
	Total	33		**Total**	30

There were three classes—primary, lower and upper—primary for children under 8, lower for between 8 and 11 and upper primary for 11 to 18.

10. *Ability grouping*: The students were divided into ability grouping according to individual differences.

11. *Teacher training*: Pestalozzi introduced teacher training at Yverdun school. Educators were attracted from Europe and America to study the working of this institution. They were so impressed that they started several schools for the training of teachers in their countries.

'Anschauung' of Pestalozzi

Meaning of Anschauung. There is no precise equivalent English word to *Anschauung*. *Anschauung* is a method of instruction teaching by experience. Usually following terms are used to convey the meaning of this concept—concrete experience, direct acquaintance, direct experience, first hand impression, personal contact experience, face to face knowledge and direct impact of persons and things. *Anschauung* may be described as: "The relations and proportions of number and form constitute the natural measures of all those impressions which the mind receives from without. They comprehend the qualities of the material world; form being the measure of space, and number the measure of time". He distinguished three aspects of *Anschauung*, namely, form, number and name.

Three-fold Principles

1. Principle of teaching children to look upon every object that is brought before them as a unit, that is separated from those with which it is connected.
2. Principle of teaching children the form of every object that is, its size and proportions.
3. Principle of recency so as to make children immediately acquainted with all the words and names descriptive of objects known to them.

Techniques of Instruction

a. He emphasised that the techniques of instruction should be directed to the primary faculties of counting, measuring and speaking which lie at the basic of accurate knowledge of objects of sense.
b. Appreciation of form was developed by Pestalozzi mainly through drawing on the basis that children are ready at an early age for getting knowledge of proportion and for using slate and pencil in making tiny letters.
c. For language teaching, he reduced language to words or names.

Pestalozzi describes his method of teaching arithmetic in these words: "For instance, when he asked in arithmetic—How many times is seven contained in sixty-three? The child has no real background for his answer, and must with great difficulty dig it out of his memory. Now, by the plan of putting nine times seven objects before his eyes, and letting him count them as nine sevens standing together, he has not to think anymore about this question; he knows from what he has already learnt, although he is asked for the first time, that seven is contained nine times in sixty-three. So it is in other subjects—this is my method". Pestalozzi explains the general principle of *Anschauung* as applied to arithmetic in these words: "That by exercising children beginning to count with real objects, or at least with dots representing them, we lay the foundation of the whole of the science of arithmetic, and secure their future progress from error and confusion.

Regarding the teaching of language, Pestalozzi wrote, "I always put the picture before the eye, then sought for a word, for the picture".

Major Contributions

1. All round and harmonious development as the aim of education.
2. Maximum freedom to the learner.
3. Analytic method of teaching.
4. Objects to come before symbols.
5. Play as the medium.

6. Stress on correlation.
7. Teacher training.
8. Ability grouping.
9. Concept of *Anschauung*.

Limitations of Pestalozzi's Educational Ideas and Practices

1. He insisted on beginning instruction with the elements of experiences but did not provide a definite idea of the elements of experiences.
2. His method of instruction was not suitable for advanced stages of learning.
3. There was no definite curriculum. Instruction was at random. Instruction was done on disconnected topics.

Some views on the His Contribution to Education Thought and Practices

Carroll Atkinson and Eurgene T. Maleska in *The Story of Education* (1962):

"Pestalozzi insisted that the natural instincts of a child should provide the motives for learning. He considered cooperation and sympathy, rather than compulsion or physical punishment, the proper means by which to achieve discipline. Influenced by Rousseau, he believed that free expression would allow the natural powers of child to develop. Since it is nature that gives the drive to life, he maintained that the teacher's responsibility is to adapt instruction to each individual according to his particular changing, unfolding nature as required at the various stages of his development. Pestalozzi looked upon the child as a unity made of moral, physical, and intellectual powers—all of which could be developed harmoniously through education."

Marlow Ediger of the Northern Missouri University, USA has summarised the views of Pestalozzi as under:

1. Reality rather than abstractions should be in evidence in the school curriculum in initial student learning.
2. The semi-concrete (models and illustrations) should follow realistic concrete experiences.
3. Students should master each step of learning prior to progressing to the next ordered activity or experience.
4. Physical punishment of pupils, in general, should be eliminated discipline based on love should be experienced by all students.
5. The use of the senses in learning is vital. These senses include the traditional utilization of touch, smell, taste, hearing, and sight. Developing the senses in learning should receive paramount emphasis.

Pestalozzi would definitely oppose:

1. Rote learning of content without students understanding what has been learned.

2. Drill and practice without developing pupil interest in ongoing activities and experiences.
3. Survey approaches in teaching-learning situations without students attaining content in depth.
4. Physical punishment of students without emphasizing students enjoying ongoing activities and experiences.
5. Forced discipline upon pupils without developing spontaneous quality behaviour within students.

The only way to correct misunderstanding between teacher and pupil, according to Pestalozzi, was for the teacher to commence with sense impressions of the object of the lesson. Only after time for these impressions to take effect had elapsed should the teacher proceed to the naming of the object. Once named, the object could be studied as to its form; that is, its various qualities could be discussed and compared. Finally, with the abstractions of its essential as against its accidental qualities, the object was ready for definition. This, in brief, is what Pestalozzi so frequently refers to as the essence of his method, teaching everything through number, form, and language. In this way language and observation or experience are always so closely linked that education should henceforth be well on its way to eliminating forever rote memory without comprehension.

Summing Up

To sum up the great German Philosopher Fichte had observed that the type of education developed by Pestalozzi would regenerate the nation. What Pestalozzi contributed to education throughout the world was a basic idea that 'Education consists of guiding children into a natural and orderly unfolding of their innate capacities'.

R. Rusk finds the following salient features of Pestalozzi's work:

1. *Anschauung* – the common starting point of all instruction.
2. Pestalozzi insistence that teaching should follow an orderly sequence.
3. Formulation of 'a method' based on psychological principles.
4. Recognition of the practical and emotional aspects of personality.
5. Laying the basis of elementary school system.
6. Reinforcing democratic tradition in education.

26

K.G. Saiyidain (1904-1971)

Khwaja Ghulamus Saiyidain was one of the leading educationist of India. He came from a well-known family of intellectuals of Panipat. In India, he received his education at the Aligarh Muslim University. He obtained his M.Ed. degree from Leeds University, writing a thesis on *Modern Educational Tendencies in England and America*. On return to India, he held distinctive positions of Professor of Education, Aligarh University, Director of Education, Jammu and Kashmir and Secretary to the Ministry of Education, Government of India.

Saiyidain was associated with almost all major educational initiatives in India for over four decades. He represented India at several international conferences. He was visiting Professor at the Universities of Columbia, Wisconsin, Stanford and Hawai.

Major Publications

1. *Iqbal's Educational Philosophy.*
2. *Education of the National Character.*
3. *Problems of Educational Reconstruction.*
4. *Faith of an Educationist.*
5. *Useful Talim.*
6. *Education, Culture and Social Order.*

Extracts from his publications which have a great bearing on educational reconstruction in India and are still relevant to a great degree are given here:

Characteristics of the Social Order—Education Ought to Strive

It should be a social order which would exploit in the fullest measure the resources and possibilities of modern scientific technology and try to eliminate all avoidable poverty and insecurity which afflict mankind today and condemn a majority of men and women to a harassed striving for a miserable and insecure livelihood. The existing social system stands irrevocably condemned because it keeps a large majority of mankind in ignorance and poverty, denying to them fullness of life, while securing to a small minority—and often an undeserving minority!—all the riches and the comforts of a materially advanced civilisation. Such a socio-economic system cannot command our loyalty and allegiance as teachers or inspire our highest educational endeavour. The social order, to which we can pledge our loyalty, must attempt consciously to control the productive activities of scientific industry in the interests of society as a whole, must secure a real equality of opportunity for individuals and groups and bring about a fairer distribution of the goods of life, both material and cultural. The educative significance of a better socio-economic order lies in the fact—and this is a very significant fact—that, by securing to all the possibility of more 'abundant' life both materially and culturally, the psychological emphasis will be shifted from the possessive and the egotistical to the creative and the social motives which even today underlie and inspire higher scientific, artistic and moral effort. It is only in a society where equality of opportunity prevails and a sense of reasonable security from want is assured to all that the sublimation of motives and urges becomes possible through social and educative forces. Otherwise, as experience teaches us, the motives of fear, hatred, exploitation and revolt are too strong to be ousted from their entrenched position through the efforts of the school alone (*Education, Culture and Social Order*, Chapter 2).

Concept of New Education

I would like to share with you a very appropriate quotation from Einstein's autobiography *Out of My Later Years* which provides a welcome and authoritative confirmation of the view of New Education that I have tried to develop:

"Sometimes one sees in the school simply the instrument for transferring a maximum quantity of knowledge to the growing generation. But that is not right. Knowledge is dead; the school, however, serves the living... Words are and remain empty sound, and the road to perdition has ever been accompanied by lip service to an ideal. Personalities are not formed by what is heard and said, but by labour and activity.

"The most important method of education accordingly has always consisted of that in which the pupil is urged to actual performance... Behind every achievement exists the motivation. The same work may owe its origin to fear and compulsion, or to ambitious desire for authority and distinction or to loving interest in the object and a desire for truth and understanding, and thus to that divine curiosity which every healthy child possesses, but which is often early weakened.

"Darwin's theory of the struggle for existence and the selectivity connected with it has been cited by many persons as authorisation for encouragement of the competitive spirit. They have tried to prove pseudo-scientifically the necessity of the destructive economic struggle of competition between individuals. But this is wrong, because man owes his strength in the struggle for existence to the fact that he is a socially living animal.

"Therefore one should guard against preaching to the young man success, in the customary sense, as the aim of life. For a successful man is he who receives a great deal from his fellowmen, usually incomparably more than his corresponding service to them. The value of a man, however, should be seen in what he gives and not in what he is able to receive.

"The most important motive for work in the school and in life is the pleasure in work, pleasure in its result, and the knowledge of the value of the result to the community. Such a psychological foundation leads to a joyous desire for the highest possessions of man—knowledge and artist like workmanship.

"The awakening of these productive psychological powers is certainly less easy than is the practice of force or the awakening of individual ambition, but is the more valuable for it. The point is to develop the childlike inclination for play and the childlike desire for recognition and to guide the child over to important fields for society. If a school succeeds in working successfully from such points of view, it will be highly honoured by the rising generation, and the tasks given by the school will be gladly submitted to as a sort of gift. I have known children who prefer school time to vacations. The wit was not wrong who said: 'Education is that which remains, even if one has forgotten everything he learned in school'." (*Ibid*, Chapter 16)

Central Objective of Education in India

If I were asked to define broadly the main objective of our educational reconstruction, I would say that we are trying to build a bridge between education and life and make our educational ideology responsive both to the new urges and aspirations of the people and the age, as well as the older, basic values of our culture. This is, in fact, the inspiration of our entire programme of national reconstruction. In dealing with this problem we have to reckon with the pull of the opposing forces of revivalism and modernism, which operate in every sphere of our life. In this battle, we have to adopt a critical, rather than a doctrinaire, approach to both, with greater emphasis on the capacity to meet the new challenges. There are some valuable elements of our cultural heritage which we must guard and cherish with solicitude but we should also have the resolute courage to discard whatever is reactionary or obscurantist and stands in the way of our going forward. (*Problems of Educational Reconstruction*, Chapter 5)

Education for Emotional Integration

What does this Emotional Integration precisely imply? It does not mean a levelling down of differences for they are part of the nature of man and society. Where it has been achieved, it means that the people have the right to differ and express their differences reasonably and fearlessly within the larger framework of national unity and basic loyalties. This involves the cultivation of the precious quality of tolerance and charity as a supreme value, for it is a basic condition of civilised life in a culture which values variety. The right approach here is neither a levelling down of all differences so that there will be nothing to integrate, nor the encouragement of an attitude of indifference to the special values of different religions or group cultures and traditions. Tolerance is essentially a tolerance of differences. It means the right to hold to one's conviction firmly and frankly and a readiness to give others the right to do the same. It means in the classic words of Voltaire: "I differ profoundly with what you say but will give my life to safeguard your right to say so". Democracy is essentially a process of give-and-take and "emotional integration" is meant to prepare the right climate for the functioning of democracy. There are many elements in our cultural foundations which are favourable to the development of such a climate of opinion—a tolerance of points of view other than one's own, a rejection of what Dr. Radhakrishnan has called the "either-or" attitude, a spirit of assimilation which has been responsible for the gradual emergence of our present composite culture. We must remember that healthy plants cannot survive, unless we make an effort to weed out the rank, poisonous growth which takes root more quickly, is more hardy and thrives more vigorously. There is no easy recipe to ensure the survival of the worthy values. It is essentially an uphill task which involves really the changing of the whole man from within and, therefore, calls for the reorientation of the entire educational process in its widest sense. We must utilise the various sources of inspiration in human life— religion, literature, science, philosophy, social sciences etc., which appeal to different persons, depending on their mental and emotional make up. We have also at our disposal the powerful modern media of mass communication through which we can direct, to some extent, the thinking and behaviour of children and adults into healthy channels. (*Education, Culture and Social Order*. Chapter 4)

The School as an Activity Environment

What are the outstanding differences between the 'new' school and the traditional school as it exists today? It differs from the traditional school both in its attitude towards the child and its attitude towards the world of everyday affairs and problems. It attaches great value to the freedom of the child and takes its stand on indisputable psychological evidence. It is inspired by the faith that a child's development can be secured only if his native powers and capacities are given free play to interact fruitfully with his environment. It does not visualise its work as consisting in a constant repression of the child's energies and activities in all directions except scholastic learning. Its attempt is to provide for the child an environment that is as rich and active and joyous as possible—with opportunities for play, social cooperation, manual work, creative and constructive activities, study of spontaneously chosen books and subjects—and, when the environment has been planned, to let the child participate fully in its manifold activities which are congenial to his age and interests. It is by living, here and now, a life that is worthwhile and immediately satisfying and meaningful that the child can be best prepared for his duties and functions as an adult. This attitude demands a genuine faith on the part of the teacher that the natural impulses of the child are the chief instrument and raw material of his education. Education is not synonymous with the pouring in of readymade knowledge; it is rather the disciplining, the organisation and the coordination of his powers and capacities towards valuable and significant ends. The essence of modern teaching, on the intellectual side, is to give the child a mastery over the tools of learning and a lively curiosity and hunger for the acquisition of knowledge. For, scientific knowledge has grown so remarkably and rapidly during the last two centuries that no education, however thorough and prolonged, can expect to make the pupil a master of all or even a considerable part of the available learning. Instead, therefore, of giving him a superficial acquaintance with many scattered and disconnected topics, it is more useful to deal thoroughly and leisurely with a small number of significant experiences, making him master the instruments of learning incidentally and purposefully and whetting his intellectual appetite all the time. Thus the modern 'progressive' school seeks to replace information by experience and chooses the most significant and abiding aspects of experience for its subject matter and thereby makes school life active and meaningful. (*Problems of Educational Reconstructions*. Chapter 1)

The School as the Centre of Community Life

Education is essentially a social affair and the school is charged by society with the duty of training and bringing up the youth so that they may be able to participate effectively in the life of the group to which they belong. They cannot inherit automatically their social heritage as they might their father's property They have to learn how to come into active possession of the cultural and institutional heritage which has been bequeathed to them by their predecessors. Without the light of experience stored up in books, in work and in social contacts they will grope in the dark and waste their efforts. Nor will they be in a position to evaluate intelligently and reconstruct this culture in the light of their present needs. This point of approach indicates the true conception of school work. We are far too apt to consider and decide educational problems from an exclusively individualistic point of view, neglecting the social relationships and bearings of education. We forget that education—whether in schools or colleges—is after all not an isolated activity but related at all points to life and responsive to all the forces that play on it. The school is—or rather should be—'an idealised epitome' of social life, reflecting within it the elements of all the worthful major activities that make up the work of society. The notion that the school just 'trains' an individual—trains his 'faculties', his senses, his mind—is entirely inadequate. For, it leads one naturally to ask: "Trains with reference to what?" and provides no clue to a satisfactory answer. The individual has certainly to be trained, but with reference to, and partly for the sake of, the needs, demands and ideals of the bigger society outside. And since these demands are always changing, enlarging and modifying themselves, it is necessary that the school should be in vital rapport with the life outside school and should educate children for a changing and dynamic environment.

In order to sum up this discussion about the 'School of the Future' and bring before the readers something like a diagrammatic sketch, I reproduce below three diagrams borrowed from *Dewey School and Society*, how it will be organically connected with the life of the community, how its internal life will be organised on the basis of productive and constructive social activities and how it will, in consequence be transformed into a vitalising and creative environment where children can live in stimulating contact with all that is of permanent and abiding value in the achievement of the human race and thus grow in understanding, appreciation and control. Brief explanatory notes are appended with each diagram to clarify the ideas underlying it.

Diagram I: The School in Relation to its Environment

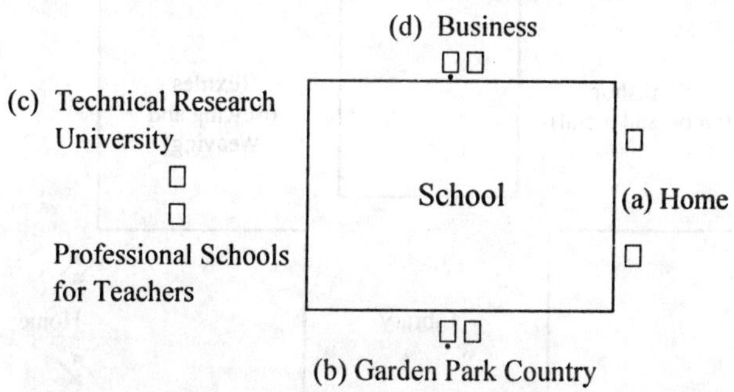

In this diagram the school is conceived of as an organic part of social life, interconnected with the various important 'institutions' of society, acting on them and being acted upon by them in return and deriving its curriculum and subject matter from the rich and varied life of adult society. The following points are specially noteworthy:

a. There is a free interplay of ideas, influences and materials between the home and the school.
b. There is a close relationship with the natural environment, the study of which develops into 'geography' and 'science'.
c. There is interaction between the highest and the lowest parts of the system. The work that is being done, in the field of Psychology,

Sociology, Biology, etc., in the Universities and the Training Colleges will enrich the understanding of school methods and problems, and the validity of their theoretical research will be tested at the touchstone of practice in schools.

d. There should be free play between the school and the problems and needs of business and industry. This involves not a preparation for one particular calling but a bringing to the child's consciousness of the business and economic relationships of society—factory, bank, labour, crafts, agriculture, etc.—as corporate activities. The task of the school will be both to provide a pre-vocational bias by offering alternative courses in the higher classes and to liberalise the vocational aspect by showing its relationship with larger and more important life purpose. This is what our reorganised secondary schools—the 'multipurpose' schools— are trying to work out.

Diagrams II and III represent not the architectural plan of the school but attempt to give an idea of the internal environment of the school and its activities in a symbolic form.

Diagram II: Lower Storey of the School

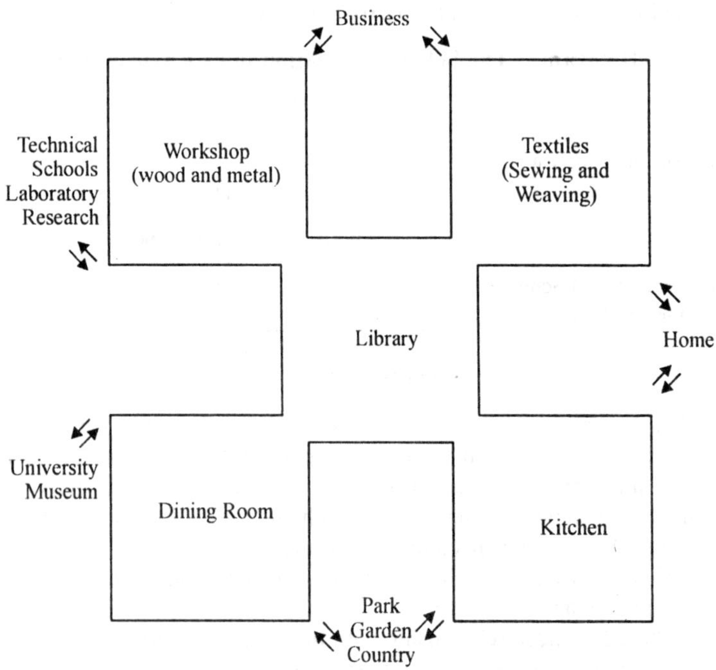

Diagram III: Upper Storey of the School

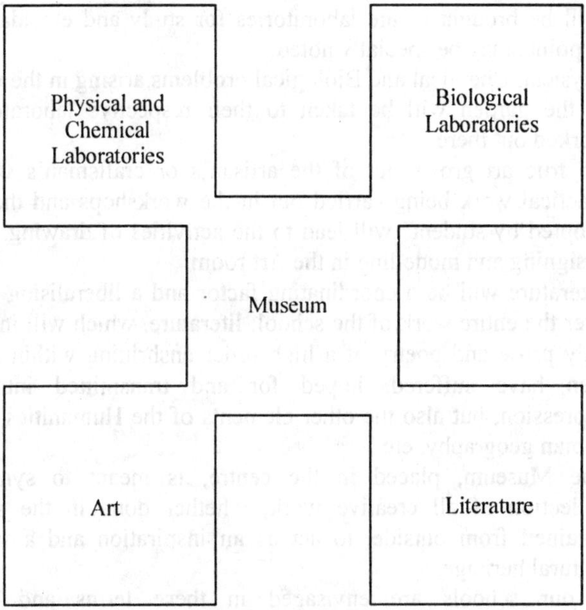

Diagram II brings out the following points:

(1) On one side are the Kitchen and the Dining Room with obvious connections between them and the home activities as well as the physical environment. In connection with occupations centring round them the children will learn a good deal of school geography, botany, agriculture, domestic science and other useful knowledge.

(2) On the other side are the wood and metal workshops as well as rooms for weaving and sewing which, between them, represent some of the most important occupations of civilised life, involving acquaintance with tools and industrial processes and products, and drawing in its train knowledge belonging to arithmetic, geometry, mechanics, etc. The mutual interaction between the school and business life is indicated by two-way arrows.

(3) The Library, situated in the centre, indicates that all these activities will be illumined, liberalised and given an enriched significance through the widening and systematisation of knowledge that will occur as a result of self-initiated or teacher-guided study. The library stands for classes, discussion groups, theoretical explorations arising out of felt needs of practical activity. It also shows that, while book knowledge is subsidiary to activity, it is all-important as interpreting and expanding knowledge and increasing the children's power and control.

Diagram III is a symbolic representation of the theoretical side of school activities, showing how theory will grow out of practice, how problems created will be brought to the laboratories for study and elucidation. The following points may be specially noted:

a. Physical, Chemical and Biological problems arising in the workshop or the garden will be taken to their respective laboratories and worked out there.
b. All true art grows out of the artisan's or craftsman's work. The practical work being carried out in the workshops and the hobbies adopted by students will lead to the activities of drawing, painting, designing and modelling in the Art room.
c. Literature will be a coordinating factor and a liberalising influence over the entire work of the school: literature, which will include not only prose and poetry of a high order enshrining within it all that men have suffered, hoped for and transmitted into artistic expression, but also the other elements of the Humanities—history, human geography, etc.
d. The Museum, placed in the centre, is meant to symbolise a collection of all creative work, whether done in the school or obtained from outside, to act as an inspiration and a vehicle of cultural heritage.

When our schools are envisaged in these terms and patterned accordingly, when they break the four walls around them and let the currents of life play on them, we shall bring about an educational revolution of enormous potential, such as we may find difficult to envisage. (*Problems of Educational Reconstruction*, Chapter 4)

27

Leo Tolstoy (1828-1910)

Tolstoy, a Russian educator-cum novelist has made a unique contribution to educational thinking. His fame as a novelist has to some extent obscured his writings on education. His writings are based on his first hand experiences.

At the age of 21, *i.e.*, in 1849 Tolstoy opened a school on his ancestral estate at Yasnaya Polyana, for the education of peasant children. However, he was not successful. During 1851 to 1856, he served in the army. After retirement from army he, once more took up teaching at his native place with a large number of peasant children. With a view to gain more knowledge on the various dimensions of teaching, he visited several countries of Europe including France, Germany and Switzerland during 1857 to 1862.

Tolstoy was keenly interested in restructuring the national system of education in Russia.

In the 1870s, he worked on the compilation of school textbooks.

Gandhiji was greatly impressed by his work on education. *War and Peace* is the monumental work of Tolstoy.

Educational Thought

In his first book *The Four Periods of Development* he described the process by which human character is formed from early childhood to youth. He highlighted the need for a respectful attitude towards the child's personality and this idea became the cornerstone of his educational work.

Freedom in School

Tolstoy called freedom 'the one and only criterion of education'. On account of this, he is compared with Rousseau. He said that a child is by nature a perfect and innocent creature whose free development should not be hindered. Tolstoy's concept of freedom is explained by Prof. Semion Filippovitch Yegoror as under:

"In Tolstoy's view, freedom in education was a gnoseological and moral principle which had to be put into practice; it was the antithesis of authoritarian teaching, and essential for a humane attitude to the pupil and respect for his or her dignity as a human being. Freedom in education was a principle which stemmed from the internal laws of cognitive activity.

Cognition could not be other than free. In the absence of that condition, activity, initiative, consistency, system and all the other tenets of traditional, classical education were of no use, lacking meaning and purpose. The more firmly education was based on that law, the more successful and fruitful it was. Knowledge which had been assimilated could not simply be transmitted and could certainly not be thrust on pupils if they did not want it. Pupils had to apply their own efforts and engage in independent cognitive activity. This they could do best of all by not being forced by a teacher but guided by their own free will".

Holistic View of Child Study

The chief method of child study for Tolstoy was that of many-sided analysis, covering psychological as well as sociological aspects.

Functioning of Yasnaya Polyana School Opened by Tolstoy

The school catered to the boys and girls from 7 to 13. L.N. Tolstoy, Son of Tolstoy describes the chief features of the school in these words:

"Lessons began between 8 and 9 o'clock in the morning. At noon, there was a break for lunch and a rest. Lessons then continued another three to four hours. Every teacher gave five to six lessons every day. According to their age. readiness and progress, the children were divided into three groups: junior, middle and senior. Pupils did not have places strictly allotted to them. They sat where they liked. No homework was given. The commonest form of educational activity was not the lesson in the usual sense of the word but a free conversation with the pupils during which the children learned reading, writing and arithmetic, their catechism, the rules of grammar, and facts adapted to their age about history, geography and nature study. They also learned to draw and sing.

"The content of the education given, like its external organisation, was not immutable but changed in accordance with the children's development, the capacities of the school and the teachers, and the wishes of the parents. Tolstoy himself taught mathematics, physics, history and other subjects to the senior group. Most frequently, he told stories in order to teach the fundamentals of science. The children were punished neither for their behaviour nor for poor progress. The requirement that the personality of pupils should be treated with respect pre-supposed that, without punishment or coercion on the part of the adults, they would move towards a recognition of the need to submit to the order on which success at school depended. 'Schoolchildren', said Tolstoy, 'are people, even though they are small. They are people with the same needs as ourselves, who think in the same way as we do. They all want to learn; that is why they go to school and that is why they will have no trouble in understanding that they must submit to certain conditions in order to learn".

Role of the Teachers

The duties of a teacher at Yasnaya Polyana were much more complex than at a school with a strict timetable, coercive discipline, a range of set methods of encouragement and punishment, and a strictly limited volume of knowledge to be studied. Here, the teacher's moral and intellectual faculties were constantly being stretched. They were required at all times to take into consideration of the situation and abilities of each of their charges. In fact, what is known as educational creativity was demanded of the teacher. But the results achieved at the school at Yasnaya Polyana were also different from those at other schools. As a former teacher at Yasnaya Polyana, Yevgeni Markov, said: "We were able to observe the extraordinary progress of Tolstoy's pupils, among whom were some bright little boys who had been taken straight from harrowing or looking after the sheep and after just a few months were able to write quite literate compositions."

Educational Journal 'Yasnaya Polyana'

Tolstoy published this journal primarily with the following objectives:

(a) New educational methods; (b) New principles of administration for people's education; (c) New ways of organising the learning process; (d) Experiments with out-of-school education involving the circulation of books among the people; (e) Monographs describing schools which had come into being spontaneously, with an examination of their achievements and shortcomings, etc.

Tolstoy saw the journal's most important task as studying spontaneous educational activity, throwing light on the underlying links in the process of education, a knowledge of which would be of inestimable value for education as a science and for the teacher as a practitioner. He sought a wide range of contributors to the journal, stipulating only that they must be teachers who looked on their work not only as a means of existence or even as a duty to children, but as a field of experiment to advance the science of education.

Tolstoy himself published the following types of articles in the journal:

- People's Education
- Methods of Teaching How to Read and Write
- A Draft Central Plan for the Organisation of People's Schools
- Who Should be Taught to Write and by Whom
- Progress and the Definition of Education

The Tsar authorities (rulers of Russia) did not like the educational views contained in these articles and they considered the journal as 'subverting the fundamental tenets of religion and morality'. Accordingly Tolstoy was prosecuted and the journal ceased publication.

'The Primer'

Tolstoy wrote a textbook for the very young. Its overall plan, content and logical structure were worked out over a prolonged period. Tolstoy was so much excited with this project that he said, "Now I have written the *Primer*, I can die in peace".

Ethical and Moral Teaching

Tolstoy extensively wrote articles on ethical and moral teaching.

Education for All

In the mid-nineteenth century Russia, the majority of the population of the peasants, were still not only uneducated but illiterate. Tolstoy was deeply conscious of the chasm in the society of his time between the cultural achievements and education of the privileged classes and the educational deprivation of the majority of the population. In this tragic division, he saw the source of many social antagonisms and troubles. He felt that education should be available to everyone. If it were made available in equal measure to all sections of the population, it could eliminate despotism and violence, superstition and injustice. "The most pressing need of the Russian people is for education", he declared. (Based on the Article of Semion Filippovitch Yegorov, *Prospects* 24(3/4), 1994)

28

M.K. Gandhi (1869-1948)

Basic Tenets of Basic Education

Mohandas Karam Chand Gandhi (Karam Chand was his father), popularly known as *Bapu* out of affection and reverence by the people, *Mahatma*, on account of his saintly nature and 'Father of the Nation' for the regeneration of the Indian nation, *free* from the British rule, was a great educator, a nation builder, a political leader, a social worker, a statesman and a writer. Gandhiji had a charismatic appeal and he attracted thousands of devoted workers hailing from all sections of the society. He took up cases which ultimately touched the life of the common man.

Early Life and Education: Gandhiji was born on October 2, 1869, at Porbandar in Gujarat. His father was a Dewan (Chief Administrator and Chief Revenue Officer) of a small state. At school, he was slow, hesitant and shy. He was married to Kasturba at the age of thirteen. His mother was very pious and he was greatly influenced by her.

Education in England: When 18 years old, he was sent to London to study law where he remained for three years. His mother made him promise that in England he would not take meat and alcohol and indulge in sex. Gandhiji kept his promise.

Work in South Africa: After returning from England, he started his law practice at Bombay. However, he was not very successful.

In April, 1893, he went to South Africa in connection with a civil law case of a firm. In 1893 itself, he was thrown out of a first class compartment in Durban (South Africa) for he was a coloured man. He stayed there for about 20 years. This was a turning point in his life. Gandhiji found that the Indians in South Africa were treated very cruelly and in fact like animals. They had no political rights. Gandhiji took up cases which were not entirely political but touched intimately the life of the people. Gandhiji gave up his legal practice. He completely devoted himself to the service of the people. He put into practice *Satyagraha* and *Ahimsa*.

Gandhiji's Publications on Education

Important publications on education and having bearing on education are:

1. *My Experiments with Truth. (Autobiography)*
2. *Basic Education*

3. *Towards Need Education*
4. *True Education*
5. *To the Students*
6. *Task Before Indian Students*
7. *India of My Dreams*
8. *Medium of Instruction*
9. *Tasks before India*

Gandhiji also wrote extensively on education in *Harijan* — a paper founded by him.

Principal Features of Gandhiji's Philosophy of Life

1. *Supreme God*: He said, "God pervades everything. God is life, Truth and Light".
2. *Truth and Ahimsa (Non-violence)*: According to Gandhiji, "Truth and Ahimsa are the two sides of a coin. They are intertwined and it is practically impossible to separate them". *Satyagraha* implies holding of truth through love and purity.
3. *Service of Humanity*: Gandhiji observed: "The immediate service of all human beings becomes a necessary part because it is the only way to see Him in his creation".
4. *Self-discipline and Self-purification*: Gandhi always held the high ideals of purity, sacrifice and service.
5. *Righteousness and truth as the highest religion*: Gandhiji was of the firm view that "true religion and true morality are inseparably bound up with each other".
6. *Ram Rajya as the Concept of a Society*: He wanted to establish Ram Rajya which he identified with justice, peace, happiness and welfare of all.

According to Gandhiji, man's ultimate aim is the realisation of God and all his endeavour—political, religious and social—must be guided to this end: "The immediate service of all human beings becomes a necessary part of the endeavour, simply because the only way to find God is to see Him in His creation and be one with it—I am a part and parcel of the whole and I cannot find Him apart from the rest of humanity". For Gandhiji, God lives in the temple of humanity and man becomes great exactly in the degree to which he works for the welfare of his fellow men.

Factors that Influenced Gandhiji's Philosophy of Life and Philosophy of Education

Following were the chief influences which had a great effect on Gandhiji's philosophy of life and philosophy of education.

1. *Mother's Influence*: Gandhiji's mother taught him the lessons of simplicity and piety.
2. *Three Great Thinkers*:

(i) Rayachand Bhai Patel who taught Gandhiji the first lesson in non-violence.
(ii) Ruskin, through his book *Unto the Last* drew his attention to the principle of dignity of labour.
(iii) Leo Tolstoy's *The Kingdom of the God is within you* greatly influenced his spiritual outlook.

3. *The Phoenix Settlement* (South Africa) where Gandhiji conducted early experiments.
4. *The Tolstoy Farm*: In 1911, Gandhiji started an Ashram in Transwal. It was here that Gandhiji helped children in their all round development. He taught vocations such as cooking, digging and massage work. The medium of instruction was mother-tongue. English was also taught. Children learnt by doing. Textbooks were not used. No punishment was administered. Creed of non-violence was put into practice in letter and spirit.
5. *The Sabarmati Ashram*: After returning to India in 1914, Gandhiji started the Sabarmati Ashram. A school was attached with the Ashram which Gandhiji wanted to become a model school.

Thoughts on Various Dimensions of Education in His Own Words

Meaning of Education

Real Education has to draw out the best from the boys and girls to be educated. This can never be done by packing ill-assorted and unwanted information into the heads of the students. It becomes a dead weight crushing all originality in them and turning them into mere automata. (*Harijan*, December 1, 1933)

By education I mean an all-round drawing out of the best in child and man—body, mind and spirit. (*Harijan*, July 31, 1937)

Literacy is not the end of education not even the beginning. It is only one of the means whereby men and women can be educated. Literacy in itself is no education. (*Harijan*, July 31, 1937)

I would develop in the child his hands, his brain and his soul. (*Basic Education*, p. 23)

Purity of personal life is the one indispensable condition for building a sound education. (*Towards New Education*, p. 31)

I hold that true education of the intellect can only come through a proper exercise and training of the bodily organs, e.g., hands, feet, eyes, ears, nose, etc. (*Basic Education*, p. 123)

True education is that which draws out and stimulates the spiritual, the intellectual and physical faculties of the children. (Tendulkar, *Mahatma*, Vol. IV, p. 187)

Education and Character

The end of all knowledge must be building up character. What is education without character and what is character without elementary purity? (*Towards New Education*, p. 301)

All our learning or recitation of the Vedas, correct knowledge of Sanskrit, Latin and Greek and what not, will avail as nothing if they do not enable us to cultivate purity of heart. The end of all knowledge may be the building of character. (*True Education*, p. 229)

The Teacher

Woe to the teacher who teaches one thing with the lips and carries another in the heart. (*To the Students*, p. 16)

The politician may succeed in his purpose even though he lacks character, but a pupils' teacher cannot do without character. If he lacks, he will be like salt without its savour. (*True Education*, p. 161)

I always felt that the true textbook for the pupils is his teacher. (*Autobiography*, p. 41)

It is possible for a teacher living miles away to affect the spirit of the pupils by his way of living. (*Towards New Education*, p. 44)

Education through Craft

I want the whole process of education to be imparted through some handicraft or industry. (*Basic Education*, p. 191)

My idea is not to teach a particular profession or occupation to the children, but to develop the full man through teaching that occupation. (Tendulkar, *Mahatma*, Vol. IV, p. 200)

The brain must be educated through hand. (*Basic Education*, p. 190)

The old idea was to add a craft to the ordinary curriculum of education followed in the schools. That is to say, the craft was to be taken in hand wholly separate from education. To me that seems a fatal mistake. The teacher must learn the craft and correlate his knowledge to the craft, so that he will impart all that knowledge to his pupils through the medium of the particular craft that he chooses.

Take the instance of spinning. Unless I know arithmetic I cannot report how many yards of yarn I have produced on the *takli*. I must learn addition and subtraction and multiplication and division. In dealing with complicated sums, I shall have to use symbols and so I get my algebra. Even here, I would insist on the use of Hindustani letters instead of Roman.

Takli-spinning leads me into the History of East India Company.

There is no limit to the possibilities of knowledge that can be imparted through this medium. (*Harijan*, February 18, 1939)

Methods of Teaching

It is not by making our brains a store-house for cramming facts that our understanding is opened. An intelligent approach to an industrial training is often a more valuable aid to the intellect than an indifferent reading of literature.

Pupils should know to discriminate between what should be received and what rejected. It is the duty of the teacher to teach his pupils discrimination. (*Towards New Education*, p. 34)

The utterly false idea that intelligence can be developed only through book-reading should give place to the truth that the quickest development of the mind can be achieved by artisan's work being learnt in a scientific way. (Bose, Nirmal Kumar, *Selections from Gandhiji*, p. 288)

The brain must be educated through the hand. (*Harijan*, Feb. 29, 1939)

The core of my suggestion is that handicrafts are to be taught not merely for production work but for developing the intellect. (*Basic Education*, p. 44)

I want to teach through hand-work all the subjects like History, Geography, Arithmetic, Science, Language, Painting etc. (Tendulkar, *Mahatma*, Vol. IV, p. 196)

Freedom and Discipline

The students mind must not be caged. This does not mean that they are not subject to discipline. No school can be run without it. But discipline has nothing to do with artificial restraint upon students' all round growth. (*True Education*, p. 57)

I have always been opposed to corporal punishment. (*Towards New Education*, p. 19)

The worst thing that can happen to boys in school is to have to render blind obedience to everything that the teacher says. (*True Education*, p. 88)

If the boys and girls do not learn discipline in their school days, money and time spent on their education is a national loss. (*Harijan*, Feb. 17, 1946)

Self-sufficiency in Education

Self-sufficiency is not a prior condition, but to me it is the acid test. This does not mean that Basic Education will be self-supporting from the very start. But taking the entire period of seven years, income and expenditure must balance each other. (*Basic Education*, p. 108)

Nai Talim without the self-support basis would be like a lifeless boy. (*Basic Education*, p. 108)

When I used the word self-supporting, I did not mean that all the capital expenditure would be defrayed from it, but at least the salary of the teacher would be found out of the proceeds of the articles made by our pupils. The economic aspect of the basic system of education is thus self-evident. (*Basic Education*, p. 10)

I am very keen on finding the expenses of a teacher through the product of the manual labour of his pupils because I am convinced that there is no other way to carry education to crores of our children. (*Basic Education*, p. 192)

My *Nai Talim* is not dependent on money. The running expenses of this education should come from the educational proceeds itself. (*Harijan*, March 2, 1947)

Dignity of Labour

Manual work will have to be the very centre of the whole thing. (*India of My Dreams*, p. 72)

The introduction of manual training will serve as a double purpose in a poor country like ours. It will pay for the education of our children and teach them an occupation to which they can fall back in later life. Such a system must make our children self-reliant. (*Towards New Education*, p. 42)

Useful manual labour, intelligently performed, is the means par excellence for developing the intellect. (*Basic Education*, p. 106)

Medium of Instruction

The foreign medium has made our children practically foreigners in their own land. It is the greatest tragedy of the existing system. (*Towards New Education*, p. 48)

As a result of English being medium of instruction we have lost all originality. We have become birds without wings. (*To the Students*, p. 89)

The baby takes its lesson from its mother. I therefore regard it a sin against the motherland to inflict upon her children a tongue other than their mother's for their mental development. (*Medium of Instruction*, p. 8)

The medium of instruction must be altered at any cost, the provincial languages being given this rightful place. I would prefer temporary chaos in higher education to the criminal waste that is daily accumulating. (*Towards New Education*, p. 89)

Gandhiji's Philosophy: Idealism in Gandhiji's Philosophy of Education

1. *Concept of Education*: Gandhiji summed up his ideas on education in these words: "By education I mean an all-round drawing out of the best in child and man—body, mind and spirit".

'All round' implies the harmonious development of the individual. Man is neither merely the gross animal body, nor intellectual and nor the heart and soul alone. A proper and harmonious combination of all these three is required for making the whole man. Any programme of education which puts exclusive emphasis on one of these aspects of the human personality is against the principle of education.

Drawing out of the best in child recognises a great potentiality coiled up in the child which can be released and developed to its perfection through education.

Body, mind and soul is a vision of the whole man. The first emphasis is on the body and the culmination point is the spirit.

Intellectual development is the mid-point and it is neither the beginning nor the end of education.

The best can be drawn out by touching the heart of the students. Gandhiji wrote: "If I were to be their teacher and guardian I must touch their hearts. I must share their joys and sorrows. I must help them to solve their problems that face them, and I must take along the right channel, the surging aspirations of their youth".

For Gandhiji, the potentiality of the child is the centre. The school has to help the child to realise this potentiality, to make his life better, fuller, happier-both individually and socially.

2. *Education and Character*: "The end of all knowledge must be building up character. What is education without character and what is character without elementary personal purity"?

The idealism of Gandhiji is reflected in the following words: "Long before I undertook the education of the youngsters at the Tolstoy Farm I had realised that the training of spirit was a thing by itself. To develop the spirit is to build character and to enable one to work towards a knowledge of God and self-realisation, and I held that this was an essential part of the training of the young, and that all training without culture of the spirit was of no use and might be even harmful.

Gandhiji believes in the harmonious development of personality and advocates that different types of social culture and physical activities may be undertaken to achieve this end.

3. *Spiritual Training (Training of Heart)*: "I made the children memorise and recite hymns, and read to them from books on moral training. But that was far from satisfying me. As I came into closer contact with them I saw that it was through looks that one could impart training of the spirit. Just as physical training was to be imparted through physical exercise and intellectual through intellectual exercise, even so the training of the spirit was possible only through the exercise of the spirit. And the exercise of the spirit entirely depended on the life and character of the teacher. The teacher had always to be mindful of his Ps and Qs whether he was in the midst of his boys or not".

4. *The Teacher*: Gandhiji said, "Woe to the teacher, who teaches one thing with the lips and carries another in his heart".

5. *Freedom but under discipline*: Gandhiji emphatically said, "The pupils must have initiative. They must cease to be mere imitators. They must learn to think and act for themselves and yet be thoroughly obedient and disciplined. The highest form of freedom carries with it the greatest measures of discipline and humility. Freedom that comes from discipline and humility cannot be denied, unbridled licence is a sign of vulgarity injurious alike to self and one's neighbours".

6. *Religious Education*: "To me religion means Truth and *Ahimsa* or rather Truth alone because Truth includes *Ahimsa* being the necessary and indispensable means for its discovery. Therefore, anything that promotes the practice of these virtues is a means for imparting religious education and the best way to do this, in my opinion, is for the teachers rigorously to practise these virtues in their own person. This very association with the boys, whether on the playground or in the classroom, will then give the pupils a fine training in these fundamental virtues".

Gandhiji's Pragmatism in Education

Gandhiji's pragmatism in education is reflected in his views as under:

(i) *Education for a just social order:* "The ultimate objective of the new education is not only a balanced and harmonious individual but also a balanced and harmonious society—a just social order in which there is no unnatural dividing line between the have and have-nots and everybody is assured of a living wage and right to freedom".

(ii) *Meaning of education:* "By education, I mean an all-round drawing out of the best in child and man—body, mind and spirit".

(iii) *Education through craft*: "The uniqueness of this scheme is that education is to be given 'through' village crafts. The end in view is not to be accomplished by merely adding a village craft to the current syllabus".

(iv) *Self-supporting aspect:* "You have to start with the conviction that looking to the needs of the villages of India, our education ought to be made self-supporting if it is to be compulsory. This education ought to be for them a kind of insurance against unemployment. He further said that not only from the economic point of view, the education must be self-sufficient, but also from moral and social points of view".

(v) *Dignity of labour:* "It is a crime to make education merely literary, and to unfit boys and girls for manual work in later life. Indeed I hold that as the large part of our time is devoted to labour for earning our bread, our children must from their infancy be taught dignity of such labour. Our children should not be so taught as to desist labour".

(vi) *Relationship with life*: Education should be closely related to life. Wardha Scheme unifies knowledge and does not allow division of knowledge into water-tight compartments. Everything is to be taught through the principle of correlation. There are three centres of correlation—craft, physical environment and social environment of the child. These three centres of correlation will achieve perfect integration of curriculum.

(vi) *Women's education*: "The question of the education of children cannot be solved unless efforts are made simultaneously to solve women's education. And I have no hesitation in saying that as long as we do not have real mother teachers who can successfully impart true education to our children, they will remain uneducated even though they may be going to school".

Gandhiji's Naturalism in Education

Gandhiji introduced several elements of naturalism in education and this becomes clear from the following:

(a) *Craft Work as Natural Meeting Point of All Subjects*: Craft work is the meeting point of all subjects. The correlated teaching arouses greater interest and enthusiasm because it gives teaching and learning a relevance born of practical and living purpose and need.

Craft work done under proper conditions not only makes the acquisition of much related knowledge more concrete and realistic but also adds a powerful contribution to the development of personality and character and instils respect and love for all society useful work.

(b) *Medium of Instruction*: Gandhiji wrote: "Our language is the reflection of ourselves and if you tell me that our languages are too poor to express the best thought, I say that the sooner we are wiped out of existence the better for us". About foreign medium he observed: "The foreign medium has caused a brain fag, put an undue strain upon the nerves of our children, made them crammers and imitators, unfitted them for original work and thought and disabled them for filtrating their training to their family or the masses. The foreign medium has made our children practically foreigners in their own land".

(c) *Curriculum and Spinning*: "In any curriculum of the future, spinning must be a compulsory subject. Just as we cannot live without eating, so it is impossible for us to attain economic independence and banish pauperism from the ancient land without reviving home spinning".

(d) *Correlation*: Correlation is a wonderful technique which tries to establish reciprocal relationship between the various subjects of the curriculum for the better understanding of the subjects of the curriculum for the better understanding of the subject under discussion. It draws out the points of resemblances which different studies of the child at school bear to one another. It is a wonderful device which can be employed safely for creating interest in the lesson and thus facilitate learning. Correlation selects related parts and combines them into a new piece of information which becomes a good ready-made mental food for the growth of the child's faculties. In this scheme of education, Gandhiji wished to treat knowledge as a compact whole. The modern educationists also advocate this. The basic education is, therefore, an effort to correlate the life of the child with his immediate, physical and social environments. It is an effort to make knowledge easier.

(e) *Freedom for the Child.* Like the naturalists he advocates freedom for the child: "If the children are to find themselves, they must be allowed a sufficient degree of freedom; if they are to develop their powers to the fullest, they must be prepared to accept the appropriate discipline and training".

(f) *Education in Natural Surroundings.* Gandhiji greatly stresses the importance of educating the child in natural surroundings. He expects "the teachers to educate village children in their villages so as to draw out all their faculties through some handicrafts".

(g) *Minimum Importance to Text Books.* Like all naturalists he minimises the importance of a textbook: "I do not even remember having made much use of the books that were available. I do not find it at all necessary to load the boys with quantities of books. I have always felt that the true textbooks for the pupil is the teacher. I remember very little that my teachers taught me from books, but I have even now a clear recollection of the things they taught me independently of books. Children take in much more and with less labour through their ears than through their eyes. I do not remember having read any book from cover to cover with my boys".

Formulation of Basic Systems of Education

Gandhiji realised that the prevailing system of education was unreal and outdated. He observed: "I am convinced that the present system of education is not only wasteful but positively harmful. Most of the boys are lost to the parents and to the occupations to which they were born. They pick up evil habits, effect urban ways and get a smattering of something which may be anything but education".

Gandhiji further observed: "The present system of education does not meet the requirements of the country in any shape or form. English has been made medium of education in all the highest branches of learning, and it has created a permanent bar between the highly educated few and the uneducated many".

Gandhiji went on to criticise the system: "We have up to now concentrated on stuffing children's minds with all kinds of information without even thinking or stimulating or developing them".

Gandhiji accordingly stressed, "Let us now cry a halt and concentrate on educating the child properly through manual work not as a side activity but as a prime means of intellectual activity".

Main Features of the Systems of Education based on Gandhiji's Philosophy

1. Education for a just social order.
2. Education through craft and manual work.
3. Education through mother tongue.

4. Self-sufficient education.
5. Education related to life activities and experiences.
6. Dignity of labour.
7. Correlation.
8. Religious education.
9. Spiritual training.
10. Freedom to children but under discipline.
11. Character development.
12. Mass education.
13. Women's education.

Origin of Basic Education/*Nai Taleem*/Wardha Scheme or System of Education

The origin of Basic System of Education may be traced back to July 1937 when Gandhiji wrote in *Harijan* (a journal started by him): "By education, I mean an all round development drawing out of the best in child and man—body, mind and spirit. Literacy itself is no education. I would, therefore, begin the child's education by teaching it a useful handicraft and enabling it to produce from the moment it begins its training. Thus every school can be made self-supporting, the condition being that the State takes over the manufacture of these schools".

In October, 1937 a Conference of National Workers was held at Wardha under the chairmanship of Mahatma Gandhi. His ideas were considered and the following resolutions passed:-

1. That in the opinion of this Conference free and compulsory education be provided for seven years on a nation-wide scale.
2. That the medium of instruction be the mother-tongue.
3. That the Conference endorses the proposal made by Mahatma Gandhi, that the process of education throughout this period should centre round some productive form of manual labour, and that all other abilities to be developed, or training to be given should, as far as possible, be integrally related to the environment of the child.
4. That the Conference expects that the system of education will gradually be able to cover the remuneration of teachers.

Zakir Hussain Committee on Basic Education: Formulation of the Scheme: The Conference appointed a Committee under the chairmanship of Dr. Zakir Hussain, a renowned educationist. The report of this Committee was published in 1938. The report is known as Wardha Scheme of Education. The scheme was approved by Mahatma Gandhi and accepted by the Indian National Congress.

***Summing up* Gandhiji View on Education**

It is not quite fair to limit Gandhiji's philosophy and principles of education to basic system of education. His contribution goes far beyond. Basic system of education is just one of his contributions to education. There is no dimension of life and education on which Gandhiji has not expressed his views. His views on the importance of mother tongue as medium of instruction, his emphasis on manual labour, his stress on 'Learning by Earning', his views on the significance of women's education and the role of the teacher etc. are quite relevant today.

To Gandhiji, education was an integral part of a comprehensive programme of socio-economic re-construction of Indian society.

As a political and spiritual leader and an economic and social reformer, Gandhiji was naturally concerned with education. All his constructive programmes, economic, educational, ethical, political, social and spiritual were organically interconnected. Gandhiji wrote: "My life is indivisible whole and all my activities run into one another, and they all have their rise in my insatiable love for mankind".

29

Maria Montessori (1870-1952)

Prominent Pioneer in Child Education: In Dr. Maria Montessori we hear a 'clarion call' to the adult world to pay heed to man in the making.

Dr. Maria Montessori, an Italian, who was a doctor by qualification and profession at the start of her career became one of the greatest pioneers of the education of the very young children of the pre-school age. Before her, very little attention was paid to the care and education of the children in the age group 3 to 6. Incidentally, it may be stated that she was the first woman to become a doctor in Italy.

Maria Montessori was born in Italy on August 31, 1870. While in school, she wanted to become an engineer but after her schooling, she made up her mind to become a doctor of medicine. The doors of the medical colleges were closed for women in those days. How to get admission was the problem before her? She tried a trick and was successful in getting admission. She signed herself as 'M. Montessori when she applied for admission. The authorities could never think that a lady would apply in such a manner. So they admitted her thinking she was a man. This speaks of her ingenuity!

Education of the Mentally Retarded Children

Montessori worked as a professor of Anthropology in the University of Rome from 1900 to 1907. There she was asked to supervise a ward of mentally deficient children. She took a keen interest in their education and made a deep study of their problems. She noted the following points:

1. The dullness of the senses was the reason of the mental deficiency of the children.
2. Marvellous results could be achieved through sense training.
3. If the same method of sense training is used in the education of the normal children, far better results could be achieved.

Origin of Children's House and Development of the Montessori Method

In 1907 Montessori was appointed as a Supervisor of Schools by the Director of Roman Association for Good Building. These schools were located in tenements and catered to the education of children between the ages of 3 to 7 whose parents were mostly at work. These were by and large neglected children. Side by side, her supervisory work, Montessori took interest in studying children and developed a novel method of teaching through sense training. She opened a new school on the basis of her experiment and named it 'Children's House'. Like a true scientist, she observed the real facets of child development.

Training of Teachers: The Government of Italy appointed her inspectress of infant schools in 1922. She began to train teachers for infant schools on the lines of the new method discovered by her. Teachers from several countries from Europe including England came to Italy for training.

Dictatorship of Mussolini and Running Away of Montessori from Italy: Mussolini came to power in Italy; he was a Fascist dictator. He wanted to educate children for war. Montessori, who was an ardent supporter of child's freedom, could not work under such a regime. So she was obliged to run away from there and proceeded to Holland where she founded a school.

Montessori's Work in India: She came to India in 1939 and remained here up to 1946. She spent her time training teachers for small children according to her method in Madras. She again spent sometime in India in 1950-51. She returned to Holland in 1951 and breathed her last there in 1952.

Contact Between Mahatma Gandhi and Maria Montessori

The first meeting between Mahatma Gandhi and Maria Montessori took place when Gandhiji went to London in 1931 to attend the Round Table Conference. At that time Dr. Montessori was holding International Training Courses for Teachers. Common friends brought them together. This meeting inspired Gandhiji, who was also keenly interested in education, to visit Montessori Schools in Rome on his way back. In 1939 when Dr. Montessori came to India, just after the outbreak of the First World War, Gandhiji sent her a message of welcome. They met and corresponded during the next 10 years.

It is an irony of fate that during the war years, both Gandhiji and Montessori were put under restrictions. Gandhiji expressed sympathy and regret when after Italy's entry into war, restrictions were imposed on Dr. Montessori, considered as enemy alien.

Gandhiji fought for freedom of the country from foreign repression and Montessori for freedom of the child.

Gandhiji wanted to reform the entire system of education especially elementary education whereas Montessori devoted all her energies to reform the system of education at the pre-elementary stage.

Essence of Montessori's Philosophy

"Child is a body which grows and a soul which develops—these two forms physical and psychic, have one eternal front, life itself". It follows then that "we must neither mar nor stifle the mysterious powers which lie within these two forms of growth, but we must await from them the manifestations which we know will succeed one another".

Publications of Madam Montessori

1. *The Discovery of the Child.*
2. *Education for a New Child.*
3. *To Educate the Human Potential.*
4. *The Secret of Childhood.*
5. *The Child Peace and Education.*
6. *Reconstruction in Education.*
7. *The Absorbent Mind.*
8. *What You Should Know About Your Child?*
9. *Child Training.*
10. *The Montessori Method.*

CHIEF FEATURES OF EDUCATIONAL THEORY AND PRINCIPLES

Principles of Education

Following are the main principles of Montessori's educational philosophy:

1. *Principle of development from within*: Montessori believed that the source of education of a child is within himself. She observed: "If any educational act is to be efficacious it will be only that which tends to help towards the complete unfolding of child's individuality. The child has a body which grows and a soul which develops". Education according to Montessori would be such as it helps in the complete unfolding of child's individuality. Suitable environment should be provided so that the child may grow and develop the potentialities that he has within him.

2. *Principles of individual development*: Montessori believes that every child is peculiar to himself and he progresses at his own speed and rate and collective methods of teaching crush his individuality. She treats each child as a separate individual and recommends that he should be helped and guided in a manner that helps him in his proper growth and development. The teacher is concerned with his mental as well as his physiological development. In the words of John Admas, Dr. Montessori "has rung the knell of class teaching".

3. *Principle of auto-education or self-education*: Montessori is of the firm view that self-education or auto-education is the only true education. She advocates that the child should remain undisturbed by adult interference. Accordingly, she has devised the didactic apparatus which attracts the attention of the children, keeps them busy spontaneously, leads them to learn the powers of movements, reading, writing and arithmetic, etc.

4. *Principle of sense training*: Montessori is a firm believer that our senses are the gateways of knowledge and therefore on their training and development depends the acquisition of knowledge throughout life. She points out that the senses are very active between the ages of 3 and 7 and that a lot of learning takes place during this period. She advocates that the sensory training is the key to intellectual development of children.

5. *Principle of freedom and liberty*: Montessori's belief is that there should be no interference in the way of child's growth and development. According to her, the freedom is the birthright of every individual and she advocates the spontaneous development of the child through full liberty. She does not believe in putting restraints as she thinks that these may 'mar or stifle the innate powers of the child'. She says, "The school must permit the free, natural manifestations of the child if he is to be studied in a scientific manner".

6. *Principle of no material rewards and punishments*: Her view is that rewards and punishments are incentives unnatural or forced effort and the development that comes with their help will also be unnatural. She writes, "The jockey offers a piece of sugar to his horse that he may respond to the signs given by the reins, and yet neither of these runs so superbly as the free horse of the plains".

7. *Principle of motor training or muscular training*: Montessori attaches great significance to motor training also as a part of the early education of children.

8. *Principle of no fairy tales*: According to Montessori, the fairy tales tend to confuse children and therefore, she would like to banish them from the school curriculum.

9. *Principle of reverence for the child*: To Madam Montessori "The child was God". Her school was the temple and duty of the temple was the essence of childhood. She further writes: "Today there stands forth one urgent need—the reform of methods in education and instruction, and he who struggles towards this end is struggling for the regeneration of man". The method as suggested by Montessori gives an important place to the child.

10. *Principle of individual teaching*: Individualism is the keynote of Montessori's philosophy of education.

Role and Functions of the Teacher

Case for the Soul of the Child: Madam Montessori assigns a unique role for the teacher whom she calls a 'Directress'. She emphasises that since the soul of the child is pure and very sensitive, it requires her utmost care. Her motto should be "I must diminish to let you grow".

Replacement of the word teacher by directress: She has replaced the world 'teacher' by the word 'directress' and she thinks that the primary duty of the person in authority is to direct and not to teach. She insists that the directress should have an extensive knowledge of psychology and laboratory technique.

Intimate knowledge of the child: The teacher should have an intimate knowledge of the mind and character of each individual. He should keep the physiological records of each child's development: his weight, height and other measurements.

Doctor-cum-scientist-cum-missionary: According to Montessori, the Directress should be partly doctor, partly scientist and completely religious. Like a doctor she should avoid scolding or suppressing the patient in order to avoid worse situations. Like a scientist she should wait patiently for the results and should conduct experiments with her material. Like a religious lady she should be there to serve the child.

Teacher as a gardener: She thinks that a teacher should care for the child like a gardener who cares for the plant so that the natural growth of the child is properly guided and aided in the process of unfolding itself.

Provision of suitable environment: The directress should allow the child to grow according to his own inner law. Her business is to provide for suitable environment. She should provide children with appropriate opportunities to think for themselves.

Moral values: "Virtues and not words are the main qualifications of the directress". She must banish anger which is a great sin and which prevents understanding the child.

Children's House

The first school started by Montessori in 1907 was called a 'Children's House'. It provides all the requirements of a good 'Family House'. It is a house which provides an environment in which each child may develop in the best possible manner. It has several rooms and a garden which is looked after by the children themselves.

Important feature of the Children's House is that children do everything in the House.

A Children's House has many rooms: (1) Study room. (2) Common room. (3) Lunch room. (4) Rest room. (5) Room for mental work. (6) Gymnasium. (7) Bathroom and (8) Laboratory.

The rooms are well-equipped according to the needs of the children and spirit of the Montessori Method. The tables, chairs, etc. are specially made for children. They facilitate movement from one place to another. Sofas of different shapes and long row cup-boards are also provided. The children keep their didactic apparatus in the cup-board and their things in a little drawer. The blackboards are fixed in the walls on which the children draw or paste pictures of different kinds, according to their own interests. The students are provided with flowers, toys, pictures, indoor games, etc. The lunch room contains low tables, chairs, spoons, knives, tumblers, etc. In the drawing room, the children are provided with their own little shelf, where they keep their soap and towel for washing. There is a small garden also which is looked after by the children themselves. Shelters are provided in the garden so that they can enjoy the open air, can play and work there, may take rest or sleep. They may have their lunch there.

The Children's House also contains a paedometer and a weighing machine to keep a record of the height and weight of the students.

Didactic apparatus is used to provide sensory training, motor training and for teaching language and arithmetic.

Exercises provided in Children's House: Following three types of exercises are provided:

One. Exercises in practical life.

Two. Exercises for sense training.

Three. Exercises for teaching language and arithmetic.

Training exercises in Practical Life: Children in the 'Children's House' carry out activities of everyday life. Therefore, Montessori called these exercises 'exercises in practical life. All work in the 'Children's House' is entrusted to the little ones who execute with devotion and accuracy their domestic duties, becoming singularly calm and dignified. The students are required to sweep their rooms, dust and clean the furniture and arrange it as they like. They learn dressing and undressing and washing themselves. They are expected to hang up their clothes tidily. They lay their tables. The children take turns in various household duties and learn by imitation to overcome difficulties in the process. "Enthusiasm and delight, fellow feeling and mutual aid are characteristics of the children learning the jobs". The students learn how to wash their hands. They learn how to use wash-stands with small pitchers and basins. They learn how to use their own soap and towels. They learn how to comb their hair, cut their nails and brush their teeth and other such things.

Motor education: These practical life exercises are considered to be very helpful for motor education. Muscular education takes place with the movements of walking, sitting and holding objects. The care of child's own body, managing the household affairs, gardening and manual work and rhythmic movements provide motor education. Children also learn how to walk in straight lines and to balance themselves properly.

Discipline in Children's House: Discipline comes through an indirect route, by providing activities which are of great interest to children. Every individual is expected to learn how to control himself by his own efforts which is directed towards no external aim but is meant to keep alive that inner flame on which our life depends. Montessori writes, "In truth, the 'good' are those who move forward towards the goodness which has been built up by their own efforts". Such a discipline can never be attained by way of commands, by sermons, by any of the disciplinary methods traditionally known and employed.

DIDACTIC APPARATUS

Meaning of Didactic Apparatus

The word 'didactic' means to convey instruction and information (learning) as well as pleasure. In other words, didactic denotes learning with pleasure. The didactic apparatus, therefore, implies that the apparatus (concrete material) is used to educate the young children in such a way that learning becomes joyful.

Principles of Didactic Apparatus

The Didactic Apparatus is intended to translate Montessori's principles of educational philosophy into action. It is based on the following principles:

1. Principle of development of the child from within.
2. Principle of individual differences of children.
3. Principle of auto-education or self-education.
4. Principle of sense training.
5. Principle of motor training.
6. Principle of freedom or liberty.
7. Principle of learning by doing.
8. Principle of self-discipline.
9. Principle of individual teaching.
10. Principle of excluding fairy tales.

Forms of Didactic Apparatus

(1) Didactic Apparatus for Sensory Training

(2) Didactic Apparatus for the Teaching of Language and Arithmetic

Sensory Apparatus: Purpose and Type

Purpose	*Apparatus*
1. For perception of size	1. Series of wooden cylinders varying in height only, in diameter only or in both dimensions; blocks varying in size and rods of varying lengths.
2. For perception of colour	2. Pink cubes, brown prisms, green and alternatively red and blue rods and coloured tablets etc.
3. For perception of form	3. Geometrical insets in metal, wood, a chest of drawers containing plane insets, series of cards on which are pasted geometrical forms in paper.
4. For discrimination in 'Weight'	4. Tablets of wood similar in size but different in weight

Purpose	Apparatus
5. For discrimination in 'Touch'.	5. Rectangular tablet with rough and smooth surface etc.
6. For discrimination in 'Sound'.	6. Cylindrical boxes containing different substances.

The didactic apparatus for teaching language and arithmetic:

a. Two sloping desks and various iron insets.
b. Cards on which are pasted sandpaper letters.
c. Two alphabets of coloured cardboard and of different sizes.
d. A series of cards on which are pasted sandpaper figures (1, 2, 3, etc.)
e. A series of large cards bearing the same figures in smooth paper for the enumeration of numbers above ten.
f. Two boxes with small sticks for counting.
g. The volume of drawings belonging specially to the method, and coloured pencils.
h. The frames for lacing, buttoning, etc. which are used for motor education of the hand.

Details of the Didactic Apparatus and its Application

1. Three sets of solid insets.
2. Three sets of solids in graduated size, consisting of:
   (i) Pink cubes,
   (ii) Brown prisms,
   (iii) Rods –
      a. Coloured green,
      b. Coloured alternately red and blue.
3. Various geometric solids (prism, pyramid, sphere, cylinder, cone, etc.)
4. Rectangular boards with rough and smooth surfaces.
5. A collection of various stuffs and materials.
6. Small wooden tables of different weights.
7. Two boxes, each containing sixty-four coloured tablets.
8. A chest of drawers containing plane insets.
9. Three series of cards on which are pasted geometrical forms in paper.
10. A collection of cylindrical closed boxes (sounds).
11. A double series of musical bells: wooden boards on which are painted the lines used in music; small wooden discs for the notes.

In the above apparatus, the child first uses three solid pieces of wood in each of which are inserted a row of ten small cylinders with a small button for handling. In the first piece of wood the cylinders are of the same height but varying in diameter. In the second, the cylinders vary in all dimensions. In the third, the cylinders vary in height but have the same diameter. The child takes out the cylinders, mixes them up and then puts them in their right places. His hands are exercised in handling them, and he learns how to judge their size by making trials. By repeating the process, he succeeds. This exercise trains the sense of sight and teaches the child to note the difference in dimensions. The apparatus is self-corrective, and the child knows when he wants to correct himself.

There is another piece of apparatus consisting of ten wooden cubes, coloured pink. The child builds a tower with these cubes, first laying the largest, and then on the top of it all the other cubes in their order of size. In this way his eyes are trained and he gets an idea of height. Among the apparatus, there is also a small rectangular board, divided into two parts: one rough, the other smooth. Through this the child gets an idea of different surfaces, and learns to appreciate their difference. There are also a series of materials of different kinds: satin, silk, woollen, cotton, coarse and fine cloth. There are two similar pieces of each of the materials of bright and vivid colour. The child mixes up the materials and then finds out and arranges them in pairs. Another striking piece of apparatus is a little box, containing six drawers. When they are opened the child finds six square wooden frames in each. In each frame, there is a large geometrical figure kept in the centre and provided with a small handle. When the geometrical figure is removed, the bottom is found to have exactly the same form. The geometrical figures are arranged in the drawers according to similarity of form, *i.e.,* in one drawer there are six circles decreasing in diameter, in other, six triangles. Another drawer contains various figures such as an oval, ellipse, rhombus and so on. The easy figures are presented first. The child mixes the six figures together and then puts them in their right places. His eye and sense of touch are educated through touching these forms, and recognising their proper shape. This exercise is an indirect but a very good preparation for drawing.

Madame Montessori points out that in training a particular sense, it is better to isolate the sense as far as possible, *i.e.,* to have silence and to blindfold the eyes for some exercises in which the education of the sense of sight is not being given.

Procedure of the use of Material: The use of the material employed involves three stages:

(i) Association of the sensory percept with the name, "This is red".

(ii) Recognition of the object, "Give me the red".

(iii) Recalling the name of the object, "What is this?"

Didactic Exercise for Teaching 3 R's., i.e., Writing, Reading and Arithmetic. After sensory training, children are taught reading, writing and arithmetic. In her system, writing starts before reading. For this purpose she depends upon the psychological principle of 'Transfer of Training'. In her own words: "Preparatory movement could be converted and reduced to a mechanism by means of repeated exercise, not in the work itself, but in that which prepares for it".

Teaching of Writing

The procedure of teaching consists of three steps:

(i) *Recognition of the Forms of Letters*: For this purpose letters of the alphabet are cut in sand-paper and pasted on card-board. The children are asked to pass their finger over these letters. In this way they gradually learn to manipulate a pencil. The same exercise is then practised with closed eyes.

(ii) *Learning of Phonetic Sounds*: While the pupils are tracing out letters, the teacher tells them their sounds, which they are asked to reproduce. This prepares them for reading.

(iii) *Control of Pen*: In the third step, the pupils are asked to place the metal frame on a piece of paper and draw a line round it with a coloured chalk. The same is repeated by placing the metal inset. In this way two figures are produced on the paper. The intervening figure is then filled up with another piece of chalk. While making upward and downward strokes, pupils are not allowed to move their pencil or piece of chalk outside the outline. Thus, they learn the necessary control of pen.

Teaching of Reading

About reading, Montessori says, "Reading is the interpretation of an idea from the written signs and not merely looking at print. Until the child receives a transmission of ideas from the written word, he does not read". Her material for reading consists of slips of paper or cards on which words and phrases are written in bold scripts. The child is given a card, containing the name of a familiar object. He tries to utter the sounds and then repeats them faster and faster. When the child is able to pronounce the word correctly, he is asked to place the card under the object, whose name is written on it. Similarly sentences, describing actions or expressing commands are written on paper or cards.

Evaluation of the Montessori Method and Didactic Apparatus

Merits of Montessori's Educational Thought and Practices

Montessori has ushered in a new era in child education and especially small children of the nursery stage. Her gospel of love, respect and sympathy for the child has been accepted all over the word. The chief merits of the Montessori method are:

1. Scientific base of the method.
2. Individual teaching.
3. Freedom for children.
4. Education through sense training.
5. Unique method of reading and writing.

6. Learning through living.
7. Social values.
8. Reverence for small children.

Limitations of Montessori's Educational Thought and Practice

1. Mechanical and artificial nature of the didactic apparatus.
2. More emphasis on biological aspects and less on psychological.
3. Belief in transfer of training.
4. Neglect of the training of imagination.
5. Lack of suitably trained teachers.
6. Expensive material.
7. Very little scope for correlation and projects.

Contribution to Educational Thoughts and Practices

Madam Montessori has ushered in a new era in child education, especially for small children between the ages of 3 to 6. It is not without reason that a Montessori school has become a household word. Probably there would be no village or city where there is no such school. Attempts are made to manufacture low cost material which is locally available.

To Madam Montessori "The child was God". Her school was the temple and the function of the temple was to provide a pure and virtuous environment. She writes, "Today there stands forth one urgent need. The reform of methods in education and instruction, and he who struggles towards this end is struggling for the regeneration of man".

By founding the Montessori method, Maria Montessori revolutionised the concept of child education. Her impact on educational thought and practices is universal. She has also made an important contribution to the training of teachers for the pre-primary stage. Montessori ranks among the forefront educators who advocate an environment of freedom to children.

Comparison Between Froebel and Montessori

Points of Similarity in the Philosophy and Practices of Education

1. *Philosophy of Education*: Both recognised the need for the growth and development of small children for the well-being of man. Both regarded child as divine and pure.
2. *Education as Development from Within*: Both the educators regard education as the development of the inner nature of the child. They point out that the function of the educator is to draw the inner out.
3. *Congenial Environment*: Both the educators stress the importance of providing a healthy and conducive environment in which the growth of inner nature of the child should take place in a suitable manner.
4. *Reverence and Affection for the Child*: Froebel as well as Montessori have greatly stressed that there should be an

environment of love and affection for the child. His personality should be recognised and even worshipped.

5. *Stress on Sense Training*: Both have devised apparatus for training the senses of children.
6. *Self-education*: Both advocate self-education on the part of the child with his own efforts.
7. *Recognition of the Importance of Nursery Education*: Froebel as well as Montessori have given us a method of educating the infants. They have brought about a revolutionary change in the concept of education at the pre-primary stage.

Points of Contrast between Froebel and Montessori

1. *Approach*: Kindergarten is the outcome of the thinking of a philosopher while Montessori Method is the outcome of the thinking of a doctor and a scientist.
2. *Individual vs. Social Basis*: In the Kindergarten, children are encouraged to work in group. On the other hand, individual work is encouraged in the Montessori Method.
3. *Gifts vs. Didactic Apparatus*: While in the Kindergarten, sense training is imparted through gifts, in the Montessori method, Didactic Apparatus is used for the training of senses.
4. *Play-Way vs. Self-Corrective Medium*: The Froebelian system puts more stress on play activities. All lessons are accompanied by songs, gestures and movements. In the Montessori method, self-corrective apparatus is provided to the child and the same is used in a specific way. There is less opportunity for play.
5. *Manual Activities vs. Daily Life Activities*: Manual activities like gardening, clay modelling, and nature study, etc. are emphasised in the Kindergarten. On the contrary, in the Montessori Method, besides manual activities, daily life activities like cleaning, dusting, sweeping and washing, find an important place and are considered very valuable to students for learning how to take care of themselves.
6. *Imagination vs. Lack of Imagination*: Froebel recommends the use of fairy tales for developing the imagination of the students. In the Montessori method, there is no such place for fairy tales.
7. *Sketchy vs. Detailed System Teaching-Learning*: The Kindergarten system is not a detailed system of teaching 3R's. In the Montessori system, there is a scientific system for this purpose.
8. *Dispensability/Indispensability of the Apparatus*: The Kindergarten method does not require an elaborate material. It can be made use of even without apparatus and other equipment. In the Montessori method, a good deal of equipment is needed for the 'Children's House'. It also needs an elaborate and rather costly apparatus.

9. *Classroom vs. Individual Learning*: In the Kindergarten method, classroom activities and instruction find an important place. By and large, in it, there is a fixed time-table. In the Montessori method, there is too much stress on individual development and learning; social development aspect recedes to the background.
10. *Teacher as a Leader vs. Directress*: In the Kindergarten the teacher is like a leader who guides the children to sing songs and directs their gestures and movements. In the Montessori method, the teacher is called the directress who provides apparatus to the students, watches them from a distance and comes to their assistance when it is needed by them.

30

Marshall McLuhan (1971-1980)

Medium is the Message

Marshall McLuhan, the author of two famous books namely *Gutenberg Galaxy* and *Understanding Mediatry*, dealing with the role of the media is known for the phrase 'The Medium is the Message'.

Marshall questions print culture and literacy in the electronic era, points out the characteristics of dropouts and suggests strategies for tackling this phenomenon.

According to McLuhan, the mass media are dangerous but can be utilised profitably in education, provided perception and critical awareness are developed in the young. He advises that media should not be allowed to become masters but should be made slaves.

Main Elements of the Educational Philosophy

1. Liberal education is the utmost necessity in the age of automation. Such an education would enable the youth to participate in an imaginative and meaningful way.
2. An educational system in which there is an in-depth approach to learning, a revolution in attitudes between the teacher and the taught, a recognition of the sensibilities is what is urgently needed.
3. Today children gain information and learn more 'outside' than 'inside' the classroom. Information in textbooks becomes out of date as soon as it is published, because it increases hourly and many changes occur in all fields. Reliance, therefore, on printed material alone for information in teaching, is restrictive, apart from being out of date.
4. Knowledge has been compartmentalised. Sheer specialism results in instruction by "Specialists" who have little or nothing to do with the knowledge in its broad sense. A unified approach to knowledge is the need of the day.
5. The best education is that which develops "Critical awareness".
6. Instead of learning many different subjects, a structured study of learning and knowledge itself, a knowledge of the world and of life itself should be introduced in schools and colleges, in a uniformed form.

7. The close inter-relationship between geographical facts, biological and anthropological studies, sociological and historical evidence and the overlapping between all areas of knowledge should be brought out through all sensory modes in television programmes so planned.
8. Real understanding of what is taught can best be brought about through electronic media which have the power of bringing about an interplay of the senses.
9. A great revolution in teaching-learning can be brought about by a very wide use of Telstar, teaching machines, programmed instruction and television on a massive scale. Teachers should do all they can to utilise these to the greatest extent with relevance to their teaching-learning.
10. Learning should become an exploration and a discovery, a process of play and pleasure.
11. Art should be taught to all pupils at all levels, but not as a separate subject.
12. In order to make education relevant to the students and to prevent them from becoming dropouts, the impersonal and dehumanising environment of education institutions should give way to one which is geared to their needs and problems. Let them move freely in the school to work alone or in groups.

Role of the Teacher in the Electronic Age

The teacher should enlarge his role and attempt to reach out and exert his influence far beyond the walls of the classroom and school. Instead of remaining in an ivory towers, the teacher should come out and exploit the new electronic resources and use them for the benefit of mankind.

The teacher has to be a dedicated and devoted person. The power of human navigation is in the hands of the teachers. They should be able to steer the path towards the survival of the human race.

31

Michel De Montaigne (1533-92)

Montaigne was a French essayist, moralist and educational theorist. His *Essays* are particularly a good illustration of the 'cultural mosaic' of Renaissance.

Source of Montaigne's Views on Education

Montaigne's views on education are found scattered through many of his *Essays*, but particularly in *Concerning the Education of Children.*

Training of Judgement

Montaigne believed in the training of judgement than mere book learning, because "To know by heart is not to know at all; it is merely to retain what one has entrusted to his memory".

Montaigne further stated, "I would rather prefer wisdom-judgement, civil customs and modest behaviour than base and literal learning".

Montaigne's Negative Education

Prof. Gerard Wormser explains Montaigne's negative education in an article in *prospects*, 84(1/2), Vol. 3, 1994 as: "Montaigne calls for a more radical interpretation. Learning provides no positive standard; it merely enables us to know how far the conduct of individuals departs from what a wise nature would prompt. Besides being incorrigible, faculties are distributed at random. Education serves above all to bring them out so that the best characters can be discovered. This is what Montaigne has in mind when he jestingly recommends that the tutor should quickly strangle the unworthy pupil when nobody is looking or apprentice him to some trade which will keep him occupied. Education would thus mainly serve a negative purpose, seeking to cast our vices likely to develop and become a danger to human society.

"Unconvinced of the influence education was supposed to have on us, Montaigne has no difficulty in showing how the natural disposition comes out under all circumstances or sets impassable limits to everyone's behaviour, even if that natural disposition is concealed by disguises and masks which give it false colours and belie it".

Need for Efficient Tutors from the Early Stages for Forming Moral Behaviour

The same writer explains Montaigne's views in these words: "Habit, even when based on a figment of the imagination 'gradually and stealthily... slides her authoritative foot into us; then, having by this gentle and humble beginning planted it firmly within us, helped by time she later discloses an angry tyrannous countenance, against which we are no longer allowed even to lift up our eyes'. Whereupon Montaigne concludes that 'our greatest vices do acquire their bent during our most tender infancy, so that our formation is chiefly in the hands of our wet-nurses'. The hold which imagination and habit acquire over children's attitudes can therefore be judged from their earliest expression. If children are not taught to detest their natural vices, 'whatever mask they hide behind', 'what is the use of educating them?' Whatever our opinion on the matter, we must realise that all behaviour, all value judgements, are based to some extent on habit, or custom, for the habits, or customs, of the place where you were born, widely though these may differ from one place to another, rule your conscience. This line of thought is continued in the brief essay on credulity, 'That it is madness to judge the true and the false from our own capacities': 'How many of the things which constantly come into our purview must be deemed monstrous or miraculous if we apply such terms to anything which outstrips our reason!'

"The essence of any education is thus the way in which it inculcates moral principles consistent with the goal of wisdom and calculated to develop a conscience enabling us all to bring our behaviour in line with incontestable standards. For this reason, Montaigne mercilessly mocks teachers who, unable to get the children to assimilate what they are taught, are content with puffing them up with it, making them conceited and arrogant: Learned we may be with another man's learning: we can only be wise with wisdom of our own'. Hence, since I would prefer that he turned out to be an able man nor an erudite one, I would wish you to be careful to select as guide for him a tutor with a well-formed rather than a well-filled brain'.

"Only on this condition can we rediscover the Socratic method of teaching by means of exercises in which the pupil shows his capacity for discernment".

Teaching by Dialogue

Montaigne advocates teaching by dialogue. He wrote, "To follow another is to follow nothing"... "the boy will transform his borrowings; he will confound their forms so that the end-product is entirely his: namely, his judgement, the forming of which is the only aim of his toil, his study and his education. Let him hide the help he received and put only his achievements on display".

32

Paramhansa Yogananda (1893-1952)

Shri Yogananda whose original name was Mukunda Lal Ghosh was born in a Bengali family at Gorakhpur in Uttar Pradesh. His father, Bhagabati Charan Ghosh was a kind person. He and his wife were of saintly nature.

Mukunda Lal Ghosh had three brothers and four sisters. He was told stories from the *Ramayana* and *Mahabharata* in his childhood. His name was changed to Yogananda when he entered the ancient monastic Swami Order in 1914, i.e., at the age of 21 years. He spent several years in the Himalayas and came into contact with several saints, who had attained self realisation.

Paramhansa Yogananda received his education at the Hindu High School, Calcutta, and he graduated from Serampore College.

Yogananda was the first yoga master of India to take up permanent residence in the West. Yogananda arrived in America in 1920, and travelled throughout the United States on what he called his 'spiritual campaigns'. His enthusiastic audiences filled the largest halls in America. Hundreds of thousands came to see the yogi from India. Yogananda continued to lecture and write up to his passing away in 1952.

In the words of Swami Kriyananda a disciple of Yogananda, "Yogananda's initial impact was truly impressive. But his lasting impact has been even greater. Yogananda's *Autobiography of a Yogi*, first published in 1946, helped launch a spiritual revolution throughout the world. His message was non-sectarian and universal. Yogananda's Guru, Swami Sri Yukteswar, sent him to the West with the admonition, "The West is high in material attainments, but lacking in spiritual understanding. It is God's will that you play a role in teaching mankind the value of balancing the material with an inner, spiritual life."

Essence of Yogananda's Teachings and Philosophy

"My spoken words are registered in the ether, in the spirit of God, and they shall move the West. Self-realization has come to unite all religions. We must go on—not only those who are, but thousands of youths must go North, South, East and West to cover the earth with little colonies, demonstrating that simplicity of living plus high thinking lead to the greatest happiness."

Paramhansa Yoganandas *Kriya Yoga*

Yogi Yogananda explains *Kriya* yoga in these words, "The Sanskrit root of *Kriya* is *Kri* to do, to act and react, the same root is found in the word *Karma*, the natural principle of course and effect. *Kriya Yoga* is thus Union (Yoga) with the infinite through a certain action or rite. A yogi who faithfully follows its technique is gradually free from *Karma* or the universal chain of causation."

According to Yogi Yogananda *kriya yoga* is a simple, psychological method by which the human blood is decarbonized and recharged with oxygen. The atoms of this extra oxygen are transmuted into life current to rejuvenate the brain and spinal centres. By stopping the accumulation of venous blood, the *yogi* is able to lessen or prevent the decay of tissues; the advanced *yogi* transmutes his cells into pure energy.

Kriya yoga is an ancient science. It is referred by Lord Krishna in Bhagvad Gita: "Offering inhealing breath into the outgoing breath, the *yogi* neutralises both these breaths, he thus releases the life force from the heart and brings it under his control." The *yogi* arrests decay in the body by an addition of life force and asserts the mutations of growth in the body by *apan* (eliminating current). Thus neutralizing decay and growth, by quieting the heart, the *yogi* learns life control.

The sage Patanjali mentions the *kriya yoga* twice. According to him *kriya yoga* consists of body discipline, mutual control and meditating on *Aum*.

The *kriya yogi* mentally diverts his life energy to revolve, upward and downward, arms his six spinal centres (medullary, cervical, dorsal lumbar, sacral and coccygeal plexuses) which correspond to the twelve astral signs of the zodiac, the symbolic cosmic Man. One-half minute of revolution of energy around the sensitive spinal cord of man affects subtle progress in his evolution, that half-minute of *kriya* equals one year of natural spiritual unfoldment.

The astral system of a human being, with six (twelve by plurality) inner constellations revolving around the sum of omniscient spiritual eye, is interrelated with the physical sum and the twelve zodiacal signs. All men are thus affected by an inner and an outer universe.

Kriya serves to prolong life and enlarge the consciousness to infinity.

According to Paramhansa, "Introspection" or "Sitting in the Silence", is an unscientific way of trying to force apart the mind and senses, tied together by the life force. The contemplative mind attempting its return to divinity is constantly dragged backward by the senses of the life currents. *Kriya*, controlling the mind directly through the life force, is the easiest, most effective, and most scientific avenue of approach to the Infinite. In contrast to the slow, uncertain, "bullock cart" theological path to God, *Kriya* may justly be called the "airplane" route. The *Kriya Yoga* consists of ancient yoga techniques to hasten one's spiritual evolution.

When Mukunda Lal was ordained as Yogananda by his Guru, he joyfully sang the following verses from the Sanskrit chant of Shankara.

"Mind, nor intellect, nor ego, feeling, sky nor earth nor metals am I. I am He, I am He, Blessed spirit, I am He! father, mother, have I none.

"I am He, I am He, Blessed spirit, I am He! Beyond the flights of fancy, formless am I Permeating the limbs of all life, Bondage I do not fear, I am free, ever free, I am He, I am He, Blessed spirit, I am He!"

A True Yogi according to Parmahansa

"A true yogi may remain dutifully in the world, there he is like butter on water, and not like the easily-diluted milk of unchurned and undisciplined humanity. To fulfill one's earthly responsibilities is indeed the higher path provided the yogi, maintaining a mental uninvolvement with egotistical desires, plays his part as a willing instrument of God!

True Religion

In the words of Paramhansa Yogananda, "The true basis of religion is not belief, but intuitive experience. Intitution is the soul's power of knowing God. To know what religion is really all about, one must know God."

Paramhansa's Views on Education

(1) *Concept of Education*: In his *Autobiography of a Yogi* Paramhansa writes, "The ideal of an all-sided education for youth had always been close to my heart. I saw clearly the arid results of ordinary instruction, aimed only at the development of body and intellect. Moral and spiritual values, without whose appreciation no man can approach happiness, were yet lacking in the formal curriculum. I determined to found a school where young boys could develop to the full stature of manhood. My first step in that direction was made in 1917 with seven children of Dihika, a small country site in Bengal." (p. 254).

(2) *Curriculum of the School*: A year later in 1918, he transferred his fast-growing group to Ranchi—two hundred miles from Calcutta. He named the school *Brahamachary Vidyalaya*, in accordance, with the educational ideals of the *rishis*.

At Ranchi, he organized an educational programme for both grammar and high school grades. The curriculum included agricultural, industrial, commercial and academic subjects. The students were also taught yoga, concentration and meditation and a unique system of physical development, *Yogada*, whose principles he had discovered in 1916.

(3) *Yogada System of Physical Development*: Paramhansa explained this in these words, "Realizing that man's body is like an electric battery, I reasoned that it could be recharged with energy through the direct agency of the human will. As no action, slight or large, is possible without *willing*, man cannot avail himself of his prime mover, will, to renew his bodily

tissues without burdensome apparatus or mechanical exercises. I therefore taught the Ranchi students my simple *Yogoda* teachings by which the life force, centred in man's medulla oblongata, can be consciously and instantly recharged from the unlimited supply of cosmic energy." (p. 255).

With this system of physical education, the students began to develop lot of ability to shift the life energy from one part of the body to another part and to sit in perfect poise in difficult body postures.

The school attracted attention and the application for admission reached two thousand whereas the residential school could accommodate only one hundred. Therefore, instruction for day students was added. The Paramhansa 'played father-mother' to the little children.

(4) *Outdoor work*: The school had a large fruit orchard and twenty-five fertile acres at its disposal. The students, teachers and the Paramahansa "enjoyed many happy hours of outdoor labour in these ideal surroundings". The school had pets, including a young deer who was fairly idolized by the children. "I too loved the fawn so much that I allowed it to sleep in my room. At the light of the dawn, the little creature would toddle over to my bed for morning caress."

(5) *Branches of the School*: The Ranchi School grew from small and simple beginnings to an institution which became well-known in India. Several department of the school are supported by voluntary contributions. Under the general name of *Yogada Sat-Sanga*, flourishing branch schools, came to be established at Midnapur, Lakshmanpur and Ranchi, *Yogada* comprises two words, i.e., *yoga* and *da*. Yoga, means union, harmony and equilibrium and *da* means that which imparts, *sat* means truth, *Sanga* means fellowship. In the west, the *Yogada Sat-Sanga* movement is called the 'Self-Realization Fellowship'.

(6) *Rabindranath's School at Santiniketan and the Paramahansa's School at Ranchi*. At the invitation of Rabindranath Tagore, Paramahansa visited him at Santiniketan in order to discuss their education ideals. "Tagore and I were soon in a comparative study of our schools, both founded along orthodox lines. We discovered many identical features: 'outdoor instruction, simplicity, ample scope for child's creative spirit'. Rabindranath, however, laid considerable stress on the study of literature and poetry, and the self-expression through music and song which I had already noted. The Santiniketan children observed periods of silence, but were given no special yoga training.

Education for Life

Swami Kriyananda (J. Donald Walters) who became a disciple of Yogananda at the age of 22 and served him for several years has explained the concept education for life in his writings. He has described the system of education in a book entitled *Living Wisdom School*.

Swami Kriyananda writes in the preface of the book, "The concept *Education for Life* can be understood in two ways, both of them intentionally so. Primarily, it is a system of education that will prepare children for meeting life's challenges, and not only fit them for employment or for intellectual pursuits. It is also a way to see the whole of life, beyond the years spent in school, as education.

"For if indeed, as most people deeply believe, life has purpose and meaning, then its goal must be to educate us ever-more fully to that meaning. And the true goal of the education we receive during our school years must be to help prepare us for that lifelong learning process."

Why Education for Life

Swami Kriyanand states, "What do I mean when I say "Education for Life?" I can present the problem and the solution. The problem is that people in traditional forms of education usually approach it from the standpoint of just preparing a person for a job. But one's job isn't the definition of one's life—it's only that which enables you to have enough money to meet your needs. Our lives encompass a much broader arena than one's capacity to earn money. Any educational system that teaches only job skills or offers only intellectual information is neglecting the essential needs of human beings. The solution is a form of education that trains us in that which is most relevant to us—how to find lasting happiness in life.

"We deeply need proper training in "how-to-live" skills such as how to find the right mate, how to raise our children, how to be a good employee, how to get along with our neighbours, and how to concentrate our minds so that we can draw success into all of our endeavours. There are many such skills that are essential to prepare a child for adulthood, and in traditional education many of them are completely ignored. Education of Life is a system that prepares the child to face the challenges of living as a human being, and helps him to achieve balance and harmony in all he does."

Knowing Four Tools which Relate us to Life

The Education for Life system tries to point the way to maturity. It doesn't presume to give maturity, but it creates a mind-set that will endure for the whole of life. It provides a direction of growth that people can take all the way into old age and still keep growing so that they find things to marvel at in the world around them.

We find that basically we have four tools that enable us to relate to life.

First, we have to recognize that since we live in physical bodies, we can see our bodies as tools for helping us grow. If we don't properly take care of our bodies, we may find them becoming our foes instead of our friends.

Second, we find that we respond to the world with our emotions. If our emotions are always agitated because of intense likes and dislikes, we will respond emotionally to what others say and not really hear them. We may hear our own idea of what they are saying, but if we have an emotional prejudice, we won't hear them objectively.

Third, if we don't know how to use our will-power to overcome faults in ourselves, or to set goals and accomplish them, then we will never know fulfillment in life.

Finally, if we don't develop our intellect, then we cannot understand things clearly; our life's experiences will come through our minds in a dull way. You need to have a clear intellect to really understand what's going on around you.

Four Stages and Contents of Education

So we have these four basic tools that enable us to grow toward ever-greater maturity: the body, the emotions or feelings, the will power, and the intellect.

1. *Education in First Six Years*: The first six years of a child's life tend to be the period when they have to learn how to get their bodies under control.

During this period from one to six years, it's important to teach children how to use their bodies to grow in other ways of understanding. For example, drama and dance movements, especially in the first six years, can be extremely important because children learn with their bodies at this stage. If through drama they can act out positive attitudes, or through dance they can be taught movements that help them express expansiveness, then they're learning in a way that's appropriate to that level of development. They can be shown those kinds of physical gestures that come with selfishness, for example, and those that come with being generous and kind. This can be done in an amusing way so that it's a game, and they can learn by imitation.

Later, as the child matures and the intellect is brought into play, it's also very important to understand the effect of physical posture on our mental functions. The seat of the intellect is located at the point between the eyebrows, or in the frontal lobe of the brain. Physiologists say that anatomically this is the most advanced part of the brain, and it's from here that we reason. If we can learn to bring our energy upward to this part of the brain, we find that we can think more clearly. If, however, we allow our energy to sink downward, it's much more difficult to think deeply.

2. *Curriculum for the Age group Six to Twelve: Feeling Aspect*: The next tool of maturity is the feelings, and these come into play during the next six year period form six to twelve. At this time, it's easiest to instruct children through their feelings, and to inspire them through stories of heroism and courage. It's essential to give them fitting role models to follow—to talk about people throughout history who have done inspiring, great, and beautiful deeds. There are many such stories, but in our day and age it seems to be a practice to show that these heroes weren't all that great after all. It seems to be the cynical philosophy of our time to bring people down

to the lowest common denominator, and we should explore that potential during these "feeling years."

3. *Curriculum for the Age group Twelve to Eighteen: Terrible Teens*: Then we have years from twelve to eighteen—the terrible teens! This is the time when children want to express their own individuality. In theory, at least, it could be a beautiful time, but in our culture particularly here in America, it's a period of rejecting the family, tradition, and authority on most levels. Yet it also has a positive side—affirming strength of will and independence. If we can encourage the development of will in wholesome ways through offering challenges and encouraging service to others, then we can help those children develop self-control and discipline. This will help them from falling into the habits of drugs and drinking that many acquire during their teens that weaken their will. If your affirm your ego and your own desires with the attitude of "What I want is all that's important," you become contractive and in the long run weaken your will. This self-focus and defiance may strengthen self will, but that's not the kind of will we're wanting to develop. Rather we want to help teens acquire the kind of will-power that helps them to overcome the real challenges they'll face in life.

4. *Curriculum for the Age Group Eighteen to Twenty Four: Development of Intellect*: Finally, we reach the ages from eighteen to twenty-four years when many children go on to college, and you find them sitting around coffee tables talking about life, with a capital "L," and discussing the great thinkers and philosophers throughout history. At this time, we consciously need to try to develop their intellects and help make their thinking clear.

Summing Up

It takes 24 years to get all these tools of maturity—the body, feelings, will, and intellect—developed and harmonized so that we can continue to grow throughout life. These four tools of maturity help us to grow all the way through life and not become a spent force by the time we're forty. This Education for Life system reflects an ever-expanding view of reality in which the child, the adult, and, on the deepest level, the eternal soul can grow to embrace broader and broader realities, until at last we can glimpse the infinite consciousness of God.

33

Paulo Freire (1922-1977)

Paulo Freire was a Brazilian educator who has made a profound impact not only in the field of education but also in the overall struggle for national development, in the Third World countries. For a while, the methodology he developed was considered such a threat to the established order that he was jailed for sometime and forced to leave Brazil for about twenty years.

Born in 1921 in Recife, the centre of one of the most extreme situations of poverty and underdevelopment in the Third World, he experienced the situation directly. The 'Economic Depression of the 1930s, hit Freire's middle class family, and his studies got disturbed and he fell behind in school. He was so stirred up that he took a vow at the age of eleven that he would dedicate his life to the struggle against hunger so that other children would not have to face the agony he was then experiencing.

He got his Ph.D. in 1959 from the University of Recife and later he worked as Professor of History and Philosophy of Education in the same university.

At Recife University, Freire conducted his experiments with the teaching of illiterates in the city of Recife. This methodology became very popular and began to be used widely. His views were considered such a threat to the old order that Freire was jailed immediately after the military comp in 1964. He spent seventy days in prison and thereafter he was forced to leave the country.

Freire spent five years working with UNESCO and the Children Institute for Agrarian Reform in the programmes of adult education.

Freire acted as a Consultant at Harvard University's School of Education and worked in close association with a number of groups engaged in new educational experiments in rural and urban areas.

He worked as Secretary of Education at Sao Paul city Brazil and Professor at the Pontifical Catholic University of Sao Pauló, PUC/ SP.

He served as special consultant to the Office of Education of the World Council of Churches at Geneva.

A member of UNESCO's International Jury, he received honorary degrees from twenty nine universities in Europe and North and South America.

Publications

1. *Cultural Action of Freedom.*
2. *Education. The Practice of Freedom.*
3. *A Pedagogy of Liberation.*
4. *Critical Literacy.*
5. *Education from Critical Consciousness.*
6. *Pedagogy of Home.*
7. *Pedagogy of the Heart.*
8. *Pedagogy in Process.*
9. *The Letters to Guinea-Bissau.*
10. *Learning to Question.*
11. *Pedagogy of the City.*
12. *Education as the Exercise of Freedom.*
13. *Extension or Communication.*
14. *Theory and Practice of Liberation.*
15. *The Importance of the Reading Act.*
16. *Pedagogy of the Oppressed.*
17. *Teachers as Cultural Workers.*
18. *Letters to Cristina.*
19. *Pedagogy of the Freedom.*
20. *A Revealing of the Pedagogy of the Oppressed.*

Some of Freire's books have been translated into over eighteen languages. One of his books *Pedagogy of the Oppressed*, written in 1970 became so popular that within three decades of its publication, over 5,00,000 copies had been sold world-wide.

Education as an Instrument of Liberating the Oppressed

Paul Freire is considered as a representative of the response of a creative mind and sensitive conscience to the enormous misery and suffering of the oppressed. He argues that the ignorance and lethargy of the poor are the direct result of the entire situation created by the economic, social and political domination of a few. By being kept in such a situation, the disadvantaged are kept 'submerged.' He is convinced that in some countries, the oppressors use the system of education to maintain the 'culture of silence', i.e., illiteracy and ignorance, while in others the advance of technology has adversely affected many people. He pleads that through the right kind of education, avoiding authoritarian teacher-pupil models and based on actual experience of students and on continual shared investigation, every human being, no matter how impoverished or illiterate, can develop a new awareness of self which will free him to be more than passive object responding to uncontrollable change.

According to Freire, "A humanizing education is the path through which men and women can become conscious about their presence in the world."

Paul Freire prefaced a method for teaching illiterates that has contributed to awaken them from their traditional lethargy. In the foreword to the book *Pedagogy of the Oppressed* (1970). Richard Shawl has explained this impact as: "In fact, those who, in learning to read and write, come to a new awareness of selfhood and begin to look critically at the social situation in which they find themselves, often take the initiative in acting to transform the society that has denied them the opportunity of participation. Education is once again a subversive force."

Freire is convinced that every human being, no matter how 'ignorant' or 'submerged' in the 'culture of silence' he or she may be, is capable of looking critically at the world in a 'dialogical encounter' with others. The individual provided with right tools for such an encounter can gradually perceive personal and social reality as well as the contradictions in it. He, with this, can become conscious of his or her own perception of that reality and deal critically with it. A peasant can facilitate this process for a neighbour more effectively than a 'teacher' brought from 'outside'. Freire thinks that "People educate each other through the mediation of the world."

Ira Shor, co-author of *A Pedagogy for Liberation* sums up the concept of education as seen by Freire in these words: "Teaching and learning are human experiences with profound social consequences. Education is not reducible to mechanical method of instruction. Learning is not a quantity of information to be memorised. Instead of transferring facts and skills from teacher to students, a Freirean class invites students to think critically about subject-matter, doctrines, the learning process itself, and their society."

In the liberating class-room, suggested by Freire's ideas, teachers pose problems derived from student life, social life, and academic subjects, in a mutually created dialogue.

Goals of Education. Following are the goals of education suggested by Freire:

1. Power Awareness.
2. Critical Literacy.
3. Desocialization.
4. Self-education.

Narration Sickness

Freire informs us that the "Teacher-student relationship at any level, inside or outside the school reveals its fundamentally *narrative character*. This relationship involves subjects (the teacher) and patients, listening objects (the students). The contents, whether values or empirical dimensions of reality tend, in the process of being narrated, to become lifeless and petrified. Education is suffering from narration sickness." The contents of this narration are "detached with reality, disconnected from the totality that engendered them and could give them significance. Words are emptied of their concreteness and become a hollow, alienated and alienating verbosity.". 'Repeating four times four is sixteen' without realizing the significance is merely the 'sensory' of words and not their 'transforming' power. Narration leads the students to memorise mechanically the narrated content.

Oppression of the Parents/Family

Freire points out that cultural invasion inhibits the creativity of the oppressed (invaded) by curbing their expression. Cultural invasion, whether urbane or harsh is always an act of violence against the persons of the invaded culture. According to him all domination involves invasion. The social 'I' of the invaded person is formed in the socio-cultural relations of the social structure. Homes and educational institutions from nurseries to universities are greatly affected by this cultural invasion.

The parent-child relationship in the home usually reflects the cultural condition of the surrounding social structure. The authoritarian cultural conditions penetrate the home as well as the school. The authoritarian, rigid and oppressive cultural environment determines relations between parents and children. The children increasingly view parent and teacher authoritarianism as inimical to their own freedom.

The environment of the home is prolonged in the school.

Here also Freire recommends the dialogical relationships.

Meaning of Educational Practice

Educational practice is not seen as 'extension' but as 'communication'. Extension is negative in nature and communication positive in nature.

Education is not the transfer, or transmission of knowledge or cultures. Nor is it the extension of technical knowledge. It is not the act of depositing reports or facts in the educatee. It is not the perpetuation of the values of a given culture. It is not an attempt to adapt the educatee to the milieu:

"I see education as the practice of freedom above all as a truly gnosiological situation. In the educational process for liberation, educator—educatee and educator—are both cognitive subjects before knowable objects which mediate them.

Placed face to face before themselves they investigate and question themselves. The more they ask questions the more they feel that their curiosity about the object of their knowledge is not decreasing. It only dismisses if it is isolated from human beings and the world."

Diological Method

Freire suggests the following method:

(a) Active, 'dialogical', critical and criticism—stimulating method.

(b) Change in the 'programme' and 'content' of education.

(c) Use of 'techniques' like thematic "breakdown" and "codification"

The method based on dialogue is a horizontal relationship between persons.

←— DIALOGUE

A with B = Communication

—→ Intercommunication

Relation of "empathy" between two "poles" who are engaged in joint research.

MATRIX: Loving, humble, hopeful, trusting, critical

Born of a critical matrix, dialogue creates a critical attitude, it is nourished by love, humility hope, faith, and trust. When the two "poles" of the dialogue are thus linked by love, hope and mutual trust, they can join in a critical search for something. Only dialogue truly communicates.

ANTI-DIALOGUE

A Over B = Communique

Relation of "Empathy" is broken

MATRIX: Loveless, arrogant, hopeless, mistrustful, a critical.

Teaching cannot be done from the top down but only from the inside out, by the illiterate himself with the collaboration of the educator.

The programme has the following phases:

Phase 1. Researching the vocabulary of the groups with which one is working.

Phase 2. Selection of generative words from the vocabulary which was studied on the following criteria:

a. Phonemic richness
b. Phonetic difficulty
c. Pragmatic tone, use of words in a given social, cultural and political reality.

Examples of generating words: Housing. Food, Clothing. Health Education.

Phase 3. The creation of the "codification": representation of typical existential situations of the group with which one is working.

Phase 4. The elaboration of agenda to serve as mere aids to the coordinators.

Phase 5. Preparation of cards with the breakdown of the phonemic families which correspond to the generative words. Preparation of slides.

Phase 6. Instructions to the team of coordinators, creation of a new attitude

Phase 7. Decoding by the group with the help of coordination.

Banking Concept of Education

Freire has introduced the new terminology of 'banking' concept in education. He explains this by stating that narration of the teacher turns students into "containers", into "receptacles" to be "filled". Education thus becomes an act of depositing, in which the students are the depositories and the teacher is the depositor. Instead of communicating, the teacher issues communiques and makes deposits which the students patiently receive, memorize and repeat. This is the "banking concept" of education, in which the scope of education allowed to the students extends only as far as receiving, filing and storing the deposits."

Ideology of the Oppressed. According to the banking concept of education, knowledge becomes a gift bestowed by those who regard themselves knowledgeable upon those whom they consider to know nothing. This projection of an absolute ignorance on others by the knowledgeable is a characteristic of the ideology of oppression. It negates education and knowledge as processes of enquiry. The students accept their ignorance like a slave. Freire here makes an interesting point by stating "but unlike the slave, they never discover that they educate the teacher." Education must begin with the solution of the teacher-student contradiction, by reconciling the poles of the contradiction so that both are simultaneously teachers and students.

Following are the chief characteristics of the banking education which lead to several contradictions in the system.

a. The teacher teaches and the students are taught.
b. The teacher knows everything and the students know nothing.
c. The teacher thinks and the students are thought about.
d. The teacher talks and the students listen—meekly.
e. The teacher disciplines and the students are disciplined.
f. The teacher chooses and he enforces his choice, and the students comply.
g. The teacher acts and the students have the illusion of acting through the action of the teacher.
h. The teacher chooses the programme content and the students (who are not consulted) adopt it.
i. The teacher confuses the authority of knowledge with his own professional authority which he sets in opposition to the freedom of the students.
j. The teacher is the subject of the learning process, while the pupils are mere objects.

The banking system reduces the creative power of the students. This is in the interest of the oppressors.. The oppressors, through their welfare schemes what they call 'humanitarianism' preserve their superiority. The oppressed are termed as 'marginals', incompetent' and 'lazy'.

The banking approach 'dehumanises' the students and adults in place of 'humanizing' them.

Role of Teachers

A Freirean teacher is a problem-poser who asks thought-provoking questions and encourages students to ask their questions. Teachers according to the traditional approach merely 'transfer' their knowledge. In this process, "Education consists in extending 'knowledge' to passive educatees preventing them from experiencing the development of the active, participatory conditions, characteristic of someone who knows. This false conception of education is a basic obstacle to transformation. Education systems based on this conception surround themselves with a "barricade" which inhibits creativity. Therefore, teachers make the process of education a truly 'gnosiological condition'.

"The conception of education which I present centres around the problematization of the human being and the world, not the problematization of the human being isolated from the world, nor the world isolated from the human being."

He further observes: "As we can see, education as a gnosiological condition which unites educator and educatee subjects in the process of knowing, opens for them innumerable and indispensable roads leading to their affirmation as beings of praxis."

Contribution of Freire: Significant Principles and Practices in Education

Freire's views are summarised as under:

1. The teacher must be imbued with a profound trust in the creative power of his students.

2. The teacher should become a partner of the students in his relations with them.

3. In the banking system of education there should be a two-way traffic. The roles of the depositors, the prescribers and the receivers must be exchanged to a great measure.

4. There should be true communication between the teacher and the students. A teacher cannot think for his students. He also cannot impose his thought on them.

5. Authentic thinking—thinking that is concerned with 'reality', does not take place in ivory tower isolation, but only in effective communication.

6. Problem-solving education—responding to the essence of consciousness– intentionally rejects communiques. Problem-solving 'epitomizes' the special characteristic of consciousness.

7. Dialogical relations—The 'teacher-of-the students' and the 'students-of- the-teacher' leads to a situation wherein the teacher is no longer merely the-one-who-teaches, but one who is himself taught in dialogue with the students, who in turn while being taught also teach. They become jointly responsible for a process in which all grow.

8. In the dialogical relations, arguments based on authority are no longer valid. Authority is on the 'side' of freedom, not 'against' it.

9. In the dialogical relations, no one teaches another, nor is anyone self-taught. People teach each other.

10. In the dialogical system, the students are no longer docile listeners. Now they are co-investigators in dialogue with the teacher.

11. In the dialogical system, knowledge does not remain at the 'doxs' (opinion) level but reaches the level of the 'Logos' (reason).

12. Students, as they are increasingly posed with problems relating to themselves in the world and with the world, will feel increasingly challenged and respond to the challenges resulting in development of new understandings.

13. Problem-solving in the dialogical system stimulates creativity and true reflection.

14. The movement of enquiry must be directed towards humanization. The pursuit of humanity cannot unfold in the antagonistic relation between oppressors and oppressed. No one can be authentically human while he prevents others from being so.

15. Dialogue cannot be reduced to the act of one person "depositing ideas" in another, nor can it become a simple exchange of ideas to be "consumed" by the "discussants". It must be meaningful.

16. Dialogue cannot exist without humility.

17. Faith is an '*a priori*' requirement for dialogue.

18. The task of the dialogical teacher in an interdisciplinary team working on the thematic universe is to "represent" the universe to the students not as a lecture but as a problem.

19. Some fundamental themes should be taken up for 'teaching- learning and learning-teaching' in dialogical relations. The themes may be broken up. The thematic breakdown splits the total themes in search of their fundamental nuclei, which are the partial elements.

20. Themes may be printed by means of brief dramatizations, reading and discussion of magazine articles, newspapers, book chapters (beginning with passages) and recorded interviews.

21. Teachers cannot think 'without' the pupils, nor 'for' the pupils but only 'with' the pupils.

Limitations of Freire's Educational Ideas

Freire's ideas are of a rebel and as such they are too revolutionary to be translated into practice in a democratic set-up. Theoretically they appear to be quite sound but functionally they are *Utopian* in nature. Freire has not provided any framework of a workable formal system of education. His ideas do not take into account the financial and organisational aspects of the formal system of education. Of course, his methodology of adult education can be made use of with some modifications.

34

Plato (427-347 B.C.)

Rousseau, one of the greatest philosophers of the world, has paid his tribute to Plato in these words: "If you wish to know what is meant by public education, read Plato's *Republic*. It is the finest treatise on education ever written".

In the words of Emerson, another eminent philosopher: "Out of Plato come all things that are still written and debated among men of thought".

A.N. Whitehead holds, "The whole of modern philosophy is a series of footnotes on Plato".

Bertrand Russell states that Plato had a great effect on subsequent ages.

Plato was born in Athens in 427 in a distinguished family. His father was a skilful player. At that time in Greece games were considered as an important medium of educating children. Plato too got his education through these means. Plato read poems and works of Homer (ancient Greek author). However, he could not get his early education properly.

Contact with Socrates: At the age of 20 years, Plato came into contact with Socrates, a great philosopher of his age. Socrates unlike Plato belonged to a poor family. He was poorly dressed but Plato put on beautiful and glamorous dress. Thus, there was a lot of economic difference between the two. This did not stand in their way. Socrates was in fact his ideal.

Plato's Visits to Different Countries: Socrates was concerned with probing the meaning of truth. His ideas did not find favour with the rulers. He was condemned to death and asked to take his own life by drinking poison. After the death of his teacher, Plato was greatly disturbed.

He left Athens. With the passage of time, he developed self-confidence and realised his potentialities. He went to Egypt and spent some years there. He engaged himself in search of knowledge. He was greatly influenced by the educational system of Egypt. He went to Italy where he studied the ideas of Pythagoras. He went to Sicily where he studied the administrative system by attending the court of King Dionysus.

Plato's Academy: Plato's philosophy and especially educational and political made a great mark. About 388 B.C., Plato opened his Academy. An academy is the name given to institutions in the field of arts, literature and science. This terms dates back to Plato who began teaching in an olive grove near Athens dedicated to a Greek warrior hero whose name was Academus. Aristotle was one of his students.

Publications

Plato wrote several books, all in the form of a dialogue.

The most important of his works are:

1. *Republic*
2. *Laws*

Plato enunciated his views on education in the above mentioned works. These two books provide us a lot of knowledge about his educational ideals and programmes.

Plato as an Idealist Philosopher

Plato believed that the soul is immortal. Since soul is immortal, it enters into the body even before the child is born. Thus knowledge is present in the child before birth. The process of education should refine this knowledge.

Plato considered the soul imbibed with virtues.

Wisdom is the eye of the soul. The aim of the life of man is to realise this 'spiritual wisdom'. This wisdom should be awakened through education.

The philosophy of Plato is known as the 'Theory of ideas' or 'Theory of Forms'. This is on account of the fact that Plato regards the world of ideas above the world of sense perception.

Plato emphasised the development of qualities of citizenship, *i.e.,* truth, beauty and goodness. He considered education as the most important instrument to do this task.

Views on Different Dimensions of Education: Meaning of Education

Plato was an idealist and he fully realised the needs of human body and soul. He wrote "Education consists of giving to the body and soul all the perfection of which they are susceptible".

In his book *Laws*, Plato wrote, "True education would develop brotherhood. Man is the highest creation. Still he needs education. He will become the most uncivilised living being of earth, if he is not given education".

He elaborated his views further, "Education should develop a kind of reason in children in order that they may feel a harmony between the soul and the various things of the world. This harmony is true virtue. Only that education can be regarded good which teaches the child to love that which is good and to hate that is bad".

Plato regarded education as a process of moral training. He wrote, "I mean by education that training which is given by suitable habits to the first instincts of virtue in children which leads you always to hate what you ought to hate and love what you ought to love, from the beginning of life to the end".

Morality according to Plato includes truth, control on desire, *i.e.,* self-restraint, intense comprehension, justice, memory and goodness. Justice induces a person for doing noble deeds. Goodness implies human welfare.

Objectives of Education

Following are the main objectives of education according to Plato:

1. Inculcating sentiments of love for truth, beauty and goodness.
2. Harmonising the personality of the child.
3. Producing self-governing individual.
4. Developing a spirit of harmony among children.
5. Developing wisdom.
6. Identifying conflicting elements in life and harmonising them.
7. Harmonising body, mind and soul.
8. Protecting the unity and integrity of the State.
9. Developing civil efficiency.

Education of the Classes: Equipping the three classes of the society, *i.e.,* rulers, soldiers and businessmen-with those qualities which would enable them to discharge their functions effectively. Plato did not feel the necessity of providing education to slaves who formed the fourth class of the society.

Curriculum

Most probably, Plato was the first educator in the Western world who presented some organisation of the curriculum. Curriculum was envisaged in terms of developing a balanced individual who could lead a balanced life.

Three-fold Division of the Curriculum

(1)	(2)	(3)
Subjects for Physical Development	Subjects for Intellectual Development	Subjects for Aesthetic Development

A. *Physical Development*: It included exercises and gymnastics. Balanced and nourishing diet was also recommended.

B. *Intellectual Development*. This comprised these subjects: (1) Mathematics, (2) Geometry, (3) Philosophy, (4) Languages, (5) History, (6) Polity, (7) Ethics etc. (8) Astronomy etc.

C. *Aesthetic Development*. This consisted of Aesthetics (i) Music, (ii) Painting, (iii) Literature Chart showing Stages of Education Subject and Activities

Three-fold Classification of Curriculum—Relating to Three Aspects of Idealism

Truth	*Goodness*	*Beauty*
Intellectual Development	Ethical Development	
(1) Philosophy (2) Logic (3) Mathematics (4) Languages (5) Geography, (6) History, Science, etc.	(1) Ethics (2) Religion (3) Politics	(1) Art (2) Music (3) Literature (4) Painting

Stages of Education

(1)	(2)	(3)	(4)	(5)	(6)	(7)
Infant stage from (1 to 3 years of age	Nursery stage (3 to 6 years of age)	Elementary stage (6 to 13 years of age)	Secondary stage (13 to 16 years of age)	Gymnastic stage (16 to 20 years of age)	Higher Education (20 to 30 years of age)	Highest Education (30 to 35 years of age)

Programme of studies for each stage

Sl.No.	*Stage*	*Age Group*	*Subjects/Activities*
1.	Infant stage	From birth to 3 years	Nourishing diet. Proper manner of bringing up
2.	Nursery	3 to 6 years of age	Play. Fairy tales. Normal recreational activities.
3.	Elementary stage	6 to 13 years of age	1. Separate education and curriculum for boys and girls. 2. Music. Dance. Poetry. 3. Mathematics. 4. Religion
4.	Secondary stage	13 to 16 years of age	1. Religious chorus songs. 2. Poem recitation. 3. Emphasis on principles of Mathematics. 4. Humanities.
5.	Gymnastic stage	16 to 20 years of age	Physical education. Military training. No literary education.

Sl.No.	*Stage*	*Age Group*	*Subjects/Activities*
6.	Higher education	20 to 30 years of age	1. Algebra 2. Geometry 3. Astronomy 4. Science subjects
7.	Higher Specialised Education	30 to 35 years of age:	Officers training 1. Epistemology 2. Ethics 3. Logic 4. Philosophy 5. Psychology 6. Polity 7. Oratory 8. Law

Plato's Dialectic

The term 'Dialectic' implies Platonic investigation of the eternal ideas, a critical investigation for exposing falsehood and eliciting truth through systematic reasoning. Important subjects included in 'Dialectic' were: (1) Polity, (2) Philosophy, (3) Ethics, (4) Logic, (5) Psychology. The study of these subjects was aimed at making philosophers and seekers of truth. It developed wisdom to understand complicated matters. These studies lasted for 5 years during the age group 30 to 35 years.

Importance of Mathematics: Next to philosophy, Plato considers mathematics most important. He observed, "Have you further observed that those who have natural talent for calculation are generally quick at every other kind of knowledge?" Similarly he emphasised the importance of geometry. In all departments of knowledge, an experience proves that anyone who has studied geometry is infinitely quicker in apprehension than anyone who has not.

Music Training: Plato is of the view that education should begin during infancy or early years of childhood with music. This is needed to lead a harmonious development of the body as well of the soul. He in this regard said, "Music training is a more potent instrument than any other, because rhythm and harmony find their way into the inward places of the soul, on which they fasten grace".

Physical Training: According to Plato, physical training should come after music training. On the role of physical training, he wrote, "My belief is not that the good boy by any bodily existence improves the soul, but on the contrary that the good soul by her own excellence improves the body as far as this may be possible".

Education of Women: Plato is for the education of women. He does not suggest any separate system of education for women. However, he considers women weaker than men. He writes, "For the patronage of State, men and women are equal but women, are, no doubt, weaker in strength".

Plato's Views on Industrial Education: Plato viewed industrial arts with contempt. According to him carpentry, tailoring, weaving, etc. were the occupations of slaves. These arts could be learnt through family traditions.

Contribution to Educational Thought and Practices

Plato made a deep study of the various aspects of education and keeping in view the socio-econo-politico structure of the society formulated his scheme/plan of education. He adopted idealistic approach in this. He was the first Western educator who paid so much attention to educational issues. He fully accepted the need for planning the system according to the various stages of development of the human being. While evaluating his scheme of education, it must be remembered that since then sea-change has taken place.

Plato's contribution may be summed up as:

1. Plato emphasised the balanced development of the personality.
2. He laid stress on inculcating the values of good citizenship.
3. He advanced moral training.
4. He formulated a definite system of education which included specific curriculum for specific stages.

Limitations of Plato's Views. From the present point of view, following limitations are noticed:

1. He laid too much emphasis on philosophy.
2. He neglected the education of the producing class.
3. He laid more emphasis on mathematics and less on literature.
4. His system of education was based on class system.
5. He paid no attention to the education of the slaves.

35

Rabindranath Tagore (1861-1941)

Tagore was a multi-splendoured personality and has left his deep impression on several facets of artistic, cultural, educational, intellectual, political and social life of India'. He was a great artist, an educationist, a poet and a patriot, a philosopher, and a reformer. There is no field of literature which he has not enriched by his contribution. He was a Nobel Prize winner.

Early Life and Education: Rabindranath Tagore was born in a family famous for its enlightened and progressive views. He was the fourteenth and the youngest son of Maharshi Devendranath and grandson of Dwarkanath Tagore. He was born at Calcutta on May 6, 1861. He wrote his first verse in his eighth year. He was introduced to the *Upanishads* and the *Ramayana* at a very young age. His school days were not happy.

In 1877, he went to England for becoming a barrister but soon returned to India. While still young his reputation as a poet began to spread.

Tagore settled down at Shantiniketan in 1901 and began his educational experiments with five pupils.

The partition of Bengal in 1905 drew Tagore to politics and he composed patriotic songs but after two years he withdrew to Shantiniketan.

Nobel Prize and International Fame: Tagore burst into international fame when his book *Gitanjali* won him the Nobel Prize for literature in 1913. With the award of Nobel Prize, Tagore became a world figure in his own right. He utilised the entire amount of the award of $8,000 for the upkeep of his school at Shantiniketan. This school which opened in a forest grove was patterned on the model of ancient *ashramas*. In 1921 the school grew into a University, called Visvabharati. Besides visiting England thrice, Tagore visited Europe, Japan, Russia and the United States.

Return of the Title on account of Jallianwala Bagh Massacre: The British Government made him 'Knight' in 1915 but he was so pained and stirred by Jallianwala Bagh massacre in Amritsar in 1919, that he returned the Insignia of Knighthood. At that time he wrote to the Viceroy of India, "The time has come when badges of honour make our shame glaring in their incongruous context of humiliation, and I for my part wish to stand, shorn of all special distinctions, by the side of those of my countrymen who, for their so-called insignificance, are liable to suffer a degradation not fit for human beings".

Tagore's Publications

1. *Shiksar Herpher* (Our Education and Its Incongruities)
2. *Shiksha Samasya* (The Problem of Education)
3. *Abaran* (Culture or Covering)
4. *Tapovan* (Forest Colony)
5. *Dharmashiksha* (Religious Education)
6. *Hindu Visvavidyalaya* (Hindu University)
7. *Strishiksha* (Women Education)
8. *Shiksar Bahan* (The Vehicle of Education)
9. *My School*
10. *Shiksar Milan* (The Meeting of Cultures)
11. *A Poet's School*
12. *Shiksar Vikiran* (Diffusion of Education)
13. *Ashramer Shiksha* (Education in Ashram)
14. *Bodher Sadhana* (Education of the Feeling)
15. *Several Convocation Addresses*

Factors Influencing Tagore's Philosophy of Education: Tagore's philosophy of education was influenced by the following factors:

1. Influence of the Home Environment.
2. Influence of the School Environment.
3. Love for Nature.
4. His Extensive Visits.

Influence of the Home Environment: Tagore was born in a family in which the time-honoured ways of Indian life and tradition of the land were strictly adhered to. His father taught him ancient Indian literature. He set before the family the Indian ideals by the example of his own life, by his talks and writings. After leaving the school, Rabindranath Tagore spent a good deal of his time in the company of his father. This constant companionship of his father exerted a great influence on his life.

His Extensive Travels: His wide travels and visits to different countries of the world and his contacts with people of different nations, developed in him a faith in the brotherhood of man and spiritual unity of humanity.

Tagore's Naturalism: Background of Tagore's Naturalism

By nature, Tagore had a love for nature. His love for naturalism was strengthened on account of the artificial and unnatural environment of the schools he attended.

Tagore's life in the school was not happy. He felt himself like 'a parrot in the cage'. Tagore was unable to adjust himself to the 'dead routine and the teaching' of the educational institutions. His teachers pronounced that he was 'unfit' for studies. Tagore considered himself 'fortunate to escape' from these 'book learning factories'. He observed later that "The Masters and Pandits who were charged with my education soon abandoned the thankless task... and realised that this boy could never be driven along the beaten track of learning".

Tagore considered school a place of great discomfort, "There was no particular trouble in the school. Yet after all, it was a school. The rooms were pitiless, its walls stood like sentries. There was nothing like a home in it, it was like a big box with many compartments".

Traditional school to him was like a 'prison house'. He observed, "It was more like a pigeon-holed box. The time spent had been thoroughly wasted". About his teachers he wrote, "Of the teachers, I remember only one, whose language was so foul that, out of sheer contempt for him, I steadily refused to answer any one of his questions". Further, he said, "I learnt about all the injustice, impatience, anger and partiality underlying the process of instruction, more easily than my lessons". The school according to him was "completely isolated from the surrounding life and beauty". It was a "restless nightmare like a jail... the whole thing was depressed".

"*A Poet's School*" is an important writing showing the place of Nature in life and education. Children have the gift of freshness of senses. They can become natural with Nature and human with the human society. "For our perfection we have to be vitally savage and mentally civilised". But the misery is that a child is offered crowded solitude in a city where man is everywhere, with never a gap for the immense non-human, the Nature. The inexpensive power to be happy that the children bring to this world is "Constantly worn away by friction with the brick-and-mortar arrangement of life". The city-built education does not take heed of the non-civilised in us, which thirst for colour, for music, for the movement of life. This is why Tagore tried his best to develop in the children of his school "the freshness of their feeling for nature, a sensitiveness of soul in their relationship with their human surrounding".

He pointed out the great significance of the school atmosphere in the life of children whose mind, like the tree, has the power to gather food and nourishment form its surroundings. The cultural atmosphere keeps the mind sensitive to rich racial inheritance, glorious traditions and concentrated wisdom of ages. The school atmosphere must also develop sensitiveness of soul and allow freedom to the mind from bondage of ignorance and apathy.

Main Characteristics of Naturalism in Education

1. *Aims of Education: Harmony with Nature.* According to Tagore, the highest aim of education is that which does not merely give us information but makes our life harmonious with all existence. He notes that this education of sympathy is not only systematically ignored in schools, but it is severely repressed. Tagore laments that from our very childhood habits are formed and knowledge is imparted in such a manner that our life is weaned away from nature and our mind and the world are set in opposition

from the beginning of our days. Thus, the greatest aim of education for which we come prepared, is neglected, and we are made to lose our world to find a handful of information instead. His hunger is for the Epics, but he is supplied with chronicles of facts and dates.

2. *Ideal School in Natural Surroundings: Tapovan (Forest Colony).* According to Tagore, the forests hold a message to us of peace and purity, of sublime feeling and pure joy—of austerity and renunciation. Nature in the forest Provides a grand perspective against which all objects, all feelings, lose their exaggerated shape and assume due proportions. In *Tapovan* a new idea is introduced. The message of the forest can be received and felt only through the expansion of sympathy or enlarging the feeling aspect within us. It is not the eye nor the ear, nor all the senses, not even the intellect that could read this grand message. It is only the feeling. One has to learn to feel, to enlarge the depth of feeling and the scope of sympathy. *Bodher Sadhana*, or what we may call 'Education of the Feeling'—that is really wanted. "We must constantly remember that neither the education of the senses, nor the education of the intellect, but the education of the feeling should receive the place of honour in our schools". That is why he pleads that "our true education is possible only in the forest, through intimate contact with Nature and purifying austere pursuits".

Tagore has observed, "It must be an *Ashram* where men have gathered for the highest end of life, in the peace of nature, where life is not merely meditative but fully awake in its activities". Tagore was convinced that "Our true education is possible only in the *Tapovan* (Forest) through intimate contact with nature and purifying austere pursuits". Tagore sings out:

> "I feel the tenderness of the grass in my forest walk,
> the way-side flowers startle me:
> That the gifts of the infinite are strewn in, the dust".

The school must enlarge the 'feeling' aspect. He wrote, "We must remember that neither the education of the senses, nor the education of the intellect, but the education of the feeling should receive the place of honour in our schools".

Tagore pointed out the great significance of the school atmosphere in the life of children whose mind, like the tree, has the power to gather food and nourishment from its surroundings. The cultural atmosphere keeps the mind sensitive to rich racial inheritance, glorious traditions and concentrated wisdom of ages. The school atmosphere must also develop sensitiveness of soul and allow freedom to the mind from bondage of ignorance and apathy.

There is a spiritual bondage between man and man, with ennobling effect of nature on the inmates. Music, songs, dancing, dramatics and other artistic activities are a daily routine. Tagore explains it in his own words: "Training in the use of limbs, development of the spirit of questioning, thinking and observation; cultivation of interest and enjoyment in trees, birds, the beasts and the varied phenomena of nature; experience in the making of articles of daily use, habit of keeping one's living room and surrounding clean, healthy and beautiful practice of cleanliness extending to the body, dress and personal behaviour through adequate observance of both, wholesome discipline in eating, physical exercise and rest and careful maintenance of bodily and mental strength—these are essential to the life of this *Ashrama*".

Pen Picture of an Ideal School

An ideal school, according to Tagore, should have the following characteristics; and he attempted to introduce these elements in his school at Bolpur, located at a distance of about one hundred miles from Calcutta. Later, this school became Shantiniketan and grew into Visvabharati.

1. The school should be situated in natural surroundings. There should prevail the atmosphere of nature's own beauty with her varied gifts of colours and dance, flowers and fruits, with the joy of her mornings and the peace of her starry nights.
2. It should provide an environment after the fashion of ancient *Tapovans*—forest schools about which he had read so much in the *Upanishads*.
3. It should give spiritual training to the students.
4. It should help the children in cultivation of love of nature and sympathy with all living creatures.
5. It should educate children by providing an atmosphere of freedom.
6. It should educate children by making them alive to their natural surroundings.
7. It should educate children by providing an environment of living aspiration, based upon living contact between the teacher and the taught.
8. It should impart knowledge to children through mother tongue.
9. The school should provide for manual labour.
10. It should provide for close personal contact with the teacher. The number of students in classes should be very small.
11. There should be a well-equipped library.
12. It should be a community school where there is no distinction of caste and creed.
13. It should teach crafts like sewing, book-binding, weaving, carpentry etc.
14. It should include drawing, art and music as an integral part of the curriculum.
15. It should provide students adequate opportunities for choosing their hobbies and occupations.
16. It should be a self-governing institution with a dairy farm, post office, hospital and workshop. Students should hold their own courts.

3. *Tagore's Concept of Discipline*: For Tagore, an educational institution is "an open house in which students and teachers are one. They must live their compact life together". He observes that an educational institution "must not be a dead cage in which living minds are fed with food artificially prepared". He further remarks that "students are not dancing monkeys or bears". About the discipline of the educational institution he founded, he states, "I never said to them: Don't do this, or don't do that. The boys were encouraged to manage their own affairs".

4. *Curriculum*: Tagore was for a comprehensive curriculum which should satisfy child's aesthetic, creative, spiritual and vocational needs. In his experimental school at Shantiniketan, Science (especially the experimental science) was taught to children in various classes. Shantiniketan school had a very well-equipped laboratory for performing experiments whereas in other schools, people had not even thought of this subject. Nature-study was also taught here, right in the midst of nature.

Methods of Teaching: Tagore strongly criticised the bookish and examination–oriented teaching. He stressed movement of the whole body in various learning activities. He followed the activity principle, and advocated constructive and creative activities. He believed that there should be daily practice by the pupils in expressing immediately what they are learning. The central point in educational activity according to Tagore, is joy which should pervade all types of activities; "Work should be wedded to joy". Tagore also emphasised the principle of curiosity and interest, and the spirit of play. He advocated fullness of experience-physical, mental, aesthetic and emotional. All this truly accords with the modern pedagogy.

5. *Role of the Teacher*: Tagore laid great emphasis on the attitude of the teacher. He wrote, "I have found that little children learn more quickly the attitude of the teacher than the knowledge imparted by him".

Tagore felt, "Most teachers do not know that in order to teach boys they have to be boys. Unfortunately, schoolmasters are obsessed with the consciousness of their dignity as grown up persons and as learned men, and therefore they always try to burden the children with their grown up manners and their learned manners, and that hurts the mind of the students unnecessarily". His concept of a good teacher is stated in these words, "A teacher can never truly teach unless he is still learning himself. A lamp can never light another lamp unless it continues to burn its own flame. The teacher who has come to the end of his subject, who has no living traffic with his knowledge, but merely repeats his lesson to his students, can only load their minds; he cannot quicken them. Truth not only must inform but also inspire".

Visvabharati at Shantiniketan in Natural Surroundings

Rabindranath Tagore was not a dreamer. He was a great educational practitioner who himself was closely associated with the entire educational practices at Visvabharati.

The word Visvabharti is composed of two words. In Sanskrit, the word *Visva* means 'world' and *bharti* means 'culture'. Thus *Visvabharti* would mean 'world culture'. The motto of this University is *Yatra Visvam bhavati ekamidam, i.e.,* where the world meets in one place. Through the *Visvabharti* as a whole, the poet and the seer sought "to establish a relationship between East and West, to promote inter-cultural and inter-social amity and understanding and fulfill the highest mission of the present age—the unification of mankind".

The *Visvabharti* was formally founded on 22nd December 1921. But it was not a new institution. It had grown gradually out of the Shantiniketan Ashrama. Today this *Visvabharti* is known not only all over the world, but also attracts scholars from different parts of the world.

Tagore has observed, "I have formed the nucleus of an International University, as one of the best means of promoting mutual understanding between the East and the West". It was intended to be, "Treasure of Light" not only for India but also for the world.

Tagore wanted to extend by degrees the scope of this university on simple lines, until it comprehended the whole range of eastern culture—the Aryan, Semitic, Mongolian etc. Its object was to reveal the eastern mind to the world.

Main features of Visvabharati: Tagore describes these as:

1. The institution that bore the name of *Visvabharati* was founded with the call that man had to be set free not only in the field of Nature but also among mankind.
2. The greatest distinction of our school is the direct and immediate emotional contact of pupils with their teachers and with external nature.
3. A speciality of our institution is that it wants to bring up our pupils in inseparable association with Nature.
4. It wants to hold before the world the ideal of the universality of man.
5. It is intended not only to be the intellectual centre of the intellectual life of India but also the centre of her economic life.
6. It is envisaged to be the nucleus of an international university and as one of the means of promoting mutual understanding between the East and the West.

Natural Environment at Shantiniketan

Education is imparted in the lap of natural surroundings. The influence of green trees, open fields, seasonal skies, songs and chirpings of birds and other natural phenomena, fills the pupils' mind with spiritual elevation. Tagore himself says, "Having in my mind the ideal of a school, which should be a home and a temple in one, where teaching should be a part of worshipful life. I selected this spot far away from all distraction of the town, hallowed by the memory of a pious life, whose days were passed here in communion with God".

Institutions at *Visvabharti*

Following institutions were started to carry out his experiments in education:

1. *Sisu Bhavan* (Nursery School)
2. *Path Bhavan* (School Section—Matriculation Examination)
3. *Siksha Bhavan* (Higher Secondary)
4. *Vidya Bhavan* (College of Undergraduate and Post-Graduate Studies and Research)
5. *Vinya Bhavan* (College of Teaching)
6. *Kala Bhavan* (College of Fine Arts and Crafts)
7. *Sangit Bhavan* (College of Dance)
8. *Sriniketan* (Department of Rural Reconstruction)
9. *Siksa Satra* (Rural High School)
10. *Silpa Sadana* (College of Industrial Training)
11. *Cheena Bhavan* (School of Languages, e.g., Chinese, Tibetan, etc.)

By and large, all formed part of *Visvabharti University*

Tagore's Contribution to Education

Tagore's concept of education and its practices balance the claims of different schools of educational philosophy, *i.e.*, humanism, idealism, naturalism, pragmatism, realism and supernaturalism. His philosophy is a true blend of the Eastern and Western philosophy.

The *Visvabharti* is the embodiment of his educational ideals.

Tagore is one of the very few educational philosophers whose philosophy is the outcome of his educational experiments. Simultaneously, he gave a practical shape to his ideology.

Rabindranath was a great educational practitioner. He was not a dreamer only to leave behind a legacy of the principles of life. He worked them out in a constructive way.

Setting up educational institutions in natural surroundings and the environment of freedom from fear—the two principal features of his theory and practice of education bear the mark of his naturalism.

36

Sarvepalli Radhakrishnan (Dr.) (1888-1975)

Born in 1888 in Tamil Nadu, Radhakrishnan is got early education in the Christian schools. After passing M.A. in philosophy in 1910, Sarvepalli Radhakrishnan started his teaching career as professor of philosophy in different Indian Universities. While his writing *Philosophy of Tagore's Life* earned him fame, his *Notes on Western Philosophy* attracted the Westerners. It was the golden period of his life when he served the Calcutta University for 20 years. His book *History of Indian Philosophy* won him laurels and he was invited by Oxford University to lecture on 'The Hindu View of Life'. He availed of the opportunity to visit a number of countries.

He joined as professor of Comparative Religion at Oxford University in 1929, and was appointed Vice-Chancellor Andhra University in 1931. His book *Eastern Religion and Western Thought* appeared in 1939. He won the rare distinction of being awarded the Fellowship by the British Academy of Fellowship. As Vice-Chancellor of the Benaras Hindu University, he visited China on a lecture tour.

He was the Chairman of the University Grants Commission and the leader of the first Indian team to the UNESCO (1946 to 1950).

He started his formal political career when he was appointed Indian Ambassador to the USSR, where with his sweet, learned and impressive behaviour he won the heart of Russian leaders. In 1952, he was elected as the first Vice-President and chairman of the Rajya Sabha where he established some democratic, parliamentary and national norms. In 1962, this philosopher became the second President of the Indian Republic and was awarded the 'Bharat Ratna', the highest national distinction in 1967.

Dr. Radhakrishnan's contribution to education has been unique and irreplaceable. In the early days of his career, he began as a teacher to become an educationist of great eminence. He had first hand experience of educational institutions and their multifarious problems, which he happened to study from different angles and various places.

As an educationist, administrator, renowned professor, philosopher, diplomat, statesman, and President, he commanded an excellent vantage point from where he could see that the whole human business was moving towards a fatal destiny, and only education of the right sort could save it from a tragic finale.

Major Works

1. *The Philosophy of Rabindranath Tagore,*
2. *Indian Philosophy,*
3. *The Hindu View of Life,*
4. *An Idealist View of Life,*
5. *East and West in Religion,*
6. *Future of Civilisation,*
7. *The Religion We Need,*
8. *Gautama the Buddha,*
9. *Eastern Religion and Western Thought,*
10. *Education, Politics and War,*
11. *Bhagvadgita,*
12. *Dhammapad,*
13. *The Recovery of Faith,*
14. *Brahma-Sutra,*
15. *Fellowship of the Spirit,*
16. *On Nehru,*
17. *The Concept of Man,*
18. *My Search for Truth,*
19. *The Principal Upanishads,*
20. *Religion and Society,*
21. *Freedom and Culture.*

Dr. Radhakrishnan's View of Life

Philosopher's vision and educationist's zeal make an ideal combination. In Dr. Radhakrishnan, philosophy and education go hand in hand. His educational thinking needs to be studied in the context of his view of life. Philosophy does not offer Dr. Radhakrishnan the seclusion of an ivory tower but offers him the opportunity to comprehend life and to have the vision of the realities of living. His philosophy is not removed from the truth of existence. The function of philosophy is to order life and guide action. It has the quality of ennobling life and broadening the outlook. Philosophy gives an insight into the meaning of life. Dr. Radhakrishnan's philosophy is idealism. This means that life has a purpose, and ideals and values are the dynamic forces that give direction to life and help it to achieve its goal. There are certain values which transcend man and society. The proper ends of life, and therefore of education, being inherent in the very nature of the universe, morally obligate man to discover, recognise and accept the supremacy of such values and to regulate his behaviour accordingly. This would imply an absolute reality. It is an expression of the absolute. The absolute, Dr. Radhakrishnan explains, is God. Man's inborn feeling in God, his quest for truth, his striving for perfection, his longing for goodness, his craving for beauty, all his hopes, ideals and aspirations abundantly prove man's essential divine nature. But man is a complex multi-dimensional being. He is not only spirit, he also has mind, life and body. These different levels of reality, these multiple sides of his nature are not contradictory. He is indivisible. Nothing in him can be rejected. Everything in him is expression of the Divine. "The end of man is to let the spirit in him permeate—his whole being his soul, flesh and affections. He attains his deepest self by losing his selfish ego".

Matter and spirit is a theme of great importance in the writings of Dr. Radhakrishnan. The developments of science and technology have made some to believe erroneously that matter is the most important thing in our life. But a little scrutiny would reveal that these great developments of science, if they establish anything, they establish the omnipotence of the human spirit and not the omnipotence of matter. They show the superiority of the human mind. We are not merely a part of nature; there is a non-natural element in us, an element which exceeds the quality and potentiality of matter. The element is the spirit of man. It is this spirit which is responsible for all the achievements in this world. But what is actually wrong with the world is not matter. It is neither the atom bombs nor the nuclear weapons which must be blamed, but it is this spirit of man which controls matter. Man is essentially a spiritual being. He himself is the frontier of mystery. It is he himself that can reach the frontier and make a breakthrough. If this be realised then man can rid himself of his lower passions and rise to his truer nature. But deep down, there exists some kind of crudeness that does not allow humanity to settle down in an atmosphere of freedom from fear. Men may be nuclear geniuses, but they remain ethical dwarfs. The spectacular achievements are trying to smother the spiritual breath of mankind. Man is afraid of his brother, and lives in an atmosphere of distrust and fear. This has to be changed by understanding the true nature of spirit.

Divinity of Human Soul

Spiritually, 'to be or not to be that is the question'. The world over the unleashed tendencies that crush the human spirit and degrade and dehumanise the mind are on the rampage. Humanity has been forced to become a robot. "If this human mind surrenders its humanity", says Dr. Radhakrishnan, "makes itself into an object, lapses into rigidly and routine and does not understand the boundless possibilities which are located in the creative side of human nature, it is then that we become victims of necessity, dialectical, mechanical, historical, or even providential. There is no such thing as God dictating the future of events completely. We are co-workers with the divine spirit.... The divine uses the human individual. Every human individual has in him this eternal spark, this creative element. If we overlook it, we are untrue, unfaithful, to our own education, to our own humanity. Thus, the spiritual nature of man, the essential divinity of the human soul is to be given utmost reverence. It is this Divine in man, which is behind the apparatus of body, mind, heart and intellect. It is ray of the celestial light that propels us towards complete fulfillment. Religions emphasise this aspect. This is the basis of democracy. Our spiritual being is inward and, therefore, it derives its strength from within and not from without. For the renewal of our spirit we need to get back to the shrine of inward solitude and not get lost in the worldly turmoil of materialism. In fact, man is not satisfied with what he is, for he longs to become better and nobler. He seeks and aspires. Through detachment and renunciation he makes himself the instrument of a higher purpose. This also proves that there is no such thing as inevitability so far as human beings are concerned. Man is not a helpless toy in the hands of the great cosmic forces. The invincible spirit within him must triumph over the gravitational downward pull of circumstances.

Place of Religion in Dr. Radhakrishnan's Philosophy and Action

In the philosophical and educational thoughts of Dr. Radhakrishnan, religion has a place of crucial importance, for he believes that the way of religion is the remaking of man, a complete integration of his being. Religion introduces an entirely new sense, a totally new set of values. But religion is not doctrinal conformity or ceremonial piety. It is a personal encounter of the individual with the supreme. But there was a time when it was assumed that a man could not be a true believer in his own religion unless he also believed that all other religions were false. Many wrongs were perpetrated in the name of religion. Teaching of sectarian creeds to children, instead of developing in them the spirit of brotherly love generates narrow group loyalties and sows the seed of future strife.

Secular Concept of State

All this has led to the secular conception of the State. Secularism does not mean the neglect of religion. It is not indifference to religion, but respect for all faiths, respect of everything which man holds sacred, respect for anything worthy of reverence. The fundamental principles of our Constitution call for spiritual training. All persons are equally entitled to freedom of conscience and the right to freely profess, practise and propagate religion; There is no State religion, which otherwise would have meant becoming partial to any one religion. The Constitution provides that public funds raised by taxes shall not be utilised for the benefit of any particular religion; and that no person attending any educational institution recognised by the State shall be required to take part in any religious institution without his consent.

How to Impart Religious Education?

On practical measures to be adopted for imparting religious education, the University Education Commission (1948-49) observes: "Religion cannot be imparted in the form of lessons. It is not to be treated as one of a number of subjects to be taught in measured hourly doses. Moral and religious instruction does not mean moral improvement... What we need is not the imparting of instruction but the transmitting of vitality. We must civilise the human heart". The Commission recommends a short period of silent meditation, every morning before the class work starts. It frees the mind for a few moments from the distractions of daily living. In these silent moments one transmutes the human into the spiritual, and sees the vision of the quenchless inner flame. The purpose of education is to teach the students to look within and to mould their life and action in the light of the inner spirit. Values can be built into the human mind through suggestion and persuasion, and not through instruction and imposition. Personal example, daily life and work, and great books read from day to day are methods of influencing the human mind. Great literature sets fire to the highest emotions and prompts the highest ideals and aspirations. A study of great books, books that shame our smallness, that quell our fears, that fill us with hope is essential in the University course. It has been the belief of Dr. Radhakrishnan that nothing opens out a man's mind or broadens his horizon as the study of great classics. Everyone should spend some time everyday in the company of the classics. It would take their thoughts away from the life's rough and tumble where men are lost in excitement, passion and strife. The classics endow us with new eyes to look at the world. Dr. Radhakrishnan quotes a Sanskrit verse which means: "In this poison tree or *samsara*, there are two fruits of inestimable value which have nectar-like quality: the tasting of the flavour of the classics and communion with great men". In addition to silent meditation and reading of great classics a reverent study of the essentials of all religions would be very much rewarding. It would be a step towards harmony between religions. It would show the Divine unity in the human mind in different places and times.

Religion and Science

Emphasis on religion does not belittle the role of science in our life. Science and religion are not opposed to each other. Both seek truth. The quest of truth is the quest of God. They represent the two dimensions of the human being, the rational and the spiritual. There is the need for their coordination and integration. Human despair, depressions and fears of fratricidal wars appear on the scene only when science as the pursuit of knowledge turns into the pursuit of power, and is used as a weapon of tyranny and exploitation by power seekers and selfish men. "Struggling as we are with the fateful horizons of the atomic age", says Dr. Radhakrishnan, "the achievements of science have induced in our minds a mood of despair, making us feel like homeless exiles, caught in a blind machine". This cannot be counted as the failure of science. It is, in fact, the failure of man. The fundamental problem remains whether science will be used in future for peace, prosperity and the profound increase of joys of mankind or for destruction, devastation and desolation. Whether scientifically and militarily strong people will ever unjustly dominate and tyrannise the scientifically poor and, therefore, militarily weak segments of the human race, or science will further the cause of human brotherhood. What is wrong is not the scientific discoveries or technological achievements but the outlook of man with his cult of power and selfish motives. Men sometimes become unmindful of their moral implication and social consequences. "The powers of science can be considered safe in the hands of those who have great reverence for human feelings and tenderness that colour the daily existence of our life. Any system of education must not forget that knowledge and feeling are equally important ingredients of living.

Meaning and Functions of Education

(Extracts from Occasional Speeches and Writings)

1. Education—Training of Intellect, Heart and Spirit

Education, to be complete, must be humane, it must include not only the training of the intellect but the refinement of the heart and the discipline of the spirit. No education can be regarded as complete if it neglects the heart and the spirit. We need education of the whole man—physical, vital, mental, intellectual and spiritual.

2. Humanism in Education

No nation in this world can hold its place of primacy in perpetuity. What counts is the moral contribution we make to human welfare. Let us, therefore, try and develop the qualities of charity in judgement and compassion for people who are suffering. If we adopt such an approach, the tensions of the world will diminish rapidly.

3. Education for Democracy

The cause of democracy is the cause of the human individual of the free spirit of man with its spontaneous inspiration and endeavour. Every man whose thoughts and feelings are not silted up has his own inner possession, which belongs to him alone, his holy shrine, which he has won for himself. When an individual is trained to appreciate his own holy being, he will develop a chastity of mind and spirit and approach with inner trembling another's sanctuary. Intolerance is basically unchastity. If we do not give this spiritual direction to our education, it fails in its purpose.

4. Education to Develop Scientific Spirit

A lively development and use of intellectual curiosity, imaginative power, technical skill, acceptance of goals that stretch one's talent and energy to their uttermost extent and the simultaneous rejection of all cliches of thought, sterile styles and forms and social manners that hamper individual aims and efforts, these are the characteristics of the young person who is anxious to defend his individuality against the ever-present and corrupting force of habit and tradition and social pressure for conformity. All this is possible with single minded devotion.

5. Education and Human Values

There is a great deal of intellectual and technical skill but the ethical and spiritual vitality is at a low ebb. The mind of man, ever young and eager, though standing on earth as on a footstool, stretches out its hold into the stars. There is nothing wrong about science; what is wrong is the use we make of it. Education should give us a purpose. Man's completeness results from the pursuit of truth and its application to improve human life, the influence of what is beautiful in nature, man and art, and spiritual development and its embodiment in ethical principles. Coarseness of feeling darkness of mind and the very casual way in which we inflict cruelties—all these indicate inward emptiness.

6. Education and Spiritual Values

Education is the means by which we can tide up our minds, acquire information, as well as a sense of values. Education should give us not only elements of general knowledge or technical skills but also impart to us that bent of mind, that attitude of reason, that spirit of democracy which will make us responsible citizens of our country. A true democracy is a community of citizens differing from one another but all bound to a common goal.

7. Education—A Search for Integration

Education aims at making us into civilised human beings, conscious of our moral and social obligations. We must know the world in which we live, physical, organic and social. We must have an idea of the general plan of the universe and the search for truth. When we attain truth our burdens are lightened and our difficulties are diminished. It lights up our pathway with the radiance of joy.

8. Education—A Capacity for Discernment

Education has for its aims not merely acquisition of information but the capacity for discernment. Judgement is more important than cleverness. In our country today we have many men who are clever but not many who are upright. We should cultivate respect for integrity. We must weed out corruption and clean up the nation. Purity is essential in daily life and administration.

9. Education to Develop the Spirit of Enquiry

We should develop the spirit of enquiry and dedication to the pursuit of science and scholarship. We waste our years in college in trivialities and inanities. We are misled into participation in non-academic endeavours. We should instil into our youth zeal for the advancement of knowledge. We have enough material but it is not guided properly. We need education in character.

10. Education to Train People for Freedom and Democracy

If we twist the minds of the young out of shape, they will be a danger to society. The future of democracy in Asia depends on our willingness to submit to discipline, undergo personal sacrifice ... If India is to remain free, united and democratic, educational institutions should train people for freedom not obedience, for unity and not localism, for democracy not dictatorship. Our young should have a sense of purpose.

11. Education and Self-Discipline

We must train the young to the best possible all round living, individual and social. We must make them intelligent and good. They must learn to observe spontaneously those unwritten laws or decency and honour felt by good men but not enforced by any statute.

12. Education Institutions to Preserve the Spirit of the Youth

Unless we preserve the spirit of youth, keep an open mind and change our belief and practice, we cannot endure. India has endured for centuries; it is because she has kept her spirit of youth. She can keep alive only if she does not idolise her institutions, does not turn them into ends in themselves. To preserve thought, spirit and inspiration of this ancient land and let them inform our customs and institutions are the tasks assigned to this generation of scholars.

13. Education of Women

Women are human beings and have as much right to full development as men have. In regard to opportunities for intellectual and spiritual development, we should not emphasise the sex of women even as we do not emphasise sex of men. The fact that we are human beings is infinitely more important than the physiological peculiarities which distinguish us from one another. In all human beings, irrespective of their sex, the same drama of the flesh and the spirit, of finitude and transcendence takes place.

Function of University

A University is not a mere information shop—it is a place where a man's intellect, will and emotions are disciplined. In it experience and adventure are combined... A University man should be unattached without being unconcerned, unambitious without being indolent, warm-hearted without being sentimental.

Universities—Places of Culture

Universities are expected to prepare young men and women with not only information, knowledge and skill but also spirit of dedication and detachment. These qualities are essential for the stupendous task of remaking the history of this great country... Universities are not mere places of learning. They are homes of culture. Man-making is the task that has been assigned to the Universities in our country today. Are we making men, are we merely turning out people who can repeat parrot-like certain passages, or are we giving them a refinement of feeling, a civilising of their purposes, a ripening of their understanding both of nature and of society? That is the supreme test of the functioning of any University. And if we are not able to fulfill this purpose we are responsible for the failure.

University and Teachers of High Quality

The kind of education we provide for our youth is determined overwhelmingly by the kind of men and women we secure as teachers. Magnificent buildings and equipment are no substitute for the great teacher. Every attempt should be made to draw a good proportion of the best ability in the country in the teaching profession if this country is to participate in the march of mind in science and scholarship. Universities must recruit for their staff some of the best minds of the country. The University teacher should be helped to live in comfort, if he is to devote himself to learning, teaching and research. As the young recruits to the Universities are paid low salaries they fail to appreciate intellectual values and get interested in writing textbooks or obtaining examinerships. I hope the University service will become as attractive as the all-India services, for that is the only way to recruit and retain some of the ablest persons for the Universities. As the example of the teacher has great influence on the pupils, we cannot evade our responsibility to the teaching profession.

Teachers as Removers of Spiritual Blindness

We in our country look upon teachers as *gurus*, *acharyas*: what do these words indicate? *Acharya* is one whose *achar* or conduct is exemplary, is good. If he is a victim of *durachar* then he is not an *acharya*. He must be an example of *sadachar* or good conduct. He must inspire the pupils who are entrusted to his care with love of virtue and goodness and abhorrence of cruelty and violence. That is the first essential for any kind of civilised being. We must love the good and detest the bad. Until we are able to give our youngsters that kind of outlook we cannot call ourselves good teachers. I hope that ideal of a true teacher will be remembered by us.

Andhakaranirodhata gurur ityabhidhiyate

Andhakar is not merely intellectual ignorance but spiritual blindless. He who is able to remove that kind of spiritual blindness is called a *guru*. Are we deserving of that noble appellation of an *acharya* or a *guru*? That is the first thing that everyone of us will have to realise.

Teachers—Reservoirs of New Spirit

Our teachers are the reservoirs of this new spirit, the new spirit of adventure in intellectual matters, in social matters, in political matters. If you do not have that spirit, you cannot communicate that spirit to the youth, who are entrusted to your care. Therefore, I appeal to the teachers that it is the generous youth, hospitable youth, adventurous youth, courageous youth, whom we have in our country, if they are to be utilised for building up a new country, a new India, a new society, the beginning must come from the teachers themselves. They must know what this country stands for and they must be able to communicate the vitality not merely instruction.

Teachers to Set Example

Let me tell you, the boys do not care for what you teach them but they care for the example you set. It is not merely the instruction which you impart to them in the classroom but the kind of life you lead. You think that they do not see it but they have eyes to see and ears to hear. They know everything about their teacher and if they have no respect for the teachers it is because they know more than they ought to know, more than what you expect them to know. Therefore, it is education, it is instruction, it is knowledge and it is also the example which the teachers give.

Education for Jnana, Darshana and Caritra

If you reflect on the figure of Saraswati you will have an idea of what our ancestors aimed at in education. The goddess has for her vehicle a swan, human which is endowed with the capacity of separating milk from water. Education has for its aim not merely the acquisition of information but the capacity for discernment. Judgement is more important than cleverness. In our country today we have many men who are clever but not many who are upright. We should cultivate respect for integrity. We must weed out corruption and clean up the nation. Purity is essential in daily life and administration.

The goddess of learning, her lotus seat and the vehicle swan, are all represented as white, the symbol of purity: *Sarvasukla Saraswati.*

A balanced personality is possible if we sharpen the intellect, cultivate imagination and discipline our passions. *Saraswati* is represented as playing on the *Vina.* Art and music should be regarded as essential elements of education. The discipline of our nature is an essential part of education.

Student Discipline

Dr. Radhakrishnan stresses that the students should be trained to approach life's problems with fortitude, self-control and a sense of balance which the new conditions demand. There should be adequate provision for games and other corporate activities. There is no reason why students who are physically fit should not be encouraged to join the National Cadet Corps in large numbers. Membership of the corps fosters habits of discipline, team work and dignity of labour. Methods of teaching should provide adequate opportunities to the students for conversation, debate, discussion and exchange of opinions and thoughts with their teachers.

Contribution of Dr. Radhakrishnan

The greatest contribution of Dr. Radhakrishnan to educational thought and practice is the Report of the University Education Commission 1948-49. The Report of the Commission which was presided over by Dr. S. Radhakrishnan, a distinguished scholar, is a document of great importance as it has guided the development of University education in India since independence. Its recommendations envisaged 12 years of schooling and degree course of 3 years. It also recommended that the University teaching be made more attractive by improving the conditions of service. Another important recommendation was the setting up of a Central Grants Commission. The Commission courageously tackled the problem of religious education. The Commission observed:

"Our education should encourage the development in its members fearlessness of mind, strength or conscience and integrity of purpose". It has further observed: "If we claim to be civilised, we must develop thought for the poor and the suffering, chivalrous regard and respect for women, faith in human brotherhood regardless of race or colour, nation or religion, love of peace and freedom, abhorrence of cruelty and ceaseless devotion to the claims of justice".

37

Shankara (Sankara) Acharya (788-820 A.D.)

Advait means 'monism'. Monism is the doctrine according to which there is only one reality, *i.e., Brahma*. Sankara is the principal promoter of this doctrine.

Sankara Acharya is also called by some thinkers as Jagat Guru Sankara Acharya. Sankara Acharya occupies a prominent place among the renowned philosophers of not only of India but also of the world.

Sankara was born in 788 A.D. in a village named Kaladi in the family of a *Nambudri Brahmans* of Kerala. His father's name was Shivagudi who was a Sanskrit scholar. However, he was deprived of the benefit of his learning as he was born after his death.

It is said that at the age of 2, Sanakra could read letters and words. At the age of 3, he acquired the mastery of Epics and the *Puranic* love. At the age of 5, he was sent to a Gurukul and at the age of 7 he studied all the *Vedas* and six systems of philosophy, *smrits* etc.

At the age of 8, he renounced the world and became a hermit (*Sanyasi*).

At the age of 12, Sankara wrote commentaries on *Brahmasutra*, *Upanishads*, *Gita* and other philosophical texts.

Sankara toured through India, held discussions with scholars on philosophical and spiritual issues. He established his supremacy over *anti-Vedic* doctrines.

Sankara as the Emotional and National Integrator

He spearheaded the movement of the revival of Hinduism on the basis of his philosophy based on the Vedas and the Upanishads. Sankara established four *Dhams* (Abodes of God) or four different *Mutts* (Places of pilgrimage) in four different parts of India.

1. Jagannath Puri in the East.
2. Dwarka in the West.
3. Jyoti Mutt at Badrinath in the North.
4. Shringiri in the South.

Essence of Sankara's Philosophy: Advaitvad

Sankara's views on *Adavita* are best illustrated in his classical line from his monumental work *Brahma Sutra Bhasya*: *Brahma*, *Satyam*, *Jagat Mithya*,

Jiva Brahmatiya Na Parah – The *Brahma* alone is real, the world is illusory, the individual, the universal and soul are one.

Basic Features of Advaitabad

1. *Brahma* (God – the Supreme Being):
   (i) It is above everything else. God is called by several names.
   (ii) *Brahma* is immortal.
   (iii) *Brahma* is the creator, preserver and destroyer
2. *Maya* The world is *Maya* – all creatures are created by Him. This element is known as the *Maya* (Illusion). *Brahma* alone is the reality.
3. *Moksha* (Liberation) is the attainment of liberation—ultimate aim of an individual. Salvation is achieved when the lid of *Maya* is removed and the individual becomes one with the *Brahma*.
4. *Atmabodh* (Knowledge of the self), knowledge of the self is the path to salvation. A*tmabodh* serves as a primer to those desirous of liberation, equipped with the tools of discernment and renunciation.
5. *Knowledge*: True knowledge is the cause of liberation just as fire is the direct cause of cooking. Requirements might include water, pots and pans but it is fire which actually makes cooking possible. In the same way knowledge makes *Brahma's* realisation possible.
6. *Practice of Knowledge*: The self can be known only through knowledge, just as light alone can dispel darkness. Sankara compares the *jnana abhyasa* (practice of knowledge) which purifies by removing ignorance with the traditional method of purifying muddy water in rural India with *Kataka-nut* (power). Just as the power sprinkled on the surface of water drags all the impurities to the bottom, leaving pure water on the surface, constant practice and use of knowledge removes dirt of ignorance.

   Just as the '*Kataka-nut*-power merges into the water after doing its work. Knowledge too disappears after the 'self' emerges.
7. *Freedom from Illusion*: Sankara refers to the illusion created by Oyster shells scattered along the beach in a moonlight night. We mistake them for silver, only till we recognise the reality of the Oyster shells. Similarly, the world of names and forms exist till *self-knowledge* dawns.
8. *Method of Knowing the Nature of Brahma*: According to Sankara, the phenomenal world exists in the mind of the perceiver alone and names and forms are like ornaments and *Vishnu*, the all-pervading consciousness is like the gold. Sankara reinforces the spirit of the *Upanishads* and reiterates the method of arriving at the nature of *Brahma* by practising *neti, neti* - not this, not this.
9. *Meditation*: Sankara declares that meditation is essential to refocus on the 'self'. The flame of knowledge can be kindled only by

constant meditation which he compares with the act of rubbing wood to light fire. Meditation is the friction between the mind-wood and Om-wood pieces.

10. *Wisdom*: Brahma is *Sat-chit-ananda* (Knowledge - existence bliss). Sankara exhorts, "All things, which can be perceived or heard are *Brahma* itself, and nothing else and though *Atma* is reality, it can be perceived by one who has the wisdom".

Evaluation of Sankara's Philosophy

According to Sankara *Brahma* exists in all beings. Therefore, there is no cause of conflict, envy and mutual distrust. *Vedanta* accepts the supremacy of the spiritual values and considers that material objects are subordinate to these. *Vedanta* also preaches that every being has inherent qualities to grow and these must be fully utilised.

Educational Implications of Advaitvad

1. *Principal Aim of Education*: The aim of education is to dispel ignorance or *Maya* and to enable the individual to realise the reality of the *Brahma.* True education is that which enables the individual to perceive the unity of the soul and *Brahma* and man and God.
2. *Nature of Education*: Education is a continuous process.
3. *Development of Spiritual Values*: Education should develop spiritual values.
4. *Methods of Instruction*: These include: (1) Listening to the teacher's lecture, (2) Contemplation (*Manan*), (3) Discussion, (4) Question-answer, (5) Reasoning (*Tark*), (6) Illustration (*Drishtant*), (7) Story-telling.
5. *Teacher-Pupil Relations*: Teacher is the spiritual preceptor. The teacher and the taught should live together. The teacher is expected to guide his student in such a way as to enable him to seek the path of salvation.
6. *Discipline*: The student is expected to exercise control over his senses. He should observe *Brahmacharya* (celibacy). Complete obedience to the teacher should be spontaneous.
7. *Curriculum*: Curriculum should include religious and spiritual subjects.
8. *Value Education*: Value education should find an important place in the curriculum; character building should be stressed. Life of purity and simplicity should be led by the learner or seeker of knowledge and wisdom.

38

Socrates (469-399 B.C.)

Socrates was born at Athens in Greece in 469 B.C. He belonged to a poor family. His mother was a nurse and father a sculptor. He did not receive any systematic education. It is quite surprising that without any systematic education, he became one of the greatest philosophers of the world. For sometime he served in the army. Thereafter he started teaching. He wandered and taught. He did not start any educational institution.

Socrates is known for his wisdom and his method of teaching which was a kind of dialogue with the students.

Socrates committed nothing to writing. Our knowledge of him comes from the accounts of some of his pupils, especially Plato. Aristotle was also his disciple.

Socrates was concerned with probing the meaning and truth of ideas by the technique of 'question and answer'. By doing so, he laid the foundations of systematic philosophical thought.

Socrates called into question the institutions of state. He observed, "A freeman ought to be a freeman in the acquisition of knowledge. Knowledge which is acquired under compulsion has no hold on mind".

Since Socrates' ideas were not in accord with the rulers, they became angry with him. He was charged with corrupting the minds of the youth and condemned to death. He was ordered to take his own life by drinking poison. This was the sad end of Socrates who is still remembered for his wisdom and regarded as one of the greatest philosophers of the world.

Socrates' Philosophy

To Socrates, 'Knowledge is virtue'. The knowledge can be achieved through knowing oneself. So Socrates said, 'Know thyself'.

Socrates made an intensive study of the works of philosophers and scientists to understand the riddles of life. He came to the conclusion, "Love is the hunger of human soul for divine beauty. This beauty is wisdom, virtue, honour, courage, justice and truth. Beauty is truth. And truth is the way that leads directly to God". He further concluded that the way to the real knowledge, *i.e.,* truth, lay through an intensive study of one's self and the mind of man.

Socratic Method of Instruction: Dialectic Method

Socrates devised a method of analysis and questioning, that is called the Socratic method or approach.

Socratic approach involved at first a generalisation from ordinary experiences and then a definition of the essential idea underlying the particular fact.

Socrates explained his ideas through a process of induction, rather by a process of definition or deduction.

Socrates taught in the open and not in a school.

The aim of the Socratic method was to bring the pupil to the point where he would be able to realise his ignorance and thus acquire the attitude of the true learner. As developed by Socrates, this conversation or quiz method, sometimes called the dialectic method has two stages:

1. The ironic or destructive phase in which, by skilful questioning, the pupil is brought from unconscious ignorance to conscious ignorance.
2. The constructive phase in which, by further questioning, the pupil is led from conscious ignorance to clear and rational truth.

Educational Implications of Socrates' Philosophy

The Socratic method has contributed to the teaching methodology in the following manner:

1. It has given us the inductive approach.
2. Right type of questions are very helpful in leading the learners to the desired goals.
3. Quiz technique is the outcome of the Socratic approach.

Limitations of Socratic Approach

There is always a great danger in this method that it is easier for the teacher to employ the ironic part of the Socratic quiz than the constructive phase. Many teachers lack the ability to use a series of question as a method of developing an understanding of a major concept. There is also the danger that the teacher in his zeal to breakdown unconscious ignorance, may employ sarcasm to an unwholesome extent.

Summing up: The Socratic method can be very effective in overcoming common misconceptions and prejudices, provided it leads, as Socrates would have it, to the consciousness of truth and not merely to the consciousness of ignorance.

39

Swami Dayananda (1825-1883)

Swami Dayananda was born in 1825 in a Brahmin family that lived at Tankara in the State of Morvi, Kathiawar in Gujarat. From the very beginning he was seized of the desire to fathom the mysteries of life and death. At the age of 20, he left home and for 15 years, from 1845 to 1860, young Dayananda wandered almost all over India in quest of knowledge and truth. Wherever he met one from whom he could imbibe any knowledge, he sat at his feet. At last he met Swami Virjanand Saraswati, one of the most learned and the noblest of Hindu saints. For two years and a half he waited on Swami Virjanand and learned all that he had to teach. To his master teacher he pledged to devote his life to disseminating truth, to waging unremitting warfare against falsehood and to establish the right method of education. In the first few years of his public life, he held numerous discussions and discourses to which crowds of his countrymen came to hear his outspoken views, his bold utterances and his novel exposition of the Hindu religion. Swami Dayananda's mission was for a reformed Hindu society free from cant and superstition. The first Arya Samaj was established in Bombay in 1875 and two years later in Lahore the Samaj took final shape. The rest of Swami Dayananda's life—1877 to 1883—was spent in preaching, teaching, and writing books and organising Arya Samajs throughout India.

In the Vedas, he sought a solution of the problems of human misery and final salvation. Rabindranath Tagore has paid him a glorious tribute as "the great path maker in northern India, who through bewildering tangles of creed and practice, the dense undergrowth of the degenerated days of our country—cleared a straight path that was meant to lead the Hindus to a simple life of devotion to God and service for man".

Publications

His work (Books and Periodicals) include:

1. *Sandhya* (1863), 2. *Bhagavata—Khandanam* (1864), (3) *Advaitamat—Khandanam* (1870), 4. *Satyarth Prakash* (1875), 5. *Panchama Hayajnavidhi* (1875), 6. *Veda-viruddh mat khan dana* (1875), 7. *Vedantidhwantanivarana* (1875), 8. *Shikshapatridhwantanivarana* (1876), 9. *Aryabhivinaya* (1876), 10. *Sanskarvidhi* (1877), 11. *Rigveda*

dibhashyayabhumika (1878), 12. *Bhrantinivarana* (1877), 13. *Aryoddheshya Ratnamala* (1878), 14. *Vedabhashya* (1877-1881), 15. *Autobiography* (1879), 16. *Gotama—Ahalya Ki Katha* (1879), 17. *Sanskrit Vakya Prabodh* (1880), 18. *Vyavaharabhanu* (1880), 19. *Bhramocchedan* (1880), 20. *Anubhramocchedan* (1880), 21. *Vedangaprakash* (1880-1883), and 22. *Gokarunanidhi* (1881).

Satyarth Prakash

Of all writings of Swami Dayananda, *Satyarth Prakash* is his monumental work, which consists of 14 Chapters:

Chapter 1. Deals with the Vedic concept of God.

Chapter 2. Describes the education of children.

Chapter 3. Outlines his system of education and religious and social observances.

Chapter 4. Discusses the '*varna*' or caste system.

Chapter 5, 6, 7. Contain views on '*ashrams*', government and theology.

Chapter 8. Deals with the theory of creation.

Chapter 9. Explains the knowledge, ignorance and salvation.

Chapter 10. Outlines the rules of conduct.

Chapter 11, 12, 13, 14. Contain a critical commentaries on other religious systems in India.

Philosophical Basis of Swami Dayananda

Back to the Vedas: Swami Dayananda, the founder of Arya Samaj, believes that the time-old wisdom contained in the Vedas holds the key to all our social and religious problems. His interpretation of the Vedas has brought a new vista of knowledge in the sphere of social reform and educational reconstruction. According to Swami Dayananda, the Vedas contain the truth of science as well as the truth of religion. He was convinced that the Vedas contain other truths of science, which the modern world does not possess at all. The echoes of the Vedic past reverberate in his educational discussion and thinking. He observed: "My conception of God and all other objects in the universe is founded on the teachings of the Vedas and other *Shastras* (Scriptures) and is in conformity with the beliefs in all ages from Buddha down to Jaimini. That alone I hold to be acceptable which is worthy of being believed by all men in all ages". From where should men derive courage and inspiration to attain the ideals of their lives? From the Vedas is the answer. Swami Dayananda believed that the most wonderful truths confined in these books must be brought out and scattered and broadcast all over the world. Vedas are the great mine of knowledge, wisdom and strength. Therein lies the strength to vivify and invigorate the whole world.

Staunch Devotee of Truth: "You would spread truth even at the cost of your life". This was the sermon given to Dayananda by his guru, the blind Sanyasi, Swami Virjanand, at Mathura in 1862, when the former sought leave of his teacher after completing his study of the Vedas. This simple-seeming parting advice was so wrought with deep meaning that for the next twenty years Dayananda had no rest and he waged war against falsehood and attacked every haunt of evil in society. Truth was the very breath of his life. No temptation could turn him away from truth. In his crusade for truth he remained relentless.

Swami Dayananda was a seeker after truth. His life was a vindication of truth. What a great significance he had accorded to truth in his life, and this line of action is mirrored well in the brief, but clear, pronouncements he had made in his *magnum opus Satyarth Prakash* (Light of Truth) and in his other works. He writes:

"My chief aim in writing this book is to unfold truth".

"To speak, write about and believe in a thing as it is, constitutes truth".

"I have expounded truth as truth and error as error. The exposition of error in place of truth and of truth in place of error does not constitute the unfolding of truth".

"He that is prejudiced tries to prove that even his error is truth, while the truth of his religious opponent is error. He cannot, therefore, know what the true religion is. Hence it is the bounden duty of truthful and learned men to unfold the right nature of truth and error before all men in their writings and speeches. It is not our object to hurt anybody's susceptibilities or to injure anyone. On the other hand, our aim is to further the progress and advance the well being of mankind, to help (all) men in the ascertainment of what is right and to enable them to accept truth, reject falsehood. In our opinion there is no other way of elevating human race".

Describing the sole aim of his life, Swamiji wrote: "The sole aim of my life, which I have also tried to achieve, is to help to put an end to the mutual wranglings, preach universal truth, bring all men into the fold of one religion whereby they may cease to hate each other and instead, may firmly love one another, live in peace and work for their common weal. May this doctrine, through the grace and help of God and with the support of all truthful, honest and learned men, who are devoted to the cause of humanity "Aptas" reach every nook and corner of this earth so that all may acquire righteousness and wealth, gratify legitimate desires and attain salvation and thereby elevate themselves and live in happiness. This alone is the chief object of my life".

Conception of Religion: Dayananda wrote: "I have not the least idea of founding a new religion or sect. My sole aim is to believe in truth and help others to do the same. Had I been prejudiced I would have championed the cause of any one of the religions of India. But I have not done so. On the contrary, I do not approve of what is objectionable and false in the institution of this or any other country, nor do I reject what is good and in consonance with true religion, nor have I any desire to do so, because a contrary conduct is not at all worthy of men".

His conception of '*dharma*' was very sublime. He says: "I believe in a religion based on universal and all-embracing principles which have always been accepted as true by mankind and will continue to command the allegiance of mankind in the ages to come. Hence it is that the religion in question is called the primeval Eternal Religion, which means that it is above the hostility of all human creeds whatsoever. Whatever is believed in by those who are steeped in ignorance or have been led astray by sectarians is not worthy of being accepted by the wise. That faith alone is really true and worthy of acceptance which is followed by "*Aptas*", *i.e.*, those who are true in word, deed and thought promote public good and are impartial and learned, but all that is discarded by such men must be considered as unworthy of belief and false."

Swami Dayananda Saraswati did not invent a new religion or creed, nor did he propound new dogmas or doctrines. He simply chopped off the deadwood and cleared the overgrowth that original Vedic religion was overlaid with. He exposed empty ritualism and assailed sacerdotal priest craft that had obscured the grand philosophical insights of the *Upanishads*. He recalled and expounded the amplitude of such *Upanishadic* aphorisms like "*Ekam sad viprah bahudha vadanti*" (God is one, but the wise call him by different names) and "*Ekameva advitiyam, aprameyam*" (God is one and only one, unique and limitless) and propagated the view that long-established Brahminical practices of the "*Karmakanda*" (ritualism) of the Veda, "*moortipooja*" (idol worship) and "*avatarvad*" (theory of incarnation) are not the essence of Hinduism.

Aims of Education: Character Formation—Control of Senses

Swami Dayananda believed that true education should build up character so that man may always walk in the path of righteousness. Character or righteous living is the highest virtue. This is the be-all and end-all of all reading and reciting, teaching and preaching. Character formation takes place through the control of senses. Dayananda observed: "As a skilful driver keeps the horses under his control, even so should a wise man keep his senses—which tend to lead both mind and soul into pursuits of undesirable objects—under his complete control. Truly, that map alone can achieve his heart's desire who is master of his senses, but he, who becomes their slave soon loses his character". A man of low character will never succeed in acquiring knowledge. A man of character keeps up his vows of celibacy and truthfulness, fulfills his duties towards man and God, keeps control over his passions and desires, remains steadfast in his devotion to truth and righteousness and performs good work. He who has a sweet and amiable temper serves others with his heart, continually grows in knowledge, reputation and strength and enjoys a long life. A man of character has no malice words any living soul and shows all men the path hat leads to happiness. His speech is sweet and kind. He is truthful in word, leed and thought.

Right Conduct of Life

It behoves all—*Brahmacharis*, *Grihasthis*, *Vanaprasthis* and *Sanyasis*—to follow assiduously the right conduct of life, which has ten chief characteristics:

1. The cultivation of firmness of mind and contentment.
2. The cultivation of the spirit of forgiveness under all circumstances—whether one be censured or praised, honoured or dishonoured etc.
3. Devotion of mind to virtue and abstinence from sin and vice, that is, refraining from the entertainment of sinful thoughts even for one moment.
4. The acquisition of a thing without the permission of its owner, or through fraud, hypocrisy, or breach of faith, or by teaching falsely, or in any other way that is condemned by the Vedas, is called dishonesty or theft; the reverse of it is called honesty.
5. Mental purity consists in freedom from inordinate love or hatred, from prejudice or injustice, etc. Bodily cleanliness consists in keeping the body clean with water, earth, etc.
6. Direction of the senses in the path of rectitude, and freedom from sin.
7. Development of one's intellect by abstaining from intoxicants and other articles that are prejudicial to its growth, from the company of the wicked, from sloth, negligence, etc., and by using things possessing healthful properties, associating with men of noble character, and by the practice of yoga.
8. The acquisition of correct knowledge of all things.
9. Truthfulness in the harmony of thought, word and deed.
10. Freedom from wrath and other evil habits, and the cultivation of calmness of mind and other good qualities.

Mother, Father, Teacher—Three Great Tutors

That man alone can become a great scholar who has had the advantage of three good tutors, *viz.*, father, mother and teacher. Blessed is the family and most fortunate is the child whose parents be godly and learned. The mother's influence on the education of children surpasses that of everyone else. He alone is said to have a mother whose mother is devout and learned. Blessed is the mother who never ceases to impart a religious tone to the mind of her child from the time of conception till his knowledge is perfected.

Education of the Child Starts even before Birth—'*Sanskars*'

It behoves both parents, before, during and after conception to avoid the use of such foods and drinks as are intoxicating, decomposed (foul smelling), non nutritious (dry) and prejudicial to the growth of intellect; and to use those articles that are productive of mental-tranquillity, health, strength, intellect, energy, and good temper—qualities that go to make a man refined. Such foods are milk, butter, sugar, cereals, etc., that help to make the reproductive element (both male and female) of the highest quality, free from all faults and imperfections.

Concept of Discipline

Those children alone become well-behaved, refined and scholarly, whose parents do not indulge them; but on the other hand, always reprimand them when necessary. Those parents and tutors who are not slow to reprimand their children and pupils (when needed) are as if giving them a drink of immortality; but those who indulge them are in fact, giving poison, and are thus the cause of their ruin because indulgence spoils children, whilst reprehension develops good qualities in them. Children should also feel pleased when reprimanded and feel uneasy when fondled. But parents and teachers should never reprimand them out of malice or spite, outwardly they should keep them in awe whilst inwardly they should be tender-hearted and kind to them. Likewise, they should advise them to abstain from stealing, committing adultery, contracting habits of indolence, arrogance, drunkenness, untruthfulness, malevolence, wickedness, malice, jealousy, blind-passion, and to cultivate good qualities such as, truthfulness, virtue.

Noble Examples to be Set

A broken pledge injures a man's character more than anything else. Therefore, once you make a promise, keep it; for example, you say to a man: "I will meet you at such and such a place and time", or "I will give you such and such a thing, at such and such a time. Then always keep your promise; otherwise, no one will ever trust you. All should, therefore, speak the truth and keep their word. One should never be vain. Deceitfulness, hypocrisy, and ingratitude are painful even to the soul that harbours them. It is hypocrisy to believe one thing and say another, and thus mislead people in order to gain selfish ends. Ingratitude is that condition of mind in which you do not feel thankful to one who has been good to you.

Education of Women

Though Swami Dayananda encouraged education of women and certain amount of freedom allied to it, he did not favour co-education. "As soon as they are eight years old", says Swami Dayananda "girls should be sent to girls' schools and boys to boys' schools". Thus even at the primary stage boys and girls will begin to have separate schools. "The place of study should be secluded and girls' and boys' schools should be two '*kosas*' (about 4 miles) apart. The teachers, servants and menials should all be females in girls' schools and males in boys' schools. No boy of five years of age should be allowed an entry into a girls' school, nor a girl of that age into a boys' school".

Compulsory Education

Swami Dayananda advocated that 'state should make it compulsory on all to send their children of both sexes to school at the said period and keep them there till they are thoroughly educated. It should be made a penal offence to break this law. In other words, let no child, whether a girl or a boy be allowed to stay in the house after the 8th year".

Education of the Masses

Swami Dayananda advocated that all persons of all classes should be given good and sound education and be well instructed in the principles of true religion, When all the classes are well educated and cultured, no one can set up any false, fraudulent and irreligious practices.

Physical Education

Swami Dayananda believed: "By the increase of bodily strength and activity, the intellect becomes so subtle that it can easily grasp the most abstruse and profound subject. It also helps to preserve and perfect the reproductive element in the human body, which, in turn, produces self-control, firmness of mind, strength, energy and acuteness of intellect". Swami Dayananda recommended '*pranayama*' for girls as well as boys.

Education for National Integration

Swami Dayananda realised that the greatest need of the country was national integration. He lamented that people should quarrel among themselves on matters of language, culture and customs. "It is very hard to shake off linguistic differences, cultural angularities and estrangement due to customs and manners. Unless it is done, it is difficult to derive the fullest benefit and achieve the goal in view.

Education for International Understanding

Not only national unity but also international understanding was in the mind of Swami Dayananda. He had no place for narrow loyalties. He regarded the entire people as united in the bonds of common brotherhood. He taught mankind to rise above petty individualism and to see the good of oneself in the good of all. "May we look with friendliness", says one of the verses of the Vedas, "on all living beings and may they all look upon us with friendliness"—so felt Swami Dayananda. He would like his countrymen to go on foreign travels and break their insular habits of keeping to their village or town. "If our actions are good there is no harm in going to foreign lands". He describes the advantages of foreign travel. "The bogey of untouchability and loss of religion current in these days is due to misrepresentation and ignorance. Those people who do not hesitate to go to other countries, come in contact with various people, know their customs and manners, expand their kingdom and business, acquire boldness, imbibe their merits, shake off their weaknesses and thus become powerful". Travel helps us not only to understand other people with different religion, language, custom and pattern of living but it also engenders courage and confidence within ourselves.

The Scheme of Studies

He visualised the following scheme of studies for about twenty years:

1. *Phonetics*. First of all comes Phonetics (*Shiksha*) by Panini. Parents and teachers should teach their children and pupils how to pronounce different letters in their right places, with the right amount of effort and the right accent.
2. *Grammar*. It includes *Ashtadhyayi*, *Dhatupath* (Book of Roots), *Ganapath* (Book of Groups), *Unadikosh* (Book of Prefixes and Suffixes etc). Last of all comes *Mahabhashya* (Exposition of the above four books of Panini by Patanjali).

   If the teachers and their scholars be intelligent, energetic, honest and extremely anxious to advance their knowledge, the pupils can master the Science of Grammar in three years, and thus become profound grammarians thoroughly acquainted with the construction of every word—Vedic or *Laukika* (*i.e.*, of ordinary Sanskrit literature). Other sciences are easier to learn. The amount of labour that is required to master any other subject; and the amount of knowledge acquired by the study of the above books on Grammar in three years cannot be gained by the study of such books as *Sarswata*, *Chandrika*, *Kaumidi*, and *Mansorma*, in fifty years. Because the great sages have expounded the most abstruse subjects in their books in such an easy way that it is entirely impossible for little men to approach it. The aim of those great souls in writing their books was to make the subjects so easy as to be readily grasped in the shortest possible time; whilst the object of little minds has always been to clothe their subject with such a difficult round-about style as would necessitate great labour and waste of time on the part of the students to comprehend it, whilst he would profit but very little. We can liken this to digging up a whole mountain and finding a penny—worth of gold; whilst the study of the books of the great sages can be well likened to the diving of a man into the sea and finding most valuable pearls in one plunge.

3. *Nighantu and Nirukta* (Books on Vedic Vocabulary and Philology by Yask). These should be read in six to eight months, but students should not waste years of their valuable time over '*Amarkosha*' and other such books written by atheists.
4. *Chhandograntha* (Prosody by Pingal). Thereafter this book should be studied by the students so that they may thoroughly master the rules that govern poetry—Vedic and otherwise, and be able to compose poems of their own. This can be done in four months. They should not waste their time over *Vritratnakar* and similar books written by mean scholars.
5. *Manu Smriti*: *Valmiki Ramayana, Vidurniti*, and other selections from *Mahabharata*. The tutor should teach these as poetry ought to be taught. The study of these books tends to eradicate evil habits and brings culture. It should not take the students more than a year to finish them.
6. *Six Shastras* (erroneously called six schools of Philosophy) with the expositions of *Rishis*—the enlightened great souls, the true seers of nature—as far as possible, or in the absence of these, with the help of true commentaries of other honest scholars. But before taking up *Vedanic Shastra* they should learn the ten *Upanishada*. All these books should be finished in two years.
7. *Four Vedas* with their four Brahmanas with proper accent, meanings, theoretically as well as practically. These should be studied in six years.
8. *Upvedas*. After the study of the *Vedas* they should learn the *Upvedas* (or *sub-Vedas*) which are four in number:—
   (i) *Ayurveda* (Medical Science). Herein are included the works of Charak and Sushrut, and other sages. They should learn both theory and practice, including Medicines, Therapeutics, Materia Medica, Physiology and Pathology, Hygiene with Dietetics and Climatology and the sciences of Temperaments, Anatomy and Surgery with the proper use of instruments in different operations, etc., in four years.
   (ii) *Science of Government* (*Dhanur Veda*): It consists of two parts—Civil and Military.
   Civil part is the art of governing people, protecting their lives and property, developing the wealth and resources of the country, making the people happy and contented by the right administration of justice, protecting the good and punishing the wicked etc.
   Military part comprises organisation of the army, use of fire arms and the knowledge of different kinds of drills, tactics and strategy, etc. They should learn both branches of the science of Government in two years.

(iii) *Science of Music* (*Gandharva Veda*). They should learn all the different parts of music, such as tunes, modes, modifications of modes, times, harmony, refrain. They should also learn singing, playing and dancing, etc., properly but chiefly singing and playing of the *Sama Veda Mantras* on musical instruments. But they should never sing amorous songs like Nauch-girls nor bray like sensual 'vairages'.

The books on this subject are *Narad Sanhita*, etc., composed by *Rishis*.

(iv) *Artha Veda* (Science and Practice of Mechanical Arts) is also called *shilpa vidya*. They should study the laws of matter and motion. They should also know how to make various kinds of machines etc.

In short, they should learn theoretically and practically, the nature and properties of all substances from solids to *Akasha*. This is the science that helps to increase the wealth and prosperity of a country:

Thereafter, they should thoroughly study *Jyotisha Shastra*—which includes Arithmetic, Algebra, Geometry, Geography, practical training in these sciences, learn the proper handling of instruments, master their mechanism and know how to use them. But they should regard Astrology which traces influence of stars and constellations on the destinies of man, auspiciousness of time, of horoscopes, etc., as a fraud and never learn or teach any book on this subject.

Both the teachers and their scholars should so endeavour as to be able to master all the sciences and arts, and become highly cultured in twenty one years, and thus accomplish the object of their lives and live in happiness.

The knowledge that can be acquired by following the aforesaid scheme in twenty or twenty-one years, cannot be gained in any other way even in one hundred years.

How to Arrive at Truth—Five Tests

The truth of everything that is learnt or taught should be carefully examined by the following five tests:

(i) *The Veda and nature of God*. All that conforms to the teachings of the Vedas, nature and attributes and characteristics of God is right, the reverse is wrong.

(ii) *Laws of nature*. All that tallies with the law of nature is true, the reverse untrue, e.g., the statement that a child is born without the sexual union of its parents, being opposed to the laws of nature, can never be true.

(iii) *The practice and teaching of Aptas, i.e.*, pious truthful, unprejudiced, honest and learned men. All that is unopposed to their practice and teaching is acceptable, and the reverse is unacceptable.

(iv) *The purity and conviction of one's own soul*—What is good for you, is good for the world; what is painful to you, is painful to others. This ought to be the guiding principle of one's conduct towards others.

(v) *Eight kinds of evidence, viz*., 1. Direct Cognisance, 2. Inference, 3. Analogy, 4. Testimony, 5. History, 6. Deduction, 7. Possibility, and 8. Non-existence or Negation.

1. *Direct cognisance* (*Pratyaksha*) is that knowledge which is the result of direct contact of the five senses with their objects of the mind (faculty or organ of attention) with the senses and of the soul with the mind.

2. *Inference* (*Anumona*). Literally it means that which follows direct cognisance.

The two have been observed to exist together at some time and place, when on some other occasion, one of the two is observed, the other, *i.e.*, the unknown, can be inferred.

It is not true that wherever there is no fall in barometer although the pressure may have been decreased. The mercury, through rise of temperature, expands and becomes lighter. Had the same pressure continued the column of mercury would have risen higher up, but the fall of pressure compensated for the rise and the lift of the mercury apparently where it was. The three canons of *Kashyap*, therefore, conclusively proved that the fall of barometer is not the linga of the decrease of the pressure. Similar reasoning will show that the decrease in the weight of the super incumbent column of mercury is the *linga* (inference) of the decrease of pressure.

Inference is of three kinds:

(a) '*Purvavat*' is one, in which you reason from cause to effect, e.g., of inference of coming rain from the sight of clouds; or, again, you see a wedding, you naturally infer that some day the wedded couple will have children. Or, again, you see students engaged in the pursuit of knowledge, and you infer that some day they will become men of learning.

(b) '*Sheshavat*' inference is one, in which you reason from effect to causes

Examples: You see a flood in the river, and infer that it must have rained on the mountain from which the river issues. Again, you see a child, you at once infer that the child must have had a father. Again you see this world and infer the existence of the spiritual cause—the elementary matter. Or, again, take another example. When you see a man in pleasure or pain, you at once infer that he must have done a virtuous or sinful deed before, since you have noticed that the consequence of a sinful act is pain, and that of a virtuous deed, pleasure.

(c) *Samanyatodrisha* is that kind of inference in which there is no relation of cause and effect between the known datum and the thing to be inferred, but there is some kind of similarity between the two; for example you know that no one can get to another place without moving from the first and hence if you find a person in a certain place, you can easily infer that he must have come to the latter place by moving from the first.

3. '*Upamana*' (Analogy) is the knowledge of a thing from its likeness to another. The thing which is required to be known is called '*Sadhya*', and that which becomes the means of this knowledge from one kind of likeness between the two is called '*Sadhna*'.

Example: A man says to his servant: "Go and fetch Vishnu Mitra". The latter answers that he does not know him, as he had never seen him before. Thereupon the master says, "you know Deva Datta, don't you? Upon the servant's answering in the affirmative his master continues "well, Vishnu Mitra is just like Deva Datta". So the servant went out to find Vishnu Mitra. As he was passing through a street, he saw a man very much like Deva Datta, and thought that man must be Vishnu Mitra, and forthwith brought him to his master. Or, take another example, you want to know what a Yak is. Well someone tells you, it is just like an ox. Next time you go to a jungle, you happen to see an animal very much like an ox, you at once know that it is the Yak, you asked your friend about. Now this kind of knowledge, *i.e.*, knowledge of Vishnu Mitra, from his likeness to Deva Datta, and the Yak from its likeness to an ox is called *Upamana* or knowledge by Analogy. The words Vishnu Mitra and Yak are called *Sadhya* whilst Deva Datta and ox *Sadhana*, in the above two instances.

4. *Shabda* (Testimony, literally word): The word of an *Apt* is called *Shabda*.

An *Apt* is a person who is a thorough scholar, well-versed in all the sciences and philosophies, physical and spiritual, is virtuous, truthful, active, free from passions and desires, imbued with love for others, and who is an altruistic teacher of humanity, solely actuated with the desire of benefiting the world by his knowledge, experience and convictions: God being the truest and greatest of all *Aptas*, His word the Veda, is also included in *Shabda* (Testimony).

5. *Itihas* is that which tells us that such a person was so and so, he did such and such a thing. In other words, *itihas* is the history of a country or the biography of a person. (The experience of the past recorded in history can be applied to solve many a difficult question of the day).

6. *Arthapatti* (Conclusion or Deduction): It is a conclusion which naturally follows from the statement of a fact; for instance, one says to another: "Rain falls from clouds" or "an effect follows a cause". The natural conclusion that can be drawn from the above statement is "There can be no rain when there are no clouds", or "no effect follows, when a cause does not exist".

7. *Sambhava* (Possibility): When you hear a thing, the first thing that enters your mind is whether such and such a thing is possible. Anything that runs counter to the laws of nature is not possible, and hence it can never be true; for example, if you are told that a child was born without parents, such and such a person raised the dead to life again, or made stones float on the sea, lifted mountains, broke the moon into pieces, was god incarnate, or saw

horns on the head of a man, or married a couple born of sterile mothers. You could at once know that it could not have possibly happened, being opposed to the laws of Nature. That alone is possible which is in conformity with the laws of Nature.

8. *Abhava* (Absence or Negation): You infer the existence of a thing in some other place from its absence from the place where you were told you would find it; for instance, a gentleman said to his man: "Go and bring the elephant from the elephant house". He went there but found that the elephant was not there. He naturally concluded that he must be somewhere near about. So he went out and looked about for the elephant and found him not very far from its proper place and brought him to his master.

These eight kinds of evidence have been briefly described. Their number can be reduced to four if History be included under Testimony, and Deduction, Possibility and Negation under Inference.

Six Kinds of Inferential Knowledge

There are six kinds of inferential knowledge, *i.e.*, knowledge derived from the relation of sign with the object signified:

1. That in which we proceed from causes to effects.

Example. A man at a distance sees a man, claps his hands; he at once infers that sound will be produced.

2. That in which we proceed from effects to causes.

Example. A person hears the sound (peculiar to the clapping of hands), he at once infers that there has been clapping of hand close by.

3. *Samyogi*. (Concurrent). Knowledge is that which is obtained from the concurrence of one thing with another.

Example. The mention of the word body at once suggests the existence of skin along with it.

4. *Samvayi*. (Inherent). Knowledge is that which is obtained from the inference of something (*i.e.*, an attribute substance or an action) in another.

Example. We know Extension inheres in Ether, therefore, from the mere mention of the word ether, extension is at once inferred.

5. *Ekartha Samyayi*. (Knowledge). When two things (such as attributes) reside in substances, the knowledge of one at once suggests the other. This kind of inferential knowledge is called '*Ekartha Samvayi*'.

Example: We see the orange colour of an orange and at once infer that it must be smooth to touch or sweet in taste.

6. *Virodhi*. (Antithetic). Knowledge is that which is gained from the natural opposition of ideas of things.

Example: White colour suggests black colour; sweet taste suggests bitter taste; hissing of a snake at once suggests that its natural foe, such as a mongoose, must be close by.

Summary of the Teachings of Swami Dayananda

Teachings of Swami Dayananda may be summed up in the following ten principles which are of great educational value. These principles sum up his philosophy which should guide every individual in his daily life.

1. God is the primary source of all true knowledge and of all that is known by its means.
2. God is Existent, Conscious, All-beatitude, Formless, Almighty, Just, Merciful, Unbegotten, Infinite, Unchangeable, Beginningless, Incomparable, the support of all, the lord of all, all pervading, Omniscient and Controller of all from within, Evermature, Imperishable, Fearless, Eternal and Creator of the Universe. To him alone is worship due.
3. The Vedas are the scriptures of all true knowledge. It is the paramount duty of all *Aryas* to read them, to teach them (to others) and to hear them read, to recite them (to others).
4. All persons should be ever ready to accept truth and renounce untruth.
5. All facts ought to be performed, in conformity to *Dharma*, *i.e.*, after due consideration of right and wrong.
6. The prime object is to do good to the world, *i.e.*, to ameliorate physical, spiritual and social conditions of all men.
7. All ought to be treated with love, justice, righteousness and due regard to their merits.
8. Ignorance ought to be dispelled and knowledge disseminated.
9. No one should remain content with his own well-being but on the contrary he should regard his well-being lying in the well-being of others.
10. In matters affecting well-being of the society (all others), individual should subordinate his personal likings, in matters affecting him alone, he is to enjoy the freedom of action.

Contribution of Dayananda

a. Swami Dayananda took upon himself to bring to the world the truth contained in the *Vedas*. He wrote commentaries noted for their lucidness and authenticity. He regarded the *Vedas* as the source of all true knowledge.

b. Swami Dayananda declared that women were entitled to social and legal rights at par with men. He championed the cause of their education, their right to study the *Vedas*. He brought them out from the seclusion of the '*purdah*' and held them in great esteem.

c. He categorically condemned the caste system based on birth. He exhorted people to uproot it as it has no sanction of the *Vedas* and is harmful. He declared that the social status of a man should be determined on the basis of his attainments and performance. As a consequence of this teaching, inter-dining and inter-caste marriages among the Hindus came into vogue.

d. He directed people to revive the *Gurukula* system of education based on self-discipline. This was his significant contribution to national education. *Gurukula* Kangri was the first and the foremost experiment in this direction where children from all classes and walks of life lived and studied together undergoing a rigorous discipline.

e. As a protagonist of Hindi and Sanskrit his achievements were notable. He proclaimed that Hindi could and should be the *lingua franca* of India as well as the basic link for national integration.

Evaluation of the Work of Dayananda

Rabindranath Tagore has paid his homage in these words:

"I offer my homage of veneration to Swami Dayananda, the great Pathmaker who through bewildering angles of creeds and practices, the dense undergrowth of the degenerate days of our counting, cleared a straight path that was meant to lead the Hindus to a simple and rational life of devotion to God and service for man".

"My reverence to the great teacher Dayananda, whose vision found unity and truth in India's spiritual history, whose mind luminously comprehended all departments of India's life; whose call to India is the call of awakening to truth and purity".

A French scholar Romain Rolland has paid the following tribute to Swami Dayananda:

"Dayananda transferred into the lifeless body of India, his formidable energy, his certainty, his lion's blood".

"Dayananda would not tolerate the abominable injustice of untouchables and nobody has been a more ardent champion on their rights".

"Dayananda was no less generous and no less bold in his crusade to improve the condition of women, a deplorable one in India. He was one of the most decent prophets of reconstruction and of national organisation".

Dr. Radhakrishnan assigns Swami Dayananda 'the chief place among the makers of modern India'. He has observed "At a time when there was spiritual confusion in our country, when many of our social practices were in the melting pot, when we were overcome by superstition and obscurantism, this great soul came forward with staunch devotion to truth and a passion for social equality and enthusiasm, and worked for the emancipation of our country".

About the work of Dayananda, Sir Jadunath Sarkar says: "He is a true statesman who can legislate for the future, who can set a force at work which will go on influencing the lives and thoughts of unborn generations. When the history of India's growth comes to be written, that high rank will be adjudged to the 'naked *faquir*' Dayananda Saraswati. He rescued the heart of Hinduism from atrophy; he linked it with the spirit of eternal progression ruling the outer world; he proved that whatever is best and truest in the legacy of ancient ages of *Aryavarta* is a possession open to the entire human race and not confined to any twice-born caste or the sacred soil.

Romain Rolland says, "This man (Dayananda) with the nature of a lion is one of those whom Europe is too apt to forget when she judges India. He was that rare combination, a thinker of action with a genius for leadership. He was the hero of the *Iliad* or the *Gita* with the athletic strength of a Hercules, who thundered against all forms of thought other than his own, the only true one. He was so successful, that in five years Northern India was completely changed."

After comparing Dayananda with other reformers like Ranade, Vivekanand etc., Sri Aurobindo says, "Very different was the manner of the working of Dayananda... Here was one who knew definitely and clearly the work he was sent to do, chose his materials, determined his conditions with a sovereign clairvoyance of the spirit and executed his conception with a mastery of the born worker.

"As I regarded the figure of this formidable artisan in God's workshop, images crowd on me which are all of battle and work and conquest and triumphant labour. Here, I say to myself, was the very soldier of Light, a warrior in God's world, a sculptor of men and institution, a bold and rugged victor of difficulties. And the whole sums itself upon me in a powerful impression of spiritual practicality".

T.L. Vaswani writes: "Not many in India today seem to be aware of Rishi Dayananda's achievements. He found the people forgetful of their ancient heritage. He found scepticism among the educated and superstition among the masses. He found nationwide ignorance of the *Aryan* ideal. And he moved from place to place with the healing message of the seers and the sages of India. His lectures arrested attention. They were a challenge at once to Hindu ecclesiasticism and western externalism. He held high the torch of the ancient wisdom at a time when India's millions wandered in the night. Rishi Dayananda will attract attention in the coming days. His life and message have a world value". Again: "Rishi Dayananda was tremendously real. Therefore, I feel drawn to him. Dayananda was an inspirer of his race, a nation builder, a preacher of the ancient ideal. Therefore, I offer him the homage of my heart. Dayananda was a *Tapasvin* (ascetic), a *Balbrahmachari*. Therefore, I bow to him in affectionate reverence".

Justice Ranade wrote about him on the occasion of his death: "Religious fervour, ... a daring and adventurous spirit born of a confidence that a higher power than man's protected him and his work, the magnetism of superior genius ... a rare insight into the needs of the times and a steadfastness of purpose which no adverse turn of fortune could conquer, a readiness and resourcefulness rarely met with, ... true patriotism which was far in advance of the times, and a sense of justice tempered with mercy—these were the sources of strength which enabled him to organise a great movement like the Arya Samaj".

C.F. Andrew says, "For Dayananda's personality and character there may well be almost unqualified admiration. He was a puritan to the backbone, and lived up to his creed. He was a fighter, strong, virile, independent, if somewhat imperious in behaviour... His courage in facing his own countrymen through years of contumely and persecution was nothing less than heroic. He was a passionate lover of truth".

Madame Blavasky writes, "It is perfectly certain that India never saw a more learned Sanskrit scholar, a deeper metaphysician, a more wonderful orator, and a more fearless denunciator of any evil, than Dayananda, since the time of Sankarachary".

Colonel H.S. Olcott, President of the Theosophical Society, wrote about Dayananda on his death, "A master spirit has passed away from India. Pandit Dayananda Saraswati ... is gone, the irresponsible, energetic reformer, whose mighty voice and passionate eloquence for the last few years raised thousands of people in India from lethargic indifference and stupor into active patriotism, is no more".

"*Do mortuis nil nisi bonum*. All our differences have been burnt with the body... We remember only the grand virtues and noble qualities of our former colleague and teacher, and late antagonist. We bear in mind but his life-long devotion to the cause of Aryan regeneration, his ardent love for the grand philosophy of his forefathers, his relentless, untiring zeal in the work of the projected social and religious reforms, and it is with unfeigned sorrow that we now hasten to join the ranks of his many mourners. In him, India has lost one of her noblest sons. A patriot in the true sense of the word, Swami Dayananda laboured from his earliest years for the recovery of the lost treasure of Indian intellect. His zeal for the Reformation of his motherland was exceeded only by his undoubted learning. There can be but one opinion as to his knowledge of Sanskrit, and the impetus to the study of both received at his hand. There are few towns and but one province we believe, namely, Madras—that Pandit Dayananda did not visit in furtherance of his missionary work, and fewer still where he has not left the impress of his remarkable mind behind him. He regenerated Hinduism, and fired with love for the teachings of the *Rishis* and *Vedic* learning the hearts of all who were drawn within the influence of his eloquent oratory. Certainly, there was no better or greater orator in Hindi and Sanskrit than Dayananda throughout the length and breadth of this land".

Dayananda a Precursor of Gandhiji. Dr. V.D. Mahajan has observed that in a way Dayananda can be called a 'precursor of Gandhiji'. There is a similarity between the two in many things. Gandhiji carried forward the movements started by Dayananda. In the matter of advocating Hindi as the national language, Dayananda went even further than Gandhiji. Whereas Gandhiji continued to use Gujarati both in speech and writing with his

Gujarati relatives and friends, Dayananda gave up the use of Gujarati altogether and carried on all his activities through Hindi. Both of them were lovers of *Ahimsa*. Gandhiji disregarded violence in all fields, including political; Dayananda recognised the principle of *Ahimsa* as taught by the Indian seers who did not condemn violence outright in all circumstances. Both Gandhiji and Dayananda stood for social reform as a prerequisite for political reform. Both of them were advocates of purity of character. Whereas Gandhiji devoted himself clearly to the liberation of his country from the foreign yoke, Dayananda put all his energy to liberate the people from all sorts of superstition and ignorance. By doing so, Dayananda tried to make them physically, intellectually, spiritually strong and thereby enabled them to achieve political independence. In a way, Dayananda prepared the ground for Gandhiji. If Gandhiji is called the father of the nation, Dayananda can be called "the grandfather of the nation".

Philosophy of Action

After centuries, the people heard in the Hindu society that all were equal; that even the non-Hindus had the right to study the *Vedas*; that all had the right to receive education. The mist of spirits, ghosts and incantations began to clear up. He preached that the amulets, the rosary, the images, the rituals would not help. Only good actions and pure and sound thinking were the remedies. Everything must relate to logic.

In Swami Dayananda Saraswati, spiritualism assumed its most practical form. Through him the philosophy of a nation became related to action. A rich past was awakened to fashion anew the temple of society. A reformed nation became fit and confident to wage and win the battle for freedom.

There is no doubt that Swami Dayananda was a pioneer in social and educational reforms in India.

Legacy of Swami Dayananda

The force of his logic, the power of his oration, the depth of his scholarship, the dazzle of his intellect, the sincerity of his purpose, the overpowering personality, his profound mastery over the language and above all his simplicity and noble life attracted a band of devoted workers and promoted his teachings.

The Arya Samaj founded by him has been doing a very useful work in the field of education.

On June 1, 1886, the followers of Swami Dayananda founded the D.A.V. School, Lahore, in his memory. At present there is a long chain of D.A.V. (Dayanand Anglo-Vedic) educational institutions spanning the country.

Swami Shraddhananda (1857-1926), a devoted follower of Swami Dayananda, chose to establish a *Gurukula*, patterned on the system of *Ashrams* near Haridwar. Now about hundred *Gurukulas*, separate for boys and girls are dotted all over the country.

40

Swami Vivekananda (1863-1902)

Early Life: Vivekananda's original name was Narendranath Dutt. He acquired the new name in 1886 when he took '*Sanyasa*'.

He was born in Calcutta in 1863. His father was a practicing lawyer at Calcutta High Court. Under the influence of his mother he made a deep study of Hindu scriptures. At college he was adept in boxing, riding, swimming and wrestling. He was an ardent student of philosophy and poetry. He graduated with honours from Calcutta University.

Education: He had an excellent command over Bengali, English and Sanskrit. He was a voracious reader and had a sharp memory. He could often display a verbatim familiarity with the *Encyclopaedia Britannica*. His principal Rev. W.W. Hastie once remarked, "Narendranath is really a genius. I have travelled far and wide but I have never yet come across a lad of his talents and possibilities, even in German Universities, among philosophical students".

Meeting with Shri Ramakrishna—A Turning Point in Life

He was deeply interested in the study of philosophy and religion. For sometime he was a classroom teacher also. His search for truth led him to Ramakrishna Paramhansa, at Dakshineswar in 1882. Though not literate, Swami Ramakrishna was an enlightened soul. During the next six years of his association with the master, he had a spiritual transformation and emerged as Swami Vivekananda. He left home and travelled all over India. His wandering left him deeply affected by the despair and poverty of the masses of India.

Swami Vivekananda organised the Ramakrishna Mission in 1886, after the passing away of his master.

In 1888, 2 years after his master's death, he set out to the Himalayas. He wandered for 2 years through deserts and forests. In Kanyakumari, after worshipping in the temple, Vivekananda sat on a rock, and meditated for sometime. He went to America in 1893.

Soul-stirring Address at the World Parliament of Religions at Chicago (USA) in 1893: On September 11, 1893, on the opening day of the Parliament, he sat rapt in silent meditation. In the afternoon session he rose to speak. He bowed down to *Saraswati*, the Devi (goddess of learning) and addressed the audience as "Sisters and brothers of America". Before he could utter another word, people were so much mesmerised that there was applause for full two minutes. When silence was restored, he began his address. His wisdom coupled with universal message of love and tolerance made him a world teacher. In his address, he said that upon the banner of every religion will soon be written, "HELP and not FIGHT", "ASSIMILATION and not DESTRUCTION", "HARMONY and PEACE and not DISSENSION". The Parliament of Religion lasted seventeen days and Swamiji addressed six times.

Message of Spirituality and Social Service: He addressed several meetings in the USA, UK, Sri Lanka and spread the spiritual message.

Swami Vivekananda devoted the rest of his strenuous life in communicating his message of unity and tolerance.

In India, he organised social work also in addition to spiritual pursuits.

Principal Features of Philosophy

1. God resides in every human heart.
2. The best worship of God is service to mankind.
3. Ethics and morality should be the real basis of life.
4. Love and renunciation should permeate the universe.
5. Religion means self-realisation through self-control.

Philosophy of Education

Following are the main elements of the philosophy of Swami Vivekananda:

1. All knowledge is in the human mind.
2. Education is the manifestation of the perfection already in man.
3. Knowledge is inherent in man. No knowledge comes from outside.
4. Like fire in a piece of flint, knowledge exists in the mind. Man discovers it.
5. The infinite library of the universe is in our mind.

Swami Vivekananda explains this as, "We say Newton discovered gravitation. The falling of an apple gave the suggestion to Newton and then he studied his own mind. He rearranged all the previous links of thought in his mind and discovered a link among them, which we call the law of gravitation".

Swami Vivekananda on Various Aspects of Education

(i) *Aim of Education*: Man-Making

(ii) *Role of the Teacher*: Vivekananda laid stress on the following qualities that a teacher should have:

1. The first condition is that he should be sinless.
2. The second condition is that he should know the spirit of scriptures.
3. The third condition is the spiritual force of the teacher should be based on love for the students.

4. The fourth condition is that the teacher should think that he is only helping the child to grow. He is the external teacher and he offers the suggestion which arouses the internal teacher, *i.e.,* the mind of the child.

(iii) *Principles of teaching-learning*: Swami Vivekananda emphasised the following:

1. *Self-teaching*—"No one was ever taught by another. Each of us has to teach himself. A child educates itself".
2. *Living Examples of Teacher*—"Words even thoughts, contribute only one-third of the influence in making an impression—the man two-thirds".
3. *Teaching through Positive Suggestions*—"We should give positive ideas. Negative ideas only weaken men. If you speak kind words to them and encourage them, they are bound to improve in time".
4. *Concentration as the only method of education*—"The power of concentration is the only key to the treasure-house of knowledge".
5. *Qualities of the Learner*: "The conditions necessary for the taught are purity, a real thirst after knowledge and perseverance".

(iv) *Physical and Health Education*: "Be strong, my young friends… you will be nearer to Heaven through football than through the study of Gita". *Education to be based on Western Science coupled with Vedanta:* "Living with the Guru and a similar system of imparting education are needed. What we want is Western science coupled with *Vedanta—Brahmacharya* as the guiding motto and also *Shraddha* (faith) in one's own self".

(v) *Education of the Masses*: Vivekananda gave prime importance to the education of the masses. He asserted, "The chief cause of India's ruin has been the monopolising of the whole education of the land, by dint of pride and royal authority, among a handful of men". He further observed, "If we are to rise again, we shall have to do it in the same way, that is, by spreading education among the masses". He considers that "The great national sin is the neglect of the masses, and that is one of the chief causes of our downfall. No amount of politics would be of any avail until the masses in India are once more well-educated, well-fed, and cared for. They pay for our education, they build our temples, but in return they get kicks. They are practically our slaves, if we want to regenerate India, we must work for them".

(vi) *Women's Education*: Vivekananda was an ardent champion of the education of women. He remarked, "Women have many and grave problems but none that cannot be solved by that magic word: education!"

(vii) *Secular Education*: Vivekananda had great regard for all religions: "Let us take in all that has been in the past, enjoy the light of the present and open every window of the heart for all that will come in the future. Salutation to all the prophets of the past, to all the great ones of the present and to all that are to come in the future".

Contribution: Relevance of His Views Today

1. He laid stress on the character development education.
2. He advocated the education of the masses which implies adult education and free and compulsory education regardless of caste, creed or colour. He said, "I consider that the greatest national sin is the neglect of the masses".
3. He revived the spirit of humanism in education.
4. His clarion call to the educated people was, "So long as the millions live in hunger and ignorance, I hold every man a traitor who, having been educated at their expense, pays not the least heed to them".
5. He considered the education of women as the chief instrument of national regeneration.

Summing up. Educational needs of modern India are reflected in the Preamble to our Constitution. It is clear that educational aims, contents and methods of teaching and in fact the entire process of education must be based on these pillars—Secularism, Socialism and Democracy. From the educational philosophy of Swami Vivekananda, as stated above, it is clear that he visualised the needs of independent India and accordingly he set forth his philosophical thought. His views are quite relevant today. He was for a liberal approach to religion and accordingly advocated values of secularism. He believed that ignorance was the most important evil of the society. He advocated mass education, *i.e.,* free and compulsory education as well as adult education. His advocacy of women's education is in accordance with the present day needs. His stress on child-centred education is another remarkable aspect of his educational philosophy. He advocated a system of education that was egalitarian.

Swami Vivekananda's views on education may be summed up in his own words, "We want that education by which character is formed, strength of mind is increased, the intellect is expanded and by which one stands on one's own feet".

Man-Making Education: Concept

Swami Vivekananda saw the 'Divine' in the form of the poor whom he called *Daridra Narayan.*

Swami Vivekananda saw the 'Divine' in the form of the poor whom he called *Daridra Narayan.* This denotes the direction of 'Man-making' education. It implies that education should develop a spirit of service, and the poor and the needy must be helped to raise themselves.

Man-making education also brings out the significance of the famous words said by Vivekananda at the Parliament of Religions held in 1893 at Chicago. These were: HELP, ASSIMILATION, HARMONY and PEACE. Accordingly education should develop these qualities in man.

Man-making education is inherent in character development as well as vocational development. Man-making education is a very comprehensive concept.

Main Elements of Man-Making Education

Following are the chief elements of man-making concept for which education should be directed to:

1. Swami Vivekananda believed in the *Vedanata* philosophy which considers that the ultimate goal of human life is to attain 'Unity with the Creator'. An individual must fully understand this.
2. Service to man is equated with devotion to God. According to Swami Vivekananda, God resides in every human heart. Thus man should develop the spirit of service to his fellow beings.
3. Swami Vivekananda believed in the liberal concept of religion. Essential elements of all religions are the same. No religion is inferior to any other religion. Man should follow an attitude of respect for all religions.
4. According to Vivekananda, love is the highest goal of religion. Man should imbibe love for all and hatred for none.
5. Swami Vivekananda developed a synthesis between science and spirituality. Man should attain knowledge of science and spirituality.
6. Swami Vivekananda was a prophet of humanity. His concept of man transcends the cultural boundaries of the East and the West. He was a rationalist and a man must develop rational attitude in life.

Educational Implications of Man-Making Education

Meaning of Education: According to Swamiji, education is the manifestation of divinity already existing in man. Education is not the imparting of facts. "If education were identical with information, the libraries would be the greatest sages in the world and encyclopaedias the Rishis". He further observed, "Will you consider a man as educated if only he can pass some examinations and deliver good lectures?. The education which does not help the common mass of people to equip themselves for the struggle for life, which does not bring out strength of character, a spirit of philanthropy, and the courage of a lion—is it worth the name?

Aims of Education

(i) *Character Development:* Man-making Education implies that education which builds character. Swamiji states, "We want that education, by which character is formed, strength of mind is increased, the intellect is expanded and by which one can stand on one's feet".

Vivekananda was a firm believer in education as an instrument of human betterment. He was greatly distressed to see the degradation in which the masses had fallen because of the denial of literacy and education to them. He was highly critical of the educational system itself with its Western bias and lack of attention to the development of the mental ability and moral character in its pupils. He wanted a thorough reorientation of the educational system. He declared, "We must have life-building, man-making, character-making assimilation of ideas". He quoted an old Sanskrit saying "*yatha kharaschandanabharavahi bharasya yetta na tu chandanasya*" which means "The ass carrying its load of sandalwood knows only the weight and not the value of the sandalwood". Vivekananda scoffed at the importance being given by the educational system to book-learning and memory training. "Education", he said, "is not the amount of information that is put in your brain and run-riots there, undigested all your life".

Vivekananda said, "If you really want to judge the character of man, look not at his great performances; watch a man do his most common actions. Those are indeed the things which will tell you the real character of the great man". 'Intellectuality' is not the highest good. 'Morality' and 'spirituality' are the things for which we strive'. "Our women are not so learned, but they are more pure". He does not consider a man as educated if he can only pass some examination and deliver good lectures. The basis of all system, social or political, rests upon the goodness of man. No nation is great or good because its Parliament enacts this or that, but because its men are great and good.

(ii) *Education for the Development of Spirit of Social Service in Man*: Swami Vivekananda's wide travels in India gave him first hand knowledge of the socio-economic conditions of the people of India. He was deeply moved at the utter poverty and backwardness of the masses. He observed, "So long as the millions live in hunger and ignorance, I hold every man a traitor who, having been educated at their expense, pays not the least heed to them ... I call him a *mahatma* who feels for the poor. Let these people be your God—think of them, work for them".

'Selflessness' is the essence of Indian philosophy and its main concern is '*Sarvajana Sukhino Bhavantu*' (happiness for all) and education's function is to serve this end. Man-making education must inculcate the spirit of selfless service.

(iii) *Mental Development of Man:* Swamiji laid stress on developing strong mind.

(iv) *Rational Development of Man:* Swamiji believed in the unity of all religions.

Curriculum Development and Man-Making

Curriculum should synthesise the knowledge and wisdom of the East and the West.

Swamiji also attached great importance to the physical development of the individual for which he wanted to include physical education as an integral part of the curriculum.

Methods of Instruction of Man-Making

Vivekananda observes, "You can supply the growing seed with the materials for the making up of its body, bringing to it the earth, the water, the air that it wants. And there your work stops. It will take all that it wants by its own nature. So is with the education of the child. A child educates itself. The teacher spoils everything by thinking that he is teaching. Within man is all knowledge, and it requires only an awakening, and that much is the work of the teacher. We have to do only so much for the boys that they may learn to apply their intellect to the proper use of their hands, legs, ears, eyes, etc. and finally everything will become easy". He was against the uncritical acceptance of any form of knowledge. This implies that education must develop reasoning power.

Swami Vivekananda laid stress on the following elements of methods of instruction:

1. A child educates itself. We have to do only so much for the boys that they may learn to apply their intellect to the proper use of their hands, legs, ears, eyes, etc. and finally everything will become easy: "Like fire in a piece of flint, knowledge exists in the mind; suggestion is the friction which brings it out".
2. The mind works through various stages to attain its fuller development. First it lays hold of the concrete, and only gradually deals with abstractions.
3. The teaching must be modified according to the needs of the taught. The true teacher is one who can immediately come down to the level of the student and transfer his soul to the student's soul and see through and understand through his mind.
4. Positive suggestions encourage learning. Negative thoughts only weaken them.
5. Concentration is the best method and is the key to the treasure-house of knowledge. Vivekananda observed, "To me the very essence of education is the concentration of mind, not the collecting of facts". *Brahmacharya* is necessary for concentration.
6. The learner must have great power of endurance.
7. The learner must be able to control the internal and external senses. There must be a continuous struggle, a constant fight, an unremitting grappling with our lower nature, till the higher want is actually felt and victory is achieved.
8. The pupil's faith in himself will enable him to imbibe knowledge effectively.
9. Reverence for the *guru* should be inculcated in the pupil.
10. Learning and intellectual development can be fostered through frank and open discussion on all topics of study between the teacher and the taught.
11. Purity in thought, speech and act is absolutely necessary in the taught and also in the teacher.
12. Travel leads to broadening our horizon and enables us to share our knowledge with others.

Role of the Teacher in Man-Making

He says, "My idea of education is personal contact with the teacher *Gurugrihavasa*. Without the personal life of a teacher there would be no education. It is the personality of man that really impresses us and not merely his words. "Words, even thoughts contribute only one-third of the influence in making an impression, the man two-thirds. What you call the personal magnetism of the man—that is what goes out and impresses you". "It is the real man, the personality of the man, that runs through us".

Women's Education

Swami Vivekananda forcefully advocates that they should acquire the 'spirit of valour and heroism'. In the present day it has become necessary for them also to learn self-defence. Vivekananda states, "If you do not raise the women who are the living embodiment of the Divine Mother, don't think that you have any other way to rise". He stresses that "the country and the nation which do not respect the women have never become great, nor will ever be in future". He pleaded that *Brahmcharinis* of education and character should take up the task of teaching because through such devout preachers of character, there will be the real spread of female education in the country.

History, house-keeping, the arts, sewing, upbringing of children, the duties of home life and the principles that make for the development of character are to be taught to girls.

Education of the Masses

He considered it a great national sin, if the education of the masses was neglected. He observed, "No amount of politics would be of any avail until the masses in India are once more well-educated, well-fed, and well-cared for". "If we want to regenerate India, we must work for them". Vivekananda calls him a Mahatma 'who feels for the poor'. He stated, "Let these people be your God—think of them, pray for them incessantly, the Lord will show you the way". He advocated that education must reach every home.

Man-making Education and Vocational Education

Swami Vivekananda's man-making education also included vocational self-sufficiency of man. He said, "It would be better if the people got technical education so that they might find work and earn their livelihood".

Concept of True Religious Education and Religious Man

He laid stress on practising all the good points of all religions. He said, "Salutation to all the prophets of the past".

Man-making Education: Physical and Health Education

Vivekananda was not satisfied with an education that merely looked to the development of the mind. He was also greatly concerned about the proper care of the body and the healthy development of one's physique. "Be strong, my young friends", he urged, "that is my advice to you. You will be nearer to heaven through football than through the 'Gita'. These are bold words, but I have to say them to you. I know where the shoe pinches. You will understand the Gita better, with your biceps, your muscles a little stronger. You will understand the mighty genius and the mighty strength of Krishna better with a little of strong blood in you". He emphasised repeatedly, "Strength is goodness. Weakness is sin".

Summing up: Contribution of Swami-Vivekananda in Man-Making: Vivekananda reminded that the nation lived in the cottages and therefore it was the duty of every educated young man to go from village to village and make the people understand their real condition, awake the village and make the people understand their real condition, awake them from their long slumber and advise them how to improve their own miserable lot. The sunken vitality of the helpless victims of social injustice was to be restored physically, intellectually as well as spiritually. Swami Vivekananda aimed at the removal of social injustice.

Man-making education must develop such individuals who are ethically sound, intellectually sharp, physically strong, religiously liberal, socially efficient, spiritually enlightened and vocationally self-sufficient.

Swami Vivekananda founded the Ramakrishna Mission which is engaged in the task of man-making through its multifarious activities. It has opened several educational institutions, libraries and reading rooms, hospitals and dispensaries. Hundreds of selfless workers of the Mission are working for the upliftment of masses.

Important Publications by and on Swami Vivekananda

1. *The Complete Works of Swami Vivekananda – 9 volumes.*
2. *Bhaktiyoga.*
3. *Advaita Vedanta.*
4. *Education.*
5. *Jnana Yoga.*
6. *Lectures from Colombo to Almora.*
7. *Memories of European Travels.*
8. *Philosophical and Religious Lectures of Swami Vivekananda.*
9. *Swami Vivekananda at the Parliament of Religions.*

41

T.P. Nunn (1870-1944)

T.P. Nunn, an individualist educational philosopher inclined towards idealism is considered as one of the great philosophers of England of the 20th Century. He was a Professor of Education at the London University.

Classification of Mind

Nunn has classified the mind in two *Horme* and *Mneme*, according to the process of mind.

Horme is a driver or urge and *Mneme* is a power of conservation.

Horme (Urge)

Horme keeps us active by propelling us to achieve some goal. On account of this urge, we move forward by organising and planning behaviour and experiences for reaching the goal. We shall not be motivated to move forward in the absence of this urge. This power affects our conscious mind as well as controls our unconscious mind. Since the *Horme* controls the unconscious mind, the digestive and respiratory systems of man also begin to help in keeping him active.

Mneme (Power of Concentration)

Mneme remains active in conserving experiences. The impact of the experiences changes although the experiences do not change. Though *Mneme* and memory are closely related, the area of operation of *Mneme* is wider than that of memory. The unchangeable impacts are called as engrains by Nunn and he considers them as hereditary. According to Nunn, all new experiences and ideas are influenced by these engrains.

Environment and Heredity

According to Nunn both *Horne* (environment) and *Mneme* (heredity) play an important role in the development of children.

Individual Aim in Education

According to Nunn, "Nothing good enters into the human world except in and through the free activities of individual men and women, and that education practice must be shaped to accord with that truth". He further said, "Education is the complete development of the individuality of the child so that he can make an original contribution to human life according to the best of his capacity".

Concept of Discipline

Nunn was against external restraints. He wrote, "Discipline consists in the submission of one's impulses and power to regulation which imposes firm control upon chaos and brings efficiency and economy where these would otherwise be ineffectiveness and chaos". He further observed, "The conviction that punishment and the fear of punishment are the natural foundations of school; government is generally being recognised as merely a barbarous superstition".

Publication

Education—Its Data and Principles.

42

Tarabai Modak (1892-1973)

A pioneer of the pre-school education in India, a recipient of 'Padmabhushan', Smt. Tarabai devoted nearly half a century to the cause of pre-school education. She graduated from Bombay University. While working as the Principal of Teacher's Training College for Women at Rajkot (Gujarat), she entered the field of pre-school education. She was greatly influenced by the work of Gijubhai Badeka, another pioneer in pre-primary education.

Contribution of Tarabai Modak to Pre-Primary Education

Pre-Primary Teacher's Training. Smt. Tarabai Modak went to Bhavnagar to study the Bal Mandir Scheme formulated and being run by Gijubhai. She was so impressed by the scheme that she resigned her job of the Principal of the Training College and started working with Gijubhai. This was the period when national movement in education was in full swing. There was a good deal of emphasis on Indianisation of system of education. Gijubhai and Tarabai were convinced that pre-school education could go a long way for furthering the cause of further education. They, therefore, started in right earnest the pre-school movement in India. They took great pains to prepare the necessary literature for the student-teachers and started a training college in 1925 for pre-primary teachers. It is said to be the first teachers training college of its kind in India.

Gijubhai and Tara Modak founded a society for the promotion of pre-school education. In addition, they out brought a monthly journal and published instructional material for teachers and parents.

Spread of Pre-School Movement in Maharashtra: Smt. M. Tarabai spread the movement of pre-school education in Maharashtra. She conducted successful experiments in pre-school education in a Harijanwada at Amravati.

In 1936, Tarabai opened a Shishu Vihar Kendra at Bombay which also served as a centre of pre-school teacher training.

Work in Tribal Areas

In 1945, Tarabai moved to Bordi and founded the Gram Bal Shiksha Kendra. For about 12 years, she worked there and thereafter, in 1957 she shifted the Kendra to the tribal area of Kosbad. She tried new methods of teaching-learning for the education of the most neglected tribal children. She contributed to the development of *Balwadis*.

Two Type of *Balwadis*

The *Balwadis* were run during the regular school hours.

The *Balwadi* was conducted for 5 hours while the *Angan Balwadi* for an hour and half. The *Balwadi* was fully equipped while the *Angan Balwadi* had only a few items like a mirror, combs, buckets, scissors, napkins etc. The children were brought from their homes to the *Balwadi*. An *Angan Balwadi* catered to the children of the same locality and was located near the huts of their parents.

The programme of the *Angan Balwadi* included the following:

(i) Personal cleanliness
(ii) Decoration
(iii) Craft work and handwork
(iv) Oral language
(v) Physical education
(vi) Rhythmic movements
(vii) Social activities

Emphasis was put on the manufacture and use of indigenous materials at the pre-primary stage of education. Teachers were encouraged to prepare the materials themselves.

Summing up. Tarabai has made a significant contribution to the promotion of pre-school education in India. She popularised the use of simple and inexpensive teaching-learning materials. Some educational thinkers have observed that she made attempts for the Indianisation of the Montessori method of teaching.

43

Zakir Hussain (1897-1969)

Family Background: Zakir Hussain was born at Hyderabad (now in Andhra Pradesh) on February 8, 1897. His father practised as a lawyer. He died when Zakir Hussain was barely nine years of age. At that time he was studying at the Sultan Bazar Government High School in Hyderabad. After the death of his father, the family shifted to the ancestral home at Qaimganj (U.P.). His mother greatly influenced him.

Education: In 1908, Zakir Hussain was sent to Islamia High School—a residential school at Etawah. At school, he showed keen interest in current affairs. During his school days, he came into contact with nationalist leaders. He also came under the influence of a sufi saint.

After passing the Matriculation Examination in 1913, he joined the Mohammadan Anglo-Oriental College, Aligarh. He passed the B.A. examination with Philosophy, English Literature and Economics. As a post-graduate student, he took up Economics and Law.

Zakir Hussain left the college at the call of the Non-cooperation Movement, launched by Gandhiji. Along with other students, he founded Jamia Millia Islamia (National Muslim University) in 1920 at Aligarh.

In 1922, he went to Germany to join the University of Berlin for his Ph.D. degree. He got his Ph.D. degree in 1926. His thesis was *The Agricultural Economy of India.*

Positions Held: On his return to India in 1926, he was made the Vice-Chancellor of Jamia Millia Islamia, Delhi at the age of 29 only. He stayed here for about 22 years and developed the institution into an important centre of learning.

In 1937 as desired by Gandhiji, he presided over the National Committee on Basic Education. The Committee prepared the details of the scheme of Basic Education.

In 1948, he was made the Vice-Chancellor of the Aligarh Muslim University. He remained in the post for about 8 years. He served as a member of the University Education Commission (1948-1949).

In 1952, he was nominated to the Rajya Sabha. In 1957, he became the Governor of Bihar.

In 1962, he was elected to the office of the Vice-President of India.

In 1967, he become the President of India and remained at this post till his death in 1969.

Publications on Education and Allied Subjects

1. *Shiksha* (Hindi)
2. *Educational Discourses* (Urdu)
3. *Dynamic University*
4. *Educational Reconstruction in India*
5. *Abukhan ki Bakri Aur Chandha Aur Kahaniyan* (Urdu)
6. *Kuchhwa Aur Khargosh* (Urdu)
7. Speeches, Articles and Addresses on Education

Dr. Zakir Hussain's Views on Various Aspects of Education

1. *Importance of Education*: In his speech after being sworn as the President of India, he said, "I maintain that education is a prime instrument of national purpose and that the quality of its education is inescapably involved in the quality of the nation."

2. *Aims of Education*: Dr. Zakir Hussain laid stress on the following aims of education:

(i) Education should develop a sense of common national ethos.
(ii) Education should develop higher values of life.
(iii) Education should develop qualities of citizenship.
(iv) Education should also derive inspiration from traditional knowledge and real work experience skills.
(v) Education should develop positive attitude.
(vi) Education should develop a sense of social responsibility.
(vii) Education should develop vocational efficiency.

3. *Education and Politics*: Education is the master and politics its servant.

4. *Education, Morality Science and Technology*: It is necessary to combine power with morality and science with ethics. The scientists and technologists must keep in view social welfare. Education thus should develop the totality of the child.

5. *What Education is Not?* Education is not putting information into the mind and the head of the child.

6. *What is Lacking in Indian Education?* Zakir Hussain pointed out the following major drawbacks. (i) Indian education has been like a stagnant pool for quite a while. (ii) Indian education ignores new ideas and fresh thinking in educational matters.

7. *Methods of Instruction*: (i) Instruction should be in accordance with the aptitude of the child. (ii) Child should be closely observed. (iii) Self-activity on the part of the child should be given due importance. (iv) Instruction should be work based.

8. *Concept of Work Education*: (i) Productive work must be related to mental work. (ii) Following is the chain in work education. 'Thinking and Doing' and 'Doing and Thinking'. (iii) All work is not educative. It is educated only when it is preceded by mental effort. (iv) Only that work is educative which serves value. (v) The real school work consists in training children to think before they take up an activity. (vi) Work should be properly planned and executed. Its 'why' and 'how' must be carefully considered. (vii) Work should be treated as worship.

9. *True Nature of Freedom, Discipline and Authority*: Running of the school without proper direction would be a fruitless venture. Freedom and authority in education are not opposites. There is no authority in education without the inner freedom. There is no freedom without creative work and orderly environment. The individual is helped by the school to go through certain stages. In the beginning the authority of the teachers is of their age, experience and maturity. At the end, the authority is of the values developed by the child. Responsibility, freedom and discipline go together and education should train a student in each of these.

10. *The Teacher's Role*: The teacher must make efforts to lead his pupils to acquire higher values of life. This he should do through his personal conduct.

The teacher is not to dictate or dominate. He is to help and serve the student.

The teacher must understand that the pupil has his own personality and the personality must be well looked after and nourished.

The teacher should possess limitless love and patience in dealing with children.

Characteristics of a Good School

In his speech on the Founder's Day Celebration of Modern School, New Delhi, on November 25, 1962, Zakir Hussain stated the following characteristics of a good school:

1. *Understanding of the Individuality of Each Pupil*: A true understanding of the individuality of the pupil is the first concern of the school and the teacher.

2. *Understanding of the Stages of Development*: The second concern of the school is that it always keeps in view the stages of development of the individuality of the pupil.

3. *All-Round Development*: The third concern of the school is that it devotes its efforts to the growth and development of the head, the heart and the hand of the pupil, i.e., development of the intellectual, moral and the physical side of the pupil's like.

4. *Provision for Purposeful Activities*: The fourth concern of the school is to provide purposeful activities of educationally productive work.

5. *Balanced Individual and Social Development*: The fifth concern of the school is to relate individual development of the pupil with a sense of social responsibility.

6. *Self-Education*: The sixth concern of the school is to initiate in the pupils the process of self-education.

Contribution of Dr. Zakir Hussain to Education

1. Establishment of the Jamia Milia Islamia, Okhla, New Delhi.
2. Formulation of the Wardha Scheme or Basic Education.

In July 1937, Gandhiji expressed his views on education in the *Harijan* a paper started by him. He stated, "Literacy itself is no education. I would, therefore, begin the child's education by teaching it a useful handicraft and enabling it to produce from the moment it begins its training."

The same year, in October, a Conference of National Workers was held at Wardha under the Presidentship of Gandhiji. The conference appointed a committee of eminent educationists under the Chairmanship of Dr. Zakir Hussain to prepare a detailed syllabus. The report of the Committee on education published in March 1938 came to be known as the Wardha Scheme of Education. Dr. Zakir Hussain played a notable role in the preparation of the report. It is also known as *Report of the Zakir Hussain Committee and the Detailed Syllabus* (1938).

Main outline of the Seven Years Course of Basic Education as Suggested by the Committee

1. *The Basic Craft*: It is to be chosen from the following:
   a. Spinning and Weaving
   b. Carpentry
   c. Agriculture
   d. Fruit and Vegetable Gardening
   e. Leather Work
   f. Any other craft for which local and geographical conditions permit.
2. *Mother-tongue*: This is the foundation of all education.
3. *Other subjects*: (i) Social studies, (ii) General Science, (iii) Drawing, (iv) Music, (v) Hindustani
4. *Total Duration of Elementary Education*: 7 years
5. *Distribution of Work in the Curriculum*

Item/Subject/Activity	*Daily Time to be Developed*
1. The Basic Craft	3 hours 20 minutes
2. Music, Drawing and Arithmetic	40 minutes
3. Mother-Tongue	40 minutes
4. Social Studies and General Science	30 minutes
5. Physical Training	10 minutes
6. Recess	10 minutes
Total	5 hours 30 minutes

6. Working Days in the School — 228 days.

Educationally Productive Work

In 1940, in an address at the All India Education Conference, Dr. Zakir Husain in his own choicest words gave one of the finest statements about the meaning of work in education. He placed work on the niche of honour and worship: "Let those who wish to make work the medium of education remember that work is not purposeless, that it is not content with any results that may follow. Work does not mean the passing of time by doing any haphazard thing; it is not amusement; it is not play; it is work; it is purposeful striving. Work sits in judgement on itself with the strictness of an enemy and, when it passes the test, it yields joy unparalleled and unsurpassed. Work is, worship." He has seen work and known work. His idea of work has developed across the years not through bookish devotion but through observation and experience: "I have after years of thinking on the subject come to the conviction that work is the only instrument of effective education. It may sometimes be manual work, at others non-manual work. But although it is work alone that can educate, I have also come to the conviction by long observation and experience that all work does not educate."

Dr. Zakir Husain designates such work of educational value as 'educationally productive work', work which helps in the cultivation of the mind and in the shaping of character and personality. Work that is educationally productive has normally four stages:

1. The consciousness of the problem; a clear understanding of what is to be done.
2. The formation of a plan of execution; the choice of the appropriate means and thinking out of the various steps that would be needed to complete.
3. The actual execution of the work.
4. Self-criticism of the result in relation to the objectives set earlier.

Four Values

In one of his convocation addresses Dr. Zakir Husain has suggested 'four self-evident values' for the young people to start on. These four objectives are Health, Strength, Beauty, and Cleanliness. "These simple values tend to expand as one endeavours to realize them, and the young pilgrim finds himself pursuing the objectives of a healthy body, a healthy mind, and a healthy character; the objectives of a strong, vigorous body, a strong, alert disciplined mind and a strong character—firm, efficient, thorough, and persevering; the objectives of a clean body, a clean mind, and clean life."

Teacher as the Custodian of the Highest Values

What type of man is the good teacher? Human types have been characterised by Dr. Zakir Husain on the basis of some dominating principles: "The highest principle of theoretical man is Truth, that of the imaginative man Beauty, that of the economic man Gain, that of the religious man Salvation, that of the political man Power, that of the social Love. Pure types are, of course, rare but some principle predominates. The good teacher, as I see him, is predominantly a character of the social type." The dominating note in the social type to which the teacher belongs is love for other fellowmen, a sense of solidarity with them, an urge to help them and belong to them and to experience joy in giving oneself up for them. The teacher is not to dictate or dominate, he is to help and serve, to mould and shape in faith and love. Teacher is the custodian of the highest values created and cherished by the people—values that represent a composition of most of what is best in the culture of mankind. He has to transmit these values to his pupils through the magic of his own personality. He can only do this if he has himself experienced these values.

Moral Orientation to Science and Technology: A Truly Educated Man

It is necessary to combine power with morality, science with ethics. The scientists and technologists must not forget the social reference and moral commitments. They should not remain hidden behind the growing mass of material and machines; they must come out in the open to understand and appreciate the urges and aspirations, the limitations and prejudices, the faith and hope of their fellow beings. Endeavour in the field of science and technology would need moral orientations. Dr. Zakir Husain, therefore, feels the impelling need that science colleges besides specializing in the domain of science, engineering and technology should acquaint their students with social science and humanities: "Their concern is not only to send out successful engineers and technologists, but also truly educated men. We can never forget the man in the engineer. He too should know and appreciate what life has to offer. If he can make machines, it does not follow that he need turn his mind into a machine and be incapable of appreciating the value of good poetry, good music, good books, and good human relationships." Yes, we should make all endeavour to keep awake the man in the engineer, the scientists, the doctor or whatever be the profession.

Education and Culture

Education and culture of the past, but also of the present and the future— "History is the treasure house from which we can select these educative goods, for a people's roots are, indeed, embedded in the soul of its history and they penetrate deeper and deeper and spread wider and wider into the past in order that it may shoot up higher into the future and secure for itself something like timelessness in the constant flux of time. Yes, but the past is immense. Education must select. And here is one of its difficult responsibilities. Our inheritance contains both the old and new; it contains the contributions of Dravidian, the Aryan, the Arab, the Turk, the Mongol, the European; it has contributions from the Hindu, the Buddhist, the Muslim, the Christian, the Sikh, the Parsi. In the rich treasure of our history nothing is good or bad just because it is Hindu, Buddhist, Muslim, Sikh, Christian or Parsi. It is the function of education, the thinking activity of society to sift the rich heritage and make it available for the moral and spiritual nourishment of growing generations. Education should be able to distinguish between the heritage that helps and the heritage that hampers, the tradition that undermines and the tradition that fortifies."

Summing Up. "Economist by training, educationist by profession, humanist by temperament. Dr. Zakir Husain is easily one of the most creative and distinguished living educationists of India. He has been an important liberating force in education enriching its purpose as well as contents, experimenting in methods and techniques, elucidating its true relationship not only with the national past, present and future but also with precious legacy of man as a whole. He has, on the one hand, shown sensitiveness to its social and psychological foundations and, on the other, has been deeply involved in its moral and spiritual implications." These are the words of Dr. K.G. Saiyidain, one of the India's leading educationists.

44

Brief Notes

73 Western and Indian Educational Philosophers and Thinkers

A. Western

1. Abelard, Peter (1079-1142 AD). A French philosopher and theologian. His philosophy as a practising teacher and scholar is summed up in two aphorisms:

"By doubting we are led to inquire, by inquiring we perceive the truth".

"A doctrine is not to be believed because God has said it, but because we are convinced by reason that it is so".

The university is regarded as his posthumous child. His Cathedral School of Notre Dame, after a generation developed into the '*Universitas*'.

2. Adams, John (1857-1934). Prof. of Education in the University of London. Stressed the claim of psychology in education; known for his dictum: "He (teacher) must know Latin (subject) and he must know John (student)". Important publications: *The Herbartian Psychology Applied to Education* (1897); *The Evolution of Educational Theory* (1912); *Modern Development in Educational Practice* (1922); *Errors in Schools* (1927).

3. Alcuin (735-804). An English scholar. Wrote in his *Grammar*, "The vowels are the souls and the consonants the bodies of the words. Now the soul moves both itself and the body, but the body is immovable apart from the soul. Such then are the consonants without the vowels. They may he written by themselves, but they cannot be uttered, nor have they any power apart from the vowels".

4. Adams, Henry Brooks (1838-1918). American historian. Introduced the seminar method of teaching. Wrote, "A teacher affects eternity; he can never tell where his influence stops".

5. Adams, James Truslow (1878-1949). American historian and philosopher. Wrote, "There are obviously two educations. One should teach us how to make a living, and the other how to live".

6. Aquinas, St. Thomas (1225-1274). Italian philosopher and theologian. Known for his books *De Magistro*—dealing with the role of the teacher and teaching and *The Opusculum De Eruditione*, dealing with the duties of the parents. Wrote, "Teaching is an art and the first rule of art is to follow nature; that one should begin by what is less difficult and then proceed by easy steps to more difficult questions".

7. Arnold, Thomas (1795-1842). English educator. Famous headmaster of the Rugby School in England. Often regarded as the founder of the modern public school system. Developed the perfectorial system.

8. Ascham, Roger (1515-1568). English educator. Tutor of Princess (afterwards Queen) Elizabeth. Wrote, *Schoolmaster*—a treatise on education. Condemned corporal punishment. He separates children into "quick-wit and "hard-wit".

9. Bacon, Francis (1561-1626). English man of letters, philosopher and statesman. Advised scholars to find 'better scientific method'. His *Novugum Organum* is the 'Scientific Declaration of Independence'. Wanted to 'make a small globe of the intellectual world'. Substituted induction for deduction in the study of nature, thus bringing 'sense realisation' in education.

10. Baden-Powell (1857-1941). An army officer. Founder of the Boy Scout Movement in 1907.

11. Bagley, William Chandler (1874-1946). American educator, who preferred to be listed in 'Who's Who as 'teacher', rather than 'educator' or professor; wrote, "The pupil is immature and helpless and he must not be given a long rope with which he may hang himself". Cautioned against regulated freedom and *laissez faire* in discipline.

12. Bain, Alexander (1818-1903). Scottish educator. In 'Education as a Science' shows "How education is concerned with the efforts of the grown-up part of the community to inform the intellect and mould the character of the young". However, excluded physical education, technical education and professional education from the conception of education.

13. Basedow, Johann Heinrich (1724-90). German school reformer. Voluminous writer, wrote; "All our knowledge comes from the senses, and experience of things is our teacher". Authored *Book of Method for Fathers and Mothers of Families and Nations* and *The Elementary Book.*

14. Beecher, Catherine Elizabeth (1800-1878). Pioneer in the movement for higher education of women in the United States. Organised the Women's Association 'to aid in securing to women a liberal education, honourable position and remunerative employment'. Published *The Moral Instructor* (1838); *Religious Training of Children* (1864) and *Women's Profession as Mother and Educator* (1871).

15. Bell, Andrew (1753-1832). An English scholar. While in India, founded the 'monitorial system' of instruction in which senior pupils teach junior pupils.

16. Bode, Boyd H. (1873-1953). American philosopher and educator. Contended that the 'the purpose of sound education is to emancipate the pupil from dependence on immediate interest. Claimed that 'Child-centred' method had become a cult selling up false 'absolutes'. Published *Progressive Education at the Crossroads.*

17. Conant, James Bryant (1893-1978). American diplomat, educator and scientist. Advocated that the Universities must rely upon experimental spirit. Recommended guidance facilities in School. Published, *The American High School Today*; *Education and Liberty*; *On Understanding Science and Modem Man.*

18. Confucius (551 B.C.-478 B.C.). Chinese philosopher, a born teacher and lover of morals. He said, "Learning without thought is labour lost, thought without learning is perilous". Wrote *Spring and Autumn* which was studied for several centuries by Chinese boys in their homes or schools.

19. Cunningham, W.I. (1885-1961). American educator, viewed knowledge as a divine instrument which leads to the knowledge of the Spiritual Kingdom. Maintained that "Knowledge of God is the beginning and end of education'. It (curriculum) is a tool in the hands of the artist (the teacher) to mould his material (the pupil) in accordance with his ideal in his studio (the school)". Publications *Pivotal Problems of Education*; *General Education* and *The Liberal College.*

20. Defoe (1659-1731). English journalist and novelist, author of the famous work *Robinson Crusoe*. Advocated in his *Essay upon Projects* (1697), the establishing of academics. This book led Benjamin Franklin (1706-1709) to the founding of the Academy and Charity School of Philadelphia.

21. De Garmo, Charles (1819-1934). American educator. Author of *Principles of Secondary Education* in two volumes in 1907 and 1908.

22. Dewey, John (1859-1952). See Chapter 22.

23. Diderot, Denis (1713-1784). French educator and philosopher. The first to say that the blind could be taught through the sense of touch. Author of the monumental work *Dictionnaire Encyclopedique* (1750-72) in 28 volumes and *Plan of a University* (1776).

24. Eliot, Charles William (1834-1926). American educator, prolific writer, leader of college and uniform reform. President of the Harvard University for 40 years. Published *Educational Reforms* (1898) and *University Administration* (1908).

25. Emerson, Ralph Waldo (1803-1882), American educator, essayist, moralist and poet, stated the role of education as "In order to control the minds of the people education should be one part words, one part worship, and one part work". Observed, "The secret of education lies in respecting the child". His ideas found in his *New England Reformers* and *Culture and Education*. Author of the famous quote:

"Not gold, but only men can make
A people great and strong..."

26. Erasmus, Desiderious (1466-1536). French educator and one of the greatest humanists of the Renaissance. Advocated a higher standard of qualifications and proper selection of teachers.

27. Fichte, Johann Gottlieb (1762-1814). German educator and philosopher. Pleaded for same education for both the sexes. Wrote *The Vocation of the Scholar*; *The Nature of the Scholar* and *The Address to the German Nation.*

28. Franklin, Benjamin (1706-1790). American author, educator, inventor, publisher, scientist and statesman. Founder of the first American circulating library (1731). Provided for a wide curriculum including practical and vocational activities in his academy. Wrote, "It is, therefore, proposed that they learn those things that are likely to be most useful and most ornamental". Publications: *Proposals relating to the Education of the Youth* (1749). *An Idea of the English School* (1750).

29. Gesell, Arnold (1880-1961). An American educator and psychologist. Famous for his contribution to child development, especially at the pre-primary stage. Earned his Ph.D. from Clark University (1906) and M.D. from Yale University (1915). Director Clinic of Child Development (1911-1948), was among the first to study human development from birth through adolescence. Worked with pre-school children and later extended it to ages 5 to 10 and 10 to 16. During 1940s and 1950s, was regarded as America's fore most authority on child rearing and development. Developed series of norms of infant and child behaviour. Publications: '*An Atlas of Infant Behaviour*' (1934), '*Infant and Child in the Culture of To-day*' (1943, '*The Child from 5 to 10*' (1946) and '*Youth: The Years from Ten to Sixteen*' (1956).

30. Grant, Charles (1746-1823). An English Officer in India, advocated English education in India. Chairman of the Board of Directors of the East India Company. Observed, "The true cure of darkness is the introduction of light. The Hindus err because they are ignorant… and it is perfectly in order, by degrees, to impart the Hindus of our language". Believed that "the acquisition of knowledge in English literature, philosophy and religion would silently, undermine the fabric of error".

31. Grundtvig, Nikolai Frederik Severin (1783-1872). Danish educator, historian, poet, statesman and founder of the 'Folk High Schools'. The 'Folk High School' is Denmark's most important contribution to adult education in the world.

32. Herbart, Johann Friedrich (1776-1841). German educator and philosopher, came into contact with great thinkers like Goethe, Schipper and Fichte, Met Pestalozzi when he was still teaching at an elementary school; occupied the most distinguished chair of philosophy at the University of Konigsburg in East Prussia; was against faulty psychology; advocated that human mind is one harmonious whole and not a confused mixture of many faculties; popularised terms like interest, apperception (mental process of understanding in terms of previous experience), circle of thought, concentration, correlation, culture, best known for his 'Herbartian Steps': (i) Preparation or Introduction or Motivation, (ii) Presentation, (iii) Comparison or Association, and (iv) Generalisation and Application. Publications: '*Aesthetic Presentation of the World as the Main Function of Education*' (1804); '*Critical Point of View of the Pestalozzian Method of Education*' (1804); '*Relation of School in Life*' (1818) and '*Encyclopedia of Philosophy*' (1831).

33. Huxley, Thomas (1828-1895). He was an English scientist, social reformer and educational thinker. He did much to popularise scientific educational thought. He showed great interest in questions of education.

His concept of education may be described as: "The man, I think, has liberal education whose intellect is clear, whose passions are trained, who has learnt to love beauty, whether of nature or of art, to hate all vileness and to respect others as himself".

About the prevailing system of education, he observed, the stock example of solid stupidity' of the 19th century. He vehemently criticised the classical education which in no way helped the youth of England.

His main ideas on educational reforms are as under:

1. Elements of physical science should be taught first in schools.
2. Physical training and drill should form part of regular school work.
3. Drawing and music should be included in every school course.
4. State should provide compulsory elementary education, and beyond that an individual should be left to himself to rise through his own innate capacity and efforts.

34. James, Wilnam (1842-1910): American educator and psychologist. Believed 'The great thing in all education is to make the nervous system our ally instead of our enemies'. Propounder of 'James-Lange Theory of Emotions' (1885). Published *The Principles of Psychology* (1890) and *Talks to Teaches* (1899).

35. Keller, Helen Adams (1880-1968). American educator, a pioneer in deaf education. Became deaf and blind at the age of 19. Wrote: *The Story of My Life* (1902), *The World I Live On* (1908) and *Mid Stream* (1930).

36. Kerschensteiner, George (1854-1932). German educator. Distinguished three aspects of education—the axiological, the psychological and the teleological. Publication *Theorieder Bildung* (Theory of Education).

37. Kilpatrick, William Heard (1871-1965). American educator, popular lecturer and writer. Gave a concrete shape to the Project Method. Publications: *The Montessori System Examined* (1914), *Foundations of Method* (1925), *Education for a Changing Civilisation* (1926), *Education and the Social Crisis* (1932), *Remaking the Curriculum* (1936) and *Philosophy of Education*' (1951).

38. Lane, Homer Tyrrell (1876-1925). British educator and a great champion of self-government in schools. Founded the 'Little Commonwealth', a reformatory school on a Dorest farm in 1912. Put his ideas into practice in this school. Wrote, "Faults are not corrected by, but brought about by, suppression in childhood. The free a child is, the more it be considerate and social, the more its chief interests will be progressive, the more its fundamental instincts will have valuable social status". Publication: *Talks To Parents and Teachers*.

39. Locke, John (1632-1704). English educator and philosopher. He was concerned primarily with the question of how the mind acquires knowledge, and he emphatically said, "To this I answer, in one word, from 'Experience'. In that all our knowledge is founded; fully recognised". Stressed that the business of a teacher was 'to raise in his pupil a love and esteem of knowledge, rather than to teach all that was knowledge'. Wrote *An Essay Concerning Human Understanding* and *Thoughts on Education*.

40. Macaulay, Thomas Babington (1800-1859). English essayist, historian, politician and Law Member of Governor General Lord William Bentinck. Known for his *Minutes on Education* (1835). Founder of the English system of Education in India. Chairman of the Committee of Public Instruction, made very derogatory remarks about oriental learning. Wrote, "A single shelf of a good European literature was worth the Whole Native literature of India and Arabian... False history, false astronomy, false medicine... false religion". Author of monumental work of five volumes of *History of England*.

41. Makarenko, Anton Semyonnovich (1888-1939). Russian educator. Believed that educational failures result from "poor preparedness as a teacher, an insufficient mastery of teaching techniques and a poor state of his nerves as well as desperation". He further observed, "Win over a child's soul, make him your ally, involve him in collective life".

42. McMillan, Margaret (1860-1931). Known for her contribution to nursery education (along with her sister Rachel McMillan and popularly called McMillan sisters). Lost father at the age of 5 and mother at 17. Born in USA but settled in UK. Concentrated on improving the physical and welfare of the slum children. Carried out the first medical inspection of elementary school children at Bradford in England. Began a campaign to improve the health of children and pleaded that local authorities should install bathrooms, improve ventilation and supply free school meals in 1988, began teaching working class children. Two sisters led a vigorous campaign for school meals and in 1906, the House of Commons in England (Lok Sabha) passed the 1906 Provision of School Meals Act. In 1908, opened the country's first school clinic in Bow. In 1910, another school clinic was opened at Deptford. The clinic provided dental care, surgical aid and lessons in breathing and posture. The sisters also established a night camp where slum children could wash and wear clean night clothes. The two sisters created the first nursery school in London in 1911.

In 1914, both the sisters started an Open-Air Nursery School and Training Centre in Peckham. Margaret opened in 1830 at Deptford, a college to train nurses and teachers. Also, supported the campaign for 'Universal Suffrage' in England. Wrote: '*Child Labour and Half the Time System*' (1896); '*Early Childhood*' (1900); '*Education through the Imagination*' (1904); '*The Economic Aspects of Child Labour and Education*' (1905); '*The Child and the State*' (1911).

43. McMillan, Rachel (1860-1917). (See above also.) After 1888, both the sisters remained together for most of the rest of their lives. Wrote: '*The Nursery School*' (1919) and '*Nursery Schools: A Practical Handbook*' (1920). Both placed high value on creativity and play in nursery programme.

44. Newman, Cardinal John Henry (1801-1890). English Educator. Wrote, "A habit of mind is formed which lasts through life, of which the attributes are freedom, equitableness, calmness, moderation and wisdom; or what is former discourse, I have ventured to call a philosophical habit". Delivered a series of lectures in 1852 on 'Idea of a University'.

45. Parker, Francis Wayland (1837-1902). American educational reformer, known for his *Doctrine of Concentration*: "The doctrine of concentration is itself a science of education that will absorb the attention of thoughtful teachers for centuries".

46. Parkhurst, Helen (1887-1937). American educator, author of the novel Dalton Plan or Contract Plan in the School System of Dalton, Massachusetts. Publication: *Education on the Dalton Plan* (1922).

47. Parsons, Frank (1854-1908). American educator, pioneer in the guidance movement. Organised the Boston Vocational Bureau. Author of *Our Country's Needs* (1894) and *Choosing a Vocation*.

48. Piaget, Jean (1896-1980). A Swiss educator and a naturalist and biologist by training. Worked as a Professor of Child Psychology at the University of

Geneva. Began his study of child development with the careful observation of his own three children. For over 50 years, observed, interviewed and tested children of all ages. Implications of his 'Theory of Cognitive Development' for early childhood are: (i) young children learn best through direct encounter with the environment than through formal education. (ii) play and activity should be the medium of early childhood education. (iii) the emphasis should be on giving children first hand experiences with objects. (iv) they should be encouraged to observe, describe, manipulate and experiment with them so as to develop clear and sound concepts. Publications:

1. *The Language of Thought of the Child* (1923).
2. *Judgement and Reasoning of the Child* (1924).
3. *The Child's Conception of the Physical World* (1932).
4. *The Moral Judgement of the Child* (1937).
5. *The Origin of Intelligence in the Child* (1937).
6. *The Child's Conception of Number* (1941).
7. *The Child's Conception of Physical Quantities* (1942).
8. *Play Dreams and Imitations in Childhood* (1945).
9. *The Child's Conception of Time* (1946).
10. *The Child's Conception of Movement and Speed* (1946).
11. *The Construction of Reality in the Child* (1947).
12. *The Child's Conception of Space* (1948).
13. *The Psychology of Intelligence* (1950).
14. *Logic and Psychology* (1953).
15. *The Construction of Reality in the Child* (1954).
16. *The Strategy of Genes* (1957).
17. *The Growth of Logical Thinking from Childhood to Adolescene* (1958).
18. *The Child's Conception of Geometry*.
19. *The Early Growth of Logic in the Child* (1964).
20. *Mental Imagery in the Child* (1969).
21. *The Mechanism of Perception* (1969).
22. *The Psychology of the Child* (1969).
23. *Science of Education and the Psychology of the Child* (1969).
24. *The Origin of the Idea of Chance in Children* (1975).
25. *The Grasp of Consciousness*.

49. Quintillion (38-86 A.D.). Roman teacher, lawyer, orator and senator. His ideas on education of children are as valid to-day as they were about nineteen centuries back. Education must begin at an early age, seventh year is the time of definite instructions. Whipping is unseemly. Respect for the individuality of the pupil by the teacher. Character is the end of education. Wrote *Institutes of Oratory*.

50. Ramus, Petrus (1515-1572). French educational reformer and humanist. Principal of the College of Presales. Held that the selection of subject matter should be based on the observation of nature and the arrangement of subject matter should be based on the law of truth, law of justice and the law of wisdom. Wrote 62 works covering subjects like grammar, rhetoric, dialectic mathematics and physics. *Recommendations for the Reformation of the University* (1562), one of his unique books.

51. Ratke, Wolfgang (1571-1635). German educator and one of the pioneers of the modem pedagogy. Initiated the search for the 'Method of Nature'. Advocated the method of teaching of one thing at a time, everything to be often repeated, no rote, learning things first and explanations afterwards.

52. Richter, Johann Paul Friedrich (1763-1825. German educator, humanist and prolific writer. Criticised Rousseau's Emile as a negative scheme. Pleaded for a joyous freedom in the early life of a child, underlined the educative functions of play games, dancing, music and fairy tales. Authored *Levana* (Doctrine of Education) in 1807.

53. Runkie, John Daniel (1822-1902). American educator and leader in the movement for the introduction of manual training in schools. President Massachusetts Institute (1870-1878). Publications: *Manual Elements in Education.*

54. Ruskin, John (1819-1900). English educator, social reformer and writer. Advocated manual training and craftsmanship. Gandhiji greatly influenced by his book *Unto the Last* containing outlines of his proposals for State Schools. *Time and Tide* contains letters on the general subject of education. Sesame and Lilies illustrates the place of literature in education.

55. Sadler, Michael (1861-1943). British educator and Vice-Chancellor of the University of Leeds. Headed the Calcutta University Commission in 1917. Report known as Sadler Report—a great document in the history of Indian education.

56. Sampson, George (1852-1950). British educator who coined the phrase 'Every teacher is a teacher of English'. Publication: '*English for the English*' (1921).

57. Sanderson, Frederick William (1857-1922). English educator and H.G. Well's 'great school teacher'. Said, "Education must be fitted to the boy, not the boy to education".

58. Santayana (1863-1952). American educator, critic, philosopher, poet and writer. Left America and made Europe his home. Rejected the idea that all are equal in education. Believed in a natural aristocracy of talent. Held, "A child educated only at school is an uneducated child".

59. Schiller, Friedrich (1759-1815). German educator, historian, philosopher and poet. Viewed education as a process of emotional development. Authored *Aesthetic Education of Man*; *On the Sublime*; *On the Necessary Limits in the Use of Beautiful Forms*.

60. Thring, Edward (1821-1887). English educator and famous headmaster of Uppingham School. Believed that 'everybody can do something good'. Insisted upon individual attention to the bright and dull student alike. Instituted the first gymnasium in any public school in England. Attached great importance to music. Publications: *Education and School* (1864); *Theory and Practice of Teaching* (1883); *Thoughts on Life Sciences* (1869).

61. Tolstoy, Count Leo Nikolayevich (1828-1910). Russian educator and laureate. Influenced Gandhiji. Persistent advocate of progressive ideas. Devoted much time in organising village schools. Edited an educational magazine in which explained his ideal of free education and described his teaching methods. His idea was not to force anything on the child; every pupil was free to come to school; free to sit where he liked; free to learn only when he liked and free to criticise or suggest. Freedom as the keynote of all his educational efforts. Publications: *Twenty three Tales*; *The Teaching of Jesus*; *On Popular Education*.

B. Indian

1. Banerjee, Gooro Dass (1844-1918). First Indian Vice-Chancellor and the only Hindu Member of the Indian Universities Commission (1902). Gave a note of dissent that the recommendations of the Commission would put education under the control of Government and reduce the popular element. He observed, "I have ventured to think that the solution arrived at is only a partial solution of the problem and that we should aim not only at raising the highest but also at broadening the base". Took an active part in the 'Dawn Society' for the promotion of education in the country.

2. Kabir, Humayan (1902-1969). Indian educator. Educational Adviser to the Ministry of Education, Government of India for a number of years. Union Minister; Chairman, University Grants Commission. Publications: *The Indian Heritage*; *Kant on Philosophy in General*; *Science, Democracy and Island*; *Education in New India*; and *Indian Philosophy of Education*.

3. Karve, Dhondo K. (1858-1962). Indian educator and a pioneer in the field of women education. Founded the Women's (S.N.D.T.) University (1916).

4. Khan, Sayyid Ahmad (1817-1898). Indian educator and pioneer of religious and social reform movement among the Muslims. Advocated Western learning in place of traditional learning. Took several steps for the promotion of Scientific temper of mind. Played prominent role in the founding of the Muhammadan Anglo-Oriental College, Aligarh in 1875.

5. Lajpat Rai (Lala) (1865-1928). Pragmatic educator, founder of the Servants of People Society, social reformer, writer and patriot. Closely associated with the D.A.V. College, Lahore. Observed, "The first aim of all publicly imparted education in India should be to increase the productivity capacity of its citizens. Education is the first necessity of such a nation and it should be the first charge on all national revenues". Publication: *The Problem of National Education in India*.

6. Malviya, Madan Mohan (1861-1946). Indian educator, social reformer, a statesman, founder of the famous Benaras Hindu University. President of Indian National Congress (1909, 1918, 1932 and 1938). Vice- Chancellor, Benaras Hindu University (1919-1939). Founded several daily and weekly journals in Hindi to educate the people on national issues. Closely associated with cultural and intellectual awakening.

7. Mukherjee, Satish Chandra (1865-1949). Indian educator who inaugurated the National Education Movement in India in 1905 and organised the National Council of Education in 1906. Apostle of Indian nationalism at the dawn of the 20th Century. Chief architect of the Swadeshi Movement in 1905. Founded an English Journal *Dawn* in 1897 and wrote articles in it on *A School of Reforms*; *The Fate of All Our Instruction* and *An Examination into the Present System of Education in India and Scheme of Reform.*

8. Naik, J.P. (1907-1981), Educational author and planner. Educational Advisor, Ministry of Education and Youth Services, Govt. of India. UNESCO Consultant. Member-Secretary of the Indian Education Commission (1964-66), popularly known as Kothari Commission. Founder of Indian Institute of Education, Pune. Major works on education: *A Student's History of Education in India*; *Educational Planning in India*; *The Single Teacher School*; *Training of Educational Administrators in India*; *The Role of Government of India in Education*; edited three vols. of *Selections from Educational Records, Government of India.*

9. (Raja) Roy, Rammohan (1772-1833). Indian educator and social reformer. Often called the 'Father of Indian Renaissance in Bengal'. Studied Arabic, Bengali. English, Hebrew, Persian and Sanskrit. Started the Brahmo Samaj. Pleaded for the synthesis of knowledge of the East and the West. Advocated the spread of Western Education and English in India. Opened educational institutions. Advocated liberal education. Laid stress on women's education and on raising their status. Translated the *Vedas* and some of the *Upanishads* in Bengali. Urged the Englishmen in India to learn Bengali.

10. Sen, Keshub Chander (1838-1884). Indian educator, social reformer and leader of the *Brahmo Samaj*. Wrote to the Viceroy and Governor General of India, "My Lord, India's first and chief requirement is an efficient and comprehensive system of education which will bring the light of useful knowledge to all classes of the community". Observed, "Knowledge without morality is a danger and a curse, and unquestionably it is more so in India than elsewhere". Champion of Women's education.

11. (Swami) Shraddhananda (1857-1926). Indian educator and social reformer. Founder of the Kangri Gurukula and other educational institutions on the lines of ancient Gurukulas. Like Swami Dayananda, accepted the *Vedas* as the source of knowledge and wisdom.

12. Vidya Sagar, Ishwarchandra (1821-1892). Indian educator, scholar and social reformer. Inspector of Schools. Principal of Calcutta Sanskrit College. Worked for the removal of restriction of admission on the basis of caste. Advocated the principle of making people's language as the medium of instruction including Western Sciences. Promoted Women's education. Established a number of girls schools. Founded the Vidya Sagar College. Translated a number of Sanskrit and English books into Bengali.

APPENDIX

Thinkers on Education in UNESCO Series

A. MATHEW (India), National Institute of Adult Education, Delhi (India)

Adolphe FERRIERE, Daniel HAMELINE (France), University of Geneva and Institut Jean-Jacques Rousseau (Switzerland)

Agoston TREFORT, Istvanne KISS (Hungary), Eotvos Lorand University, Budapest (Hungary)

AI-GHAZALI Nabil NOFAL (Egypt), UNESCO Regional Coordinating Unit of the Educational Innovation Programme for Development in the Arab States, Amman (Jordan)

ALAIN, Philippe FORAY (France), Institut Universitaire de Formation des Maitres, Lyon (France)

Alexander Sutherland NEILL, Jean Francois SAFFANGE (France), University of Lyon II (France)

AL-FARABI 'Ammar AL-TALBI (Algeria), University of Qatar (Qatar)

Alfred BINET, Rene ZAZZO (France), Ecole Pratique des Hautes Etudes en Sciences Sociales, Paris (France)

Andres BELLO, Gregorio WEINBERG (Argentina), University of Buenos Aires (Argentina)

Anton Semionovitch MAKARENKO G.N. FILONOV (Russian Federation), Academy of Pedagogical Sciences, Moscow (Russian Federation)

Antonio GRAMSCI, Attilio MONASTA (Italy), University of Florence (Italy)

Antonio SERGIO DE SOUZA, Antonio NOVOA (Portugal), University of Lisbon (Portugal)

ARISTOTLE Charles HUMMEL (Switzerland), Former President, Council of the International Bureau of Education, Geneva (Switzerland)

AVICENNA (Ibn Sina) 'Abd al-Rahman AL-NAQIB (Egypt), Mansuora University (Egypt)

B.F.SKINNER Louis SMITH (United States of America), Washington University, St Louis, Missouri. (United States of America)

Bogdan SUCHODOLSKI, Irena WOJNAR (Poland), University of Warsaw (Poland)

Boutros AL-BOUSTANI, Khalil ABOU-RJAILI (Lebanon), *Ministry of National Education* (Lebanon)

Bruno BETTELHEIM, Karen ZELAN (United States of America), The New School for Psychoanalysis, San Francisco (United States of America)

CAI Yuanpei, ZHANG Lizhong (China), La Trobe University (Australia)

Carl ROGERS, Fred ZIMRING (United States of America), Case Western Reserve University, Cleveland, Ohio (United States of America)

Celestin FREINET, Louis LEGRAND (France), Louis Pasteur University, Strasbourg (France)

Christen Mikkelsen KOLD, Jens BJERG (Denmark), Roskilde University Centre, Roskilde (Denmark)

COMENIUS Jean PIAGET (Switzerland), Formerly Director of the International Bureau of Education, Geneva (Switzerland)

CONDORCET Bernard JOLIBERT (France), University of Reunion (France)

CONFUCIUS YANG Huanyin (China), Central Institute of Educational Sciences, Beijing (China)

Constantin Dmitrievitch USHINSKY, Miroslav CIPRO (Czech Republic), Charles University, Prague (Czech Republic)

Davorin TRSTENJAK, Nedjeljko KUJUNDZIC (Croatia), University of Zagreb (Croatia)

Dijana PLUT (Yugoslavia), University of Belgrade (Yugoslavia)

Dimitri GLINOS, Marie ELIOU (Greece), University of Athens (Greece)

Dmitry Nikolaevich UZNADZE, Georgi Nikolaevich KETCHUACHVILI (Georgia), Tbilisi State University (Georgia)

Domingo Faustino SARMIENTO, Hector Felix BRAVO (Argentina), University of Buenos Aires (Argentina)

Edouard CLAPAREDE, Daniel HAMELINE (France), University of Geneva and Institut Jean-Jacques Rousseau (Switzerland)

Ellen KEY, Thorbjorn LENGBORN (Sweden), Stockholm University (Sweden)

Emile DURKHEIM, Jean-Claude FILLOUX (France), University of Paris X (France)

ERASMUS Jean-Claude MARGOLIN (France), University of Tours (France)

Federico von BORSTEL (United States of America), Fundacion Jose Vasconcelos, Poway, California (United States of America)

Francisco GINER DE LOS RIOS, Julio RUIZ BERRIO (Spain), Complutense University of Madrid (Spain)

Friedrich Adolph Wilhelm DIESTERWEG, Karl-Heinz GUNTHER (Germany), Former Chairman, Commission on the History of Education and the School in Germany

Friedrich FROBEL, Helmut HEILAND (Germany), Duisburg University (Germany)

FUKUZAWA Yukichi, NISHIKAWA Shunsaku (Japan), Fukuzawa Memorial Centre for Modem Japanese Studies, Keio University, Tokyo (Japan)

Gaspar Melchor de JOVELLANOS, Angeles GALINO CARRILLO (Spain), Complutense University of Madrid (Spain)

Georg HEGEL, Jurgen-Eckardt PLEINES (Germany), Karlsruhe University (Germany)

Georg KERSCHENSTEINER, Hermann ROHRS (Germany), Heidelberg University (Germany)

Georgij S. COV'JANOV (Russian Federation), Academy of Pedagogical Sciences, Moscow (Russian Federation)

Giambattista VICO, Maria Teresa MAIULLARI (Italy), The Luigi Einaudi Foundation, Turin (Italy)

Henri WALLON, Helene GRATIOT ALPHANDERY (France), Former professor at the University of Paris V and the Ecole Pratique des Hautes Etudes en Sciences Sociales, Paris (France)

Herbert READ, David THISTLEWOOD (United Kingdom), University of Liverpool (United Kingdom)

Herbert SPENCER, Brian HOLMES (United Kingdom), Formerly University of London (United Kingdom)

Hugo RODRIGUEZ ALDABALDE (Uruguay), Teacher Training Institute, Montevideo (Uruguay)

Immanuel KANT, Heinrich KANZ (Germany), Rheinische Friedrich-Wilhelms University, Bonn (Germany)

Isaac Leon KANDEL, Erwin POLLACK (United States of America), Kennedy-King College, Chicago (United States of America)

Isabel MONAL (Cuba), UNESCO Regional Office for Culture in Latin America and the Caribbean, Havana (Cuba)

Ismail AL-QABBANI, Mahmoud KOMBAR (Egypt), University of Qatar (Qatar)

Ivan ILLICH, Marcela GAJARDO (Chile), Latin-American Faculty of Social Science (FLACSO), Santiago (Chile)

J.P. NAIK, A.R. KAMAT (India), Indian Institute of Education, Kothrud, Pune (India)

Jan Wladysaw DAWID, Czeslaw KUPISIEWICZ (Poland), Warsaw University (Poland)

Jandhyala B.G. TILAK (India), National Institute of Educational Planning and Administration, New Delhi (India)

Janusz KORCZAK, Tadeusz LEWOWICKI (Poland), University of Warsaw (Poland)

Jean PIAGET, Alberto MUNARI (Switzerland), University of Geneva (Switzerland)

Jean-Jacques ROUSSEAU, Michel SOETARD (France), Catholic University of the West, Angers, and University of Lyon II (France)

Jean-Ovide DECROLY, Francine DUBREUCQ (Belgium), Centre for Decrolian Studies, Brussels (Belgium)

Johann Friedrich HERBART, Norbert HILGENHEGER (Germany), University of Cologne (Germany)

Johann Heinrich PESTALOZZI, Michel SOETARD (France), Catholic University of the West, Angers, and University of Lyon II (France)

John DEWEY. Robert WESTBROOK (United States of America), University of Rochester, New York (United States of America)

John LOCKE, Richard ALDRICH (United Kingdom) University of London (United Kingdom)

Jose MARTI, Ricardo NASSIF (Argentina), Formerly professor at the Universities of Tucuman and La Plata (Argentina)

Jose ORTEGA Y GASSET, Juan ESCAMEZ SANCHEZ (Spain), University of Valencia (Spain)

Jose Pedro VARELA, Marta DEMARCHI SCARAVINO (Uruguay), University of the Republic, Montevideo (Uruguay)

Jose VASCONCELOS, Rosario ENCINAS (Mexico), National Institute of Adult Education, Mexico City (Mexico)

Joseph PRIESTLEY, Ruth WATTS (United Kingdom), University of Birmingham (United Kingdom)

Jozsef EOTVOS, Istvan MESZAROS (Hungary), University Lorand Eotvos (Hungary)

Juan Luis VIVES, Ricardo MARIN IBANEZ (Spain), National Pedagogical University, Valencia, and National University for Distance Education, Madrid (Spain)

Julius Kambarage NYERERE, Yusuf KASSAM (United Republic of Tanzania), E.T. Jackson & Associates, Ottawa (Canada)

Karl JASPERS, Hermann HORN (Germany), Dortmund University (Germany)

Ibn KHALDUN, Abdelsselam CHEDDADI (Morocco), Mohamed V University, Rabat (Morocco)

Leo TOLSTOY, Semion Filippovitch EGOROV (Russian Federation), Academy of Pedagogical Sciences, Moscow (Russian Federation)

Lev S. VYGOTSKY, Ivan IVIC (Yugoslavia), University of Belgrade (Yugoslavia)

MAO Zedong, ZHUO Qingjun (China), China National Institute of Educational Research, Beijing (China)

Marc-Antoine JULLIEN, Jacqueline GAUTHERIN (France), University of Nantes (France)

Maria GRZEGORZEWSKA, Alicja SIEMAK-TYLIKOWSKA (Poland), University of Warsaw (Poland)

Maria MONTESSORI, Hermann ROHRS (Germany), Heidelberg University (Germany)

Martin BUBER, Kalman YARON (Israel), Hebrew University of Jerusalem (Israel)

MENCIUS (Meng Ke), GE Zhengming (China), China National Institute of Educational Research, Beijing (China)

Michael Ernest SADLER, James Henry HIGGINSON (United Kingdom), Formerly Warden of Sadler Hall, Leeds University (United Kingdom)

Michel de MONTAIGNE, Gerard WORMSER (France), Institute for Political Studies, Paris (France)

MISKAWAYH Nadia GAMAL AL-DIN (Egypt), Ayn al-Shams University, Cairo (Egypt)

Mohandas Karamchand GANDHI, Krishna KUMAR (India), University of Delhi (India)

Nadezhda Konstantinovna KRUPSKAYA, Mihail S. SKATKIN (Russian Federation), Formerly of the Academy of Pedagogical Sciences, Moscow (Russian Federation)

Nikolay GRUNDTVIG, Max LAWSON (Australia), University of New England, Armidale (Australia)

Otto SALOMON, Hans THORBJORNSSON (Sweden), Linkoping University (Sweden)

Paul GOODMAN, Edgar Z. FRIEDENBERG (United States of America), Former Professor at Dalhousie University, Halifax (Canada)

Paulo FREIRE, Heinz-Peter GERHARDT (Germany), Frankfurt University (Germany); visiting professor at the University of Rio Grande do Norte (Brazil)

Pavel Petrovitch BLONSKY, Mihail Gerasimovich DANILCHENKO, (Russian Federation) Teacher Training University, Moscow (Russian Federation)

Peter NOIKOV, Zhecho ATANASSOV (Bulgaria), Kliment Ohridsky University, Sofia (Bulgaria)

PLATO Charles HUMMEL (Switzerland), Former president, Council of the International Bureau of Education, Geneva (Switzerland)

Rabindranath TAGORE, Narmadeshwar JHA (India), Former Vice-chancellor of the University of Bihar (India)

Rif'at Rafi' AL-TAHTAWI, 'Aly SA'ID ISMA'IL (Egypt), Kuwait University (Kuwait)

Robert OWEN, Peter GORDON (United Kingdom), University of London (United Kingdom)

Roger COUSINET, Louis RAILLON (France), Former Director, Education et developpement, Paris (France)

Rudolf STEINER, Heinrich ULLRICH (Germany), Mainz University (Germany)

Sigmund FREUD, Bernard JOLIBERT (France), University of Reunion (France)

SUN Yat-sen, ZHANG Lanxin (China), China National Institute of Educational Research, Beijing (China)

Taha HUSSEIN, Abdel Fattah GALAL (Egypt), National Centre for Educational Research Development, Cairo (Egypt)

Thomas MORE, Keith WATSON (United Kingdom), University of Reading (United Kingdom)

Torsten HUSEN T., Neville POSTLETHWAITE (United Kingdom), Hamburg University (Germany)

Torsten RUDENSCHOLD, Gunnar RICHARDSON (Sweden), Linkoping University (Sweden)

Wilhelm von HUMBOLDT, Gerd HOHENDORF (Germany), Dresden University (Germany)

Yuri ALFEROV (Russian Federation), Russian Academy of Education (Russian Federation)

Source: '*Prospects*'. IBE/UNESCO.

Name Index